The Knight Triumphant

The Knight Triumphant

THE
HIGH MIDDLE AGES
1314–1485

STEPHEN TURNBULL

CASSELL&CO

Dedicated to my parents,
William and Joyce Turnbull

Cassell & Co
Wellington House, 125 Strand
London WC2R 0BB

First published 2001

The Knight Triumphant is based on the author's earlier work *The Book of the Medieval
Knight*, first published by Arms and Armour Press 1985, and now fully revised and
redesigned. It forms the second volume in his three volume history of the knight.

British Library Cataloguing-in-Publication Data
A catalogue record for this book is available from the British Library

ISBN 0-304-35971-8

Distributed in the United States by
Sterling Publishing Co Inc
387 Park Avenue South
New York NY 10016-8810

Printed and bound in Slovenia by DELO tiskarna
by arrangement with Preŝernova družba d.d., Ljubljana

Contents

PREFACE   7

1   A NEW EDWARD   9

2   KING OF ENGLAND – KING OF FRANCE   29

3   A KING'S RANSOM   53

4   THE ILL-MADE KNIGHT   71

5   THE LAST CRUSADERS   99

6   THE ITALIAN JOB   115

7   SWORDS AND PROPHECIES   131

8   THE AGINCOURT WAR   149

9   THE LONG, LOSING WAR   167

10   THE WARS OF THE ROSES   187

11   THE SUN IN SPLENDOUR   211

12   THE FADED ROSES   235

INDEX   252

Preface

WHEN Cassell invited me to revise *The Book of the Medieval Knight* I welcomed the opportunity to edit and improve a book of which I had always been proud. The suggestion was then made that the revised and edited work should eventually form the second volume of a trilogy covering the history of the knight from the Dark Ages to the beginning of the seventeenth century. The results of this work are presented here for readers to judge for themselves whether or not the effort has been worthwhile.

If this book was a computer game I could reasonably claim that it had been upgraded: the text has been fully edited and revised. One completely new chapter has been added, one has been extensively augmented, and others have been completely rewritten.

One of the most welcome compliments passed about *The Book of the Medieval Knight* was that the illustrations were not the usual picture-library fare of stylized manuscript illuminations and doubtful Victorian interpretations of siege weapons, but photographs that genuinely reflected the text they were there to illustrate. With this in mind I have used the opportunity to replace poorer-quality photographs by better ones, which my publishers have fitted into a new and much more attractive layout.

As I am now working on the other two volumes which will accompany *The Knight Triumphant*, I trust my readers will enjoy this start to the project, and will want to keep track of developments through my website, to be found at www.stephenturnbull.com.

I dedicated the original *Book of the Medieval Knight* to my father. This new trilogy is dedicated to him and, of course, to Mum too. They were the ones who first took me to castles and museums and awakened the interest herein expressed. Thank you so much!

Stephen Turnbull

Opposite: Warwick Castle, one of the finest medieval fortresses in Europe.

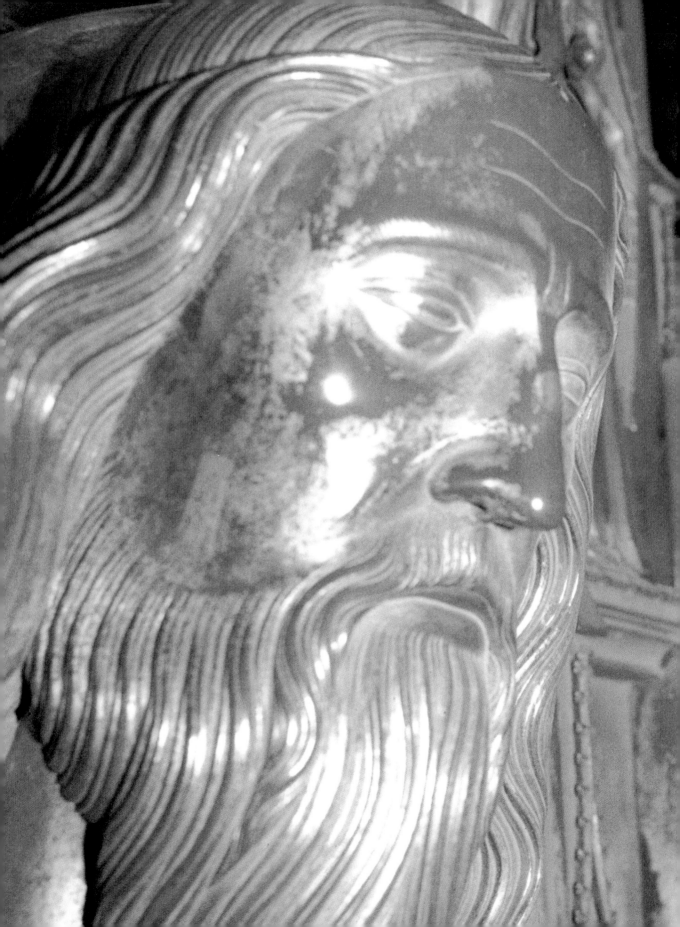

A New Edward   1

When the second English king to bear the name of Edward ended his attempt to snuff out the flame of Scottish independence by his defeat at Bannockburn, he laid his country open to a reaction unparalleled for decades. Stirling, to whose relief Edward II had marched, surrendered to the Bruce and joined Perth, Dumfries, Edinburgh and Roxburgh as lost English possessions. During the summer of 1314 the Bruce launched a series of retaliatory raids across the border, and the impotence of the English monarch allowed the Scots to penetrate more deeply into the kingdom than would have been possible a decade earlier. In August the Scots crossed the Tees and advanced to the gates of the castle of Richmond. The Bishop of Durham purchased a truce to last until January 1315. Cumberland too paid a ransom for itself, while the valleys of the North Tyne paid homage to the King of Scotland.

King Robert the Bruce, who defeated the English and maintained a strong policy against them until his death. This model was made by the sculptor who designed the statue of him at the site of his great victory at Bannockburn in 1314.

RAIDS AND REACTIONS

The year 1315 therefore opened under circumstances more depressing for England than at any time in a century. The country's rulers, mocked on the battlefield and humiliated by raiding, presented an even less impressive sight out of their armour. When they attempted to reach agreement on policy, a process from which Edward II usually absented himself, their personal rivalries prevented any agreement being reached. While the English quarrelled the Scots grew bolder, and by 1318 had completed their preparations to claim the prize that was as much symbolic as strategic – the town and castle of Berwick upon Tweed.

Berwick was what it had been and was destined to remain for centuries – a hotly disputed fortified town that was the key to the Anglo-Scottish border. With the help of a little treachery from within the garrison the Scots, under the leadership of Sir James Douglas, scaled the walls of the town in the early hours of the morning of 2 April. Six days later, after some uncontrolled plundering which allowed the defenders to counter-attack quite successfully, the main castle fell. The exultant Scots marched south, passing mighty Richmond and burning Northallerton and Boroughbridge. On 1 June the town of

Opposite: Edward III, the heir to numerous problems of state, from the effigy on his tomb in Westminster Abbey.

Skipton Castle, the final target of the deepest ever Scottish raid into England, which happened in 1315. Skipton's owner, Lord Clifford, had been killed at Bannockburn, and the castle would have fallen had it not been for its strong position high above the river.

Ripon paid protection money of £1,000, so the Scots turned on Knaresborough, and then headed off on their deepest-ever raid into England – westward up Wharfedale towards Skipton, plundering Otley on the way. Skipton's lord, Robert de Clifford, had been killed at Bannockburn, and now the fortress seemed open and undefended, but the Scottish raiders had not come prepared for a siege, so they contented themselves with plundering the town and moved on.

In July 1319 an English army of 12,000 assembled at Newcastle and marched north to recapture Berwick, in front of which they sat down and began a careful siege. Robert the Bruce responded by launching another raid deep into England that was so devastating that Edward was obliged to draw off many of his troops from Berwick and hurry south. John Randolf, Earl of Moray, and Sir James Douglas crossed the border and reached Boroughbridge without encountering any English resistance. Edward's Queen Isabella was then residing in York so a rich royal prize was almost within the Bruce's grasp. Some chroniclers suggest that the Scots had received information as to her whereabouts, but whatever treachery there may have been failed in its purpose, and the queen was hurriedly evacuated to Nottingham and safety.

Resistance to the Scots then fell upon the shoulders of Archbishop Melton of York who, perhaps, mindful of the great victory at Northallerton against the Scots two centuries previously, set out with a mixed army of clerics, citizens and some men of military experience to withstand this new onslaught. On the afternoon of 20 September the Archbishop found the Scots at Myton-on-Swale near Boroughbridge. Caught between the two schiltrons which the Scots formed like the teeth of pincers, the citizens' army was driven back into the angle where the River Swale joins the Ure, and great was the slaughter. The mayor of York was killed among countless others who were either cut down or drowned as they tried to flee. The Scots then withdrew, to discover to their delight that the siege of Berwick had been lifted and a ten-year truce proclaimed. Never had English military prowess sunk so low.

THE HEIR TO MISFORTUNE

Observing all that went on was a young boy who grew to manhood as the fierce war with Scotland raged on, and when the time came for Edward II to go it was in the name of Edward III that pressure was applied. In early 1325 the queen was in France on a diplomatic mission to her brother King Charles IV. Later in the year Prince Edward, then nearly thirteen, joined her. At that time Paris was a refuge for numbers of discontented exiles, among whom was Roger Mortimer who had escaped from the Tower of London where he had been incarcerated by Edward II following an abortive rising. The queen provided a natural focus for the development of a movement against her husband, and publicized her estrangement from him by taking Mortimer as her lover. On 23 September she and Mortimer sailed for England at the head of a band of mercenaries and landed in Suffolk. She had foreseen the effect well. The country rose in support and Edward fled to the west, where he was captured and then murdered in Berkeley Castle in a particularly unpleasant manner.

The young Edward III was crowned at Westminster on 1 February 1327, but within hours of the crown being placed on his head the Scots showed their defiance by crossing the Tweed at night, setting up scaling ladders against the walls of Norham Castle, and attempting to overpower the garrison. The surprise attack was unsuccessful but the message was clear. Truce or no truce, the Scottish people would defy any attempts at being ruled from England, either by Edward II or by his young son.

The keep of Norham Castle. Norham and Berwick were always in the front line of any Scottish advance on England, and Norham was in fact attacked on the very day that Edward III became King of England.

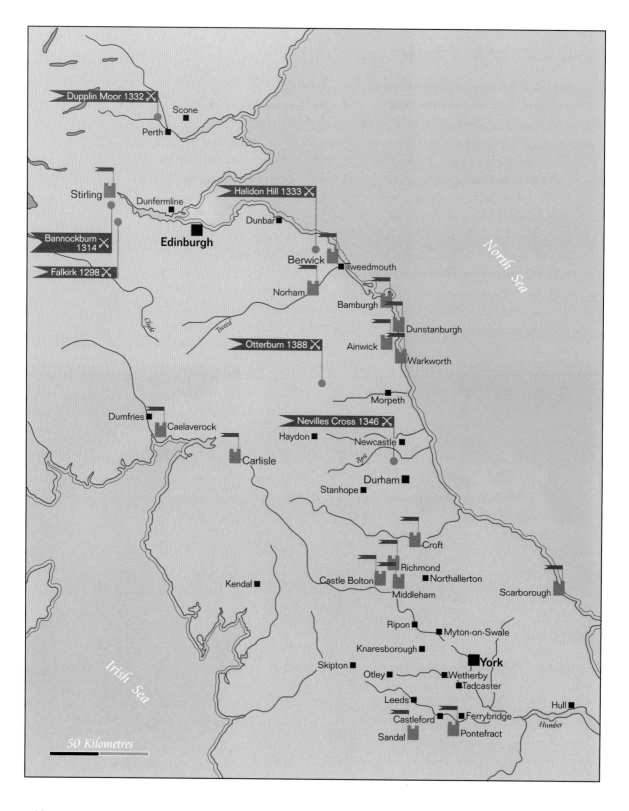

Dupplin Moor 1332

Scone

Perth

Stirling

Dunfermline

Halidon Hill 1333

Dunbar

Bannockburn 1314

Edinburgh

Falkirk 1298

Berwick

Tweedmouth

Norham

Bamburgh

Dunstanburgh

North Sea

Otterburn 1388

Ainwick

Warkworth

Clyde

Tweed

Morpeth

Dumfries

Caelaverock

Nevilles Cross 1346

Haydon

Newcastle

Carlisle

Tyne

Durham

Stanhope

Croft

Kendal

Richmond

Castle Bolton

Northallerton

Middleham

Scarborough

Irish Sea

Ripon

Myton-on-Swale

Knaresborough

Skipton

York

Otley

Wetherby

Tadcaster

Leeds

Hull

Castleford

Ferrybridge

Humber

Sandal

Pontefract

50 Kilometres

12

THE WEARDALE CAMPAIGN

To Edward III's army the paramount virtue among all their expectations of him was his prowess in the waging of war, so it was most unfortunate that the new king's first military expedition proved to be an almost total disaster. It was marred even before the English army set out, because Queen Isabella had acquired on her son's behalf the services of 500 mercenaries from Hainault. In June they were billeted in York, where quarrels broke out between them and the English archers, allegedly over a game of dice. The quarrelling became a full-scale riot, which was put down in brutal fashion by the Hainaulters, leaving 316 Lincolnshire archers dead in the streets. There were also disagreements among the English commanders as to how the campaign should be planned, a situation which the young king was unable to control.

All this gave the Scots ample opportunity to take the initiative, and at the end of June they stormed across the border and threatened Carlisle. Edward, who headed from York to meet them, halted at Durham. Only the smoke of burning villages gave any indication of where the enemy lay. The English army was accordingly deployed for battle in three divisions on foot, each flanked by mounted knights.

The Scots were almost certainly outnumbered, but were highly mobile, and Froissart gives a particularly vivid description of Scottish military techniques. They were, he writes, 'all a-horse back', the knights and squires being well horsed, while the lower ranks rode sturdy little nags, whose sole object was to transport the rider to the field of battle or convey him rapidly in a raiding party.

Opposite: Map of the Anglo-Scottish border.

> They take with them no purveyance of bread nor wine, for . . . they will pass in the journey a great long time with flesh half sodden, without bread, and drink of the river water without wine, and they neither care for pots nor pans, for they seethe beasts in their own skins . . . on their horse between the saddle and the panel they truss a broad plate of metal, and behind the saddle they will have a little sack full of oatmeal . . . they lay this plate on the fire and temper a little of the oatmeal; and when the plate is hot, they cast of the thin paste there on, and so make a little cake . . . and that they eat to comfort withal their stomachs.

The idea of mounted infantry had also been introduced into the English army by Sir Andrew Harcla, a veteran of Edward II's Scottish campaigns, and these 'hobelars' made up about a quarter of the English host in 1327, but as most of the present army were on foot the Scots evaded them completely, leaving the commanders frustrated. Then some movement by the Scots, who were apparently

English and Scottish knights skirmishing on the Tyne, from an illustration to Froissart's *Chronicles*. The incident illustrated is typical of the many encounters between the two nations during the period under discussion.

shifting camp, suggested the possibility that they were planning to withdraw, so the English attempted to cut off their retreat. Abandoning the baggage train, the English army marched overnight for the ford at Haydon, a crossing of the South Tyne near Hexham. As they crossed it began to rain, and after a few days the ford disappeared to leave the English on the northern bank, and the Scots nowhere in sight. As days passed, and morale sank lower, it was proclaimed that anyone who could find the Scottish army and lead the English to engage them would receive lands worth £100 a year and a knighthood. Fifteen men took up the challenge, and carefully recrossed the river, while the main body struck camp and headed upstream to look for a suitable ford. The promised reward was gained by Sir Thomas Rokeby, who tracked the Scots to the vicinity of Stanhope on the Wear, where they had established themselves on the southern bank, in a naturally strong position of rocky outcrops, just beyond bowshot of the northern side.

Nothing would induce the Scots to fight, and an attempt at crossing to taunt them into giving battle was summarily dealt with by Sir James Douglas's cavalry. So the English troops sat down and waited, disturbed by Scottish war cries, and exploited by the exorbitant prices for supplies brought up on packhorses by enterprising merchants. Any vague hopes that the Scots could be starved into submission were dashed when they calmly decamped for stronger positions further upstream.

The English followed, and on the first night suffered the indignity of a raid during which Sir James Douglas managed to fight his way as far as the ropes of the king's own tent. For the remainder of their stay the English were kept awake by frequent false alarms.

The knights from Hainault had even more to worry about. As well as sharing guard duties against the Scots, they had also to protect themselves from the English archers, who were thirsting for revenge for the incident at York. Within a few days news was brought to the young king that the Scots had once again slipped away entirely unnoticed. He is said to have wept tears of vexation. There was nothing to do but to head south and pay off the mercenaries, but the bill was so large that Edward III had to pawn some of his jewels to meet the first instalment.

Edward's first campaign therefore ended in humiliation. The Scots had taken the offensive, had set the pace, and had led Edward a merry dance. The use of mercenaries had also been an expensive mistake, and less had been gained from the venture than in some of the campaigns of his ill-fated father, whose military ineptitude Edward was expected to reverse. It was to the young sovereign's credit that he was to show that he differed from his father in one vital respect. He could learn from his mistakes.

The aftermath of a Scottish raid on an English border town. A woodcut from a printed edition of Holinshed's *Chronicles*.

DUPPLIN MOOR

Edward had ample time to absorb the lessons of the Weardale campaign, because in the intervening years Scottish rivalries came most splendidly to his assistance. King Robert the Bruce died in 1329, emphasizing on his deathbed the policy of defensive warfare and guerrilla attacks which his own career had done so much to establish as a success. Sir James Douglas, the hero of Weardale, then carried out

The unique triangular-plan fortress of Caerlaverock. The castle was largely dismantled early in the fourteenth century in accord with King Robert Bruce's policy of rendering defenceless all military buildings which might prove useful to the English.

the king's last request by taking his heart on a crusade against the Moors of Spain.

King Robert was succeeded by his son David Bruce, but the accession was challenged. Following Bannockburn, Robert had disinherited from their Scottish lands all those who had failed to support him, and his death enabled the disinherited to pursue their claims. The most serious challenge was their claim to the throne of Scotland for one of their number, Edward Balliol, the son of John Balliol, to whom Edward I had awarded the Scottish crown in 1292.

Edward Balliol, currently in exile, raised an army in England and travelled to Scotland by sea. He landed on 6 August 1332 in Fife, and advanced via Dunfermline towards Perth. It was the Weardale campaign in reverse, but with a much more serious objective. Opposing Balliol was a hastily assembled Scottish army of possibly 40,000 men, untrained for pitched battle, and apparently in two minds about the legitimacy of Edward Balliol's claim to the Scottish throne. This we know from an argument which took place between the Scottish leaders immediately before the Battle of Dupplin Moor began. The dispute was resolved by the rivals deciding that each would be the first to attack the English position, so both contingents lurched off in an uncoordinated advance.

Balliol's small English force (1,500 in all is the best estimate) had taken up a defensive position – they had little choice of any other – with their horses in the rear and their main defence being provided by archers. By the exigencies of his position Edward Balliol therefore anticipated what was to become the English way of fighting for the next century and a half, and demonstrated how such tactics could defeat a numerically larger host. The archers concentrated their heavy fire upon the Scottish flanks, driving them inwards. At this point Scottish reinforcements arrived, led by the Earl of Mar. Unfortunately this addition to their strength produced an advantage for the English, who had managed to trap the Scottish army in a glen. Mar charged down the narrow pass behind his comrades, making it impossible for them to move. One chronicler described the ensuing scene as being like a burial heap into which the English poured flight after flight of arrows. The panic-stricken Scots attempted to escape by climbing over one another, making the press worse, until the Scottish army had turned into a writhing heap nearly 15 feet high, on which English soldiers stood grotesquely, jabbing with their spears at any sign of life beneath them. Weardale was avenged.

THE SIEGE OF BERWICK

Edward Balliol was crowned King of Scots at Scone, but once the English military presence was removed the Scots rallied and he was forced to flee to England to seek Edward III's help once again. Weardale had shown Edward the strength of the Scots, but Dupplin Moor had exposed their weaknesses, so Balliol led where

Hermitage Castle, grimmest of the Border fortresses, was captured in 1338 by the Knight of Liddesdale, Sir William Douglas, from the English Baron, Sir Ralph Neville, who held it by gift from Edward III. Thereafter it was a Douglas stronghold until the end of the fifteenth century.

A few fragments of wall, and a precipitous flight of steps leading down to the River Tweed, are all that remain today of the once mighty fortifications of medieval Berwick-upon-Tweed. This garrison and frontier town par excellence changed hands several times, and was the scene of the first major campaign fought by the young Edward III.

Edward intended to follow, and in March 1333 the deposed monarch returned to Scotland and laid siege to Berwick-upon-Tweed. Berwick was now the only major fortification left in south-east Scotland, because Robert the Bruce had slighted all English strongholds as soon as they fell into his hands, so as to deny refuge to any English army that crossed the border. Berwick was therefore of greater importance than ever, and when the Scots recaptured it in 1318 they had strengthened its defences.

The Scots first tried their old ruse of raiding into England to draw the besiegers off from Berwick, but this time it only provoked a small but violent counter-raid that provided Edward with some useful propaganda about Scottish atrocities. Public proclamations and petitions to the clergy all served to emphasize the rightness of retaliation, and against this background of righteous indignation Edward assembled his army. The surviving records of Edward's plans show how well he had learned his lessons in Weardale. Orders were sent to the sheriffs of various midland and southern shires to supply food for men and horses, and these began to arrive at Newcastle by land and sea. He had also realized that such supplies could not be totally relied upon, for of fifteen shires responsible for deliveries to Newcastle only ten complied, and they supplied only a fifth of the amount Edward had originally demanded. The quantity, however, was found to be sufficient, prompting the suspicion that Edward had deliberately overestimated. The great religious houses were requested to supply wagons and draught-horses, but so poor was the response that the sheriff of

York requisitioned items presently in use for the construction of York Minster. As the Scots made use of a load of timber destined for the Franciscan friars of Roxburgh, ecclesiastical honours might be considered to have been equal.

By the time Edward and his army arrived at Berwick, Balliol had been conducting the siege for two months. Four conduits carrying fresh water to the town had been discovered and smashed. As the defenders had failed to adopt the scorched earth policy advocated by Bruce, the English were unhindered by shortages and raided widely to supplement their foodstuffs. The most valuable asset possessed by the English, however, was their chief adviser on siege operations, who had performed the same function for the defenders during the siege of 1319. His name was John Crabb, a Fleming who had been captured in 1332 by Sir Walter Manny and then purchased by the English king. No one knew better than Crabb how to find the weaknesses in Berwick's defences, and enormous trebuchets were directed against these softer points. Records survive of the construction of one of these machines, for which forty oak trees supplied the wood, while thirty-seven stonemasons and six quarrymen prepared hundreds of stone balls for flinging at the walls.

The bombardment of Berwick continued throughout the month of June, and on the 27th the English launched an assault on the walls by land and sea, which proved quite successful because of another failure on the part of the defence. Faggots soaked in tar had been stacked on the town walls ready to drop on to the English assault ships, but before they could be employed the flames

The counterweight trebuchet was the heavy artillery of the Middle Ages. This working replica is in action at Caerphilly Castle, where it is one of several reproduction siege engines on display.

from the burning faggots had blown back into Berwick and set a number of houses alight. A twenty-four-hour truce enabled the Scots to control the fire, but the renewed vigour of the English attack forced them to negotiate a further fifteen-day truce, which was guaranteed by giving Edward twelve hostages.

This was to be the first of several truces negotiated during the siege of Berwick, and illustrates an aspect of siege warfare every bit as important as blockading, mining or bombardment. Most medieval sieges began with a period of assessment, of trying the opponent's strength and measuring his capabilities. From these warlike experiments conclusions would be drawn about the likely outcome of the siege, which frequently hinged on an estimate of the length of time the garrison could hold out until the besieging army withdrew or a relieving army appeared. Naturally enough the besieging army would be drawing similar conclusions, so both sides were therefore able to negotiate on the basis of several presumptions, the facts of which were not in dispute.

At Berwick the first such agreement laid down that the garrison would surrender if they were not relieved by 11 July, fifteen days from the date of signing. Scottish hopes rested on Sir Archibald Douglas (the half-brother of Sir James Douglas, who had been killed in 1330), who was busily, but slowly, assembling a large army. It was unfortunate for Scotland that he had not acted sooner, for his resulting efforts, though dramatic, were not threatening enough for Edward to alter his resolve to maintain the siege unless the very letter of the agreement were followed.

Douglas in fact crossed the Tweed above Berwick, and burned Tweedmouth while Edward's army watched from the northern bank. During the afternoon of the same day, 11 July, the day mentioned in the agreement, 200 Scottish knights picked their way over the precarious ruins of the Tweed bridge and flung some supplies into Berwick, and some soldiers actually managed to enter the town. The brave force were attacked by the English as they carried out this limited operation, which Sir Archibald Douglas considered sufficient to claim that in terms of the agreement, Berwick had been relieved by the agreed date, and that the siege must therefore be concluded.

To illustrate that he had force to back his legalistic points, Douglas drew up his army on Sunnyside Hill, south of the Tweed, and threatened that unless Edward complied with the agreement the army would move off south and devastate England. His brother, Sir James Douglas, had of course adopted similar threatening postures in the Weardale campaign of 1327, but

A trebuchet is used during a siege to throw severed heads of the enemy back into the castle.

Edward's situation was now much improved. It was perhaps worrying that Edward's Queen Philippa was in Bamburgh Castle, a comparatively short journey away, but Bamburgh could withstand a siege for far longer than the time during which Berwick might now be expected to hold out.

Edward also challenged Douglas over the technicalities of the supposed relief, As far as he was concerned, a handful of soldiers climbing over a broken bridge did not constitute a relieving force. Besides, his catapults were still carrying out their destructive work, and the northern bank of the Tweed outside the walls had not felt the tread of a Scottish foot since the operation began. The town had therefore not been relieved in any sense, technical, legalistic or otherwise, and it was now Edward's turn to insist. As the siege had not been lifted the town must surrender or the twelve hostages would die.

A trebuchet loaded with a dead horse, which would spread disease in a besieged town

To show that he was in earnest Edward erected a high gallows as close to the walls of Berwick as security would allow, and the first of the hostages, Thomas Seton, was hanged before his parents' eyes, the third of their children to die in the war against England. Douglas's army stopped dead in its tracks. This was not the hesitant young monarch they had humiliated in Weardale, but a ruthless, calculating military leader, prepared to follow the military conventions of his day and to take them to their extremes. Realizing what they were now facing, the Scots returned to the negotiating table.

The resultant agreement was so complicated in its efforts to reach a definition of relief acceptable to both parties that it looks ridiculous to a modern world where warfare is instantly devastating and the opportunities for havoc elsewhere are so enormously varied. The discussions at Berwick remind one most of the patient and precise negotiations that take place when a terrorist faction take hostages, but the outcome was on a much larger scale, and was coldly calculated with an under-standing of the notion of risk that is never normally credited to the medieval mind.

The agreement that was put in writing and signed on 15 July 1333 declared a truce until sunrise on 20 July. The town and castle of Berwick would then be regarded as having been relieved if any of the following conditions had been satisfied:

1. The Scottish army crosses the Tweed by the fishery called Berwick stream to the west of the town at any time before sunrise on 20 July.

2. The Scottish army defeats the English army in battle on Scottish ground between the Tweed and the sea by Vespers on 19 July.

3. A division of the Scottish army, to include 200 men-at-arms, forces its way through the English lines into Berwick between sunrise and sunset on any of the days, with a loss of not more than thirty men-at-arms.

On fulfilment of any of the above conditions Edward would raise the siege and return the remaining hostages at sunrise on 20 July. If none of the conditions had been fulfilled the town and castle of Berwick would surrender to the English at the aforesaid time.

What delicate bargaining, what trading of numbers and locations, one wonders, took place before the above document was produced? It would appear, however, that Sir Archibald Douglas took no part in the arrangements. He had set off on a raid towards Bamburgh and the English queen, and not even the Scottish commanders had any idea where he had gone, for we know that the day after the agreement was signed three Scottish knights set out under Edward's safe conduct to find him. They tracked him down near Morpeth and persuaded him to return to try his hand at one of the Herculean tasks which the cunning Edward had forced upon Scottish pride.

THE BATTLE OF HALIDON HILL

In the absence of the able Douglas the Scottish commanders had managed to negotiate themselves into three unpalatable alternatives. The first, a crossing of the Tweed, where the English had chosen the ground and were obviously prepared to defend it with archers, was potentially suicidal and was rejected almost immediately as a means of saving Berwick. The second involved a pitched battle, the one form of encounter that the great Bruce had insisted against, but which his noble pupil, Sir James Douglas, had successfully achieved in Weardale. The third alternative could only succeed if the 200 Scots were allowed to test their mettle against the siege lines while the majority of the English army were otherwise engaged, and the only way they could be thus engaged would be for the Scottish main body to fight them.

Edward had clearly appreciated that this would be the likely choice, because his dispositions on the return of Douglas illustrate just such an expectation. He had three possible threats against which to guard: the main Scottish army, the 200 moving against his lines, and the likelihood of a sally by the defenders to help either of the other two operations towards a successful conclusion. About 200 men-at-arms were detailed to oppose a minor attack on his lines, 500 were detached to hold back any advance from the town, while the rest of the army were withdrawn 2 miles north-west of Berwick to the highest, and in the military sense, strongest, ground near to Berwick: Halidon Hill.

Douglas had by now returned to Scotland, and was camped at Duns, some 13 miles to the west of Berwick. He set out from there on the morning of 19 July, knowing that unless he achieved one of the two remaining tasks Berwick would fall as the sun rose on the following day. From the summit of Halidon Hill

Opposite: The defence of a gateway. In an attack on a castle the most hotly contested spot would be the gateway, protected by drawbridge and portcullis.

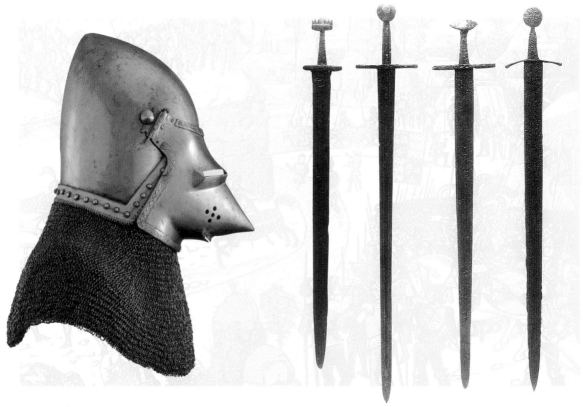

A visored bascinet with an aventail of mail, North Italian *c.*1380-1400. (Board of the Trustees of the Royal Armouries IV 470)

Various swords of the fourteenth century. (Wallace Collection, London)

Edward could follow his every movement as he approached Berwick along the direct route. Only one possible movement offered any chance of surprise: to swing to the north behind a hill now called Witches Knowle, which was higher than Halidon. This was the route Douglas chose, leaving his picked force of 200 in reserve on his left flank. Edward's scouts sighted them at midday. The stage was set for the first pitched battle of Edward's career. How much of Weardale, of Dupplin Moor, had the young king learned? There was no Bruce, but there could still be another Bannockburn.

Once the Scots had been sighted the English deployed themselves in three divisions looking across the shallow valley from Halidon Hill towards Witches Knowle and the Scots to the north. The whole area is probably very similar today to the aspect it presented on 19 July 1333. Edward led the centre division, while the victor of Dupplin Moor and recently deposed King of Scotland, Edward Balliol, took command of the left. His presence was undoubtedly decisive for the dispositions of the English army. The measures he had been forced to adopt at Dupplin Moor had to be shown to be more than merely defensive. Halidon Hill would prove whether or not such tactics would work against an army unhampered by a restricted front and impetuous support from the rear. It is not clear how Edward arranged his archers, but it would appear that they formed flanks at an angle to each of the three divisions, the idea probably being to cause in the Scottish army that same constricting, packing movement which had brought about their downfall before. As he was going to fight defensively and let the Scots come to him, there was little point in the men-at-arms remaining mounted, so the horses were sent to the rear, and kept ready for an eventual pursuit. After addressing his troops from horseback Edward himself dismounted, a move which was noted by several chroniclers as a departure from the traditions of knightly warfare.

The Scots, too, were arranged in three divisions, their men-at-arms also dismounting to support the schiltrons of pikemen with their 12-foot pikes. This decision was no doubt taken in view of the terrain, for not only were the English on a hill, where, as one chronicler relates, 'one man might discomfort three', but a treacherous bog divided the two armies. These schiltrons could have won Halidon Hill as they had won Bannockburn, but time was not on Douglas's side. If Edward was to be defeated it had to be accomplished that very afternoon. Even a delay, with the hope of an eventual victory for the Scottish army, would be immediately nullified by Edward's inevitable reaction of hanging the hostages and recommencing the bombardment of the town. The decline in Scottish morale alone would then probably serve to turn a possible victory into defeat.

Immediately prior to the battle proper there occurred one of those incidents that are as much a part of chivalry as gentlemanly agreements to surrender towns when honour has been satisfied – a single combat between champions. The one which had preceded Bannockburn proved a correct augury of that battle, and no doubt the Scots hoped the same for the one which took place before Halidon. Here the author must declare a certain personal interest. The Scottish champion was a knight of the Borders called Turnbull, who was a giant of a man according to the chronicler Baker, and is identified in Scottish legend as the first to bear the surname, having saved King Robert the Bruce from a charging bull. Whatever Turnbull's previous exploits, we are told that at Halidon he was accompanied by a large black mastiff, and was opposed by a Norfolk knight called Robert Benhale. It was perfectly natural for a Turnbull to be present, because their lands were a baronial possession of the House of Douglas, but unfortunately for Douglas the example his champion set was to prove only too accurate a prediction of the outcome of the day. The dog was first to be dispatched, cut clean in two by the Englishman's sword, and the animal was followed shortly after by Turnbull himself. Accounts vary as to whether he was hacked to death, or run through by Benhale's lance, but the outcome was the same: valuable time was lost along with the champion.

To reach the English lines the Scots had to cross the boggy ground mentioned above. Although it has since been drained, the farm presently on the site is called Bog End, and the ground is still treacherous after rain. As they

Sir John D'Aubernoun, shown in this brass of 1327, wears armour that would have been seen at the Battle of Halidon Hill in 1333. The shield is small, and fastened to the arm, and it is noticeable that a full coat of mail is worn under the gipon.

struggled through the mud and up the slope, an estimated 500 Scottish soldiers fell as flights of English arrows swept their ranks 'as thick as motes on the sun beam'. Those who got through tackled the divisions of Edward and Balliol, while Edward's right flank had to contend with the strength of Douglas's own division, which included the picked 200 whose goal was a forced entry into Berwick. They were held on the slopes of Halidon until evening, the men-at-arms balanced in the centre of each division, while the slow advantage passed to the English, the scales being gradually tipped by the volleys of arrows poured into the Scottish rear ranks coming up in support. Soon there were none to support, and the three separate Scottish formations were herded as one, and their rear ranks straggled off down the hill.

At this point the English knights mounted up and gave chase, scouring the countryside for miles around as the survivors scattered. The casualties were estimated in widely differing figures ranging from 30,000 to 60,000, with negligible losses on the English side. Among the slain were Sir Archibald Douglas and his nephew William. At Weardale the late Sir James had honoured the advice of his late king. If Archibald had had the resources to pursue such a policy to Halidon

Hill, with perhaps the moral courage to abandon the now symbolic Berwick, the eventual outcome might have been a certain shame, but no disaster. Instead, in the absence of the able Douglas, the agreement with Edward was seized upon by the defenders as being their best hope. Douglas responded as best he could to a situation that must have appeared to his experienced military mind as always hopeless.

The hanging of Thomas Seton had indicated the kind of man the Scots were up against. Following the battle few Scots escaped, and fewer were offered quarter. I can find no other battle in the whole of the period covered by this book where defeated troops committed suicide rather than be captured, but this happened at Halidon Hill. No less than four chroniclers indicate that some of the Scots flung themselves into the sea in despair. Their expectation of death was fully justified, for a disinterested chronicler confirms that on the morrow of the battle Edward ordered a hundred captives to be beheaded.

Berwick, of course, opened its gates as the sun rose, in fulfilment of the agreement. But what a new, ruthless talent had emerged from the ashes of his father's disasters – and this was just the beginning of a very long career.

The battlefield of Halidon Hill, looking across the valley to the Scottish positions on Witches Knowle. The farm visible in the middle distance is known as Bog End, testimony to the swampy nature of the ground that played a decisive part in the battle of 1333.

King of England – King of France

2

If Edward III's military operations had been confined to the Scottish border, then the Battle of Halidon Hill would have been seen merely as a rather well-fought battle and not as the precursor of events to come. But this warrior King of England is not known to posterity for his wars against Scotland. He is remembered because he, more than anyone else, was responsible for starting a conflict that was to divide France and England for more than a century – the Hundred Years' War.

I use the word 'divide' advisedly, because the Hundred Years' War embodied not a collision between elements that had always been divided, but a split between parties that were, to some extent, once united. Nowhere in France was this apparent unity more noticeable than in Gascony, the area of south-west France which a recent historian has called England's first colony. Its southern border was the Pyrenees, its western the Atlantic Ocean. On the other points of the compass its borders varied as Gascony developed to become what India was to be to a later generation of imperial administrators and rulers – the jewel in the crown.

HOMAGE FOR GASCONY

Gascony's connection with England dated back to the twelfth century, when its heiress, Eleanor of Aquitaine, one of the richest women in Europe, was divorced from her husband, Louis VII, King of France, and married a certain Henry Plantagenet. From the point of view of the King of France there could have been no worse alliance. Henry Plantagenet had recently inherited Maine, Touraine and Anjou from his father, and was already both Duke of Normandy and Suzerain of Brittany. With possession of Aquitaine (or Gascony, the names are to all intents and purposes interchangeable) he now controlled more territory in France than the King of France, and in 1154, on the death of King Stephen, Henry became King Henry II of England. The amalgamation of their territories into what was to become the Angevin Empire, the glory of the Plantagenets, would provoke the virtue of internationalism and the vice of conflict between England and France for the next three centuries.

Opposite: The city of Vannes, in Brittany, was the scene of one of the earliest sieges of the Hundred Years' War, when Robert d'Artois captured it on behalf of the English King, only to lose it in 1343 to Olivier de Clisson.

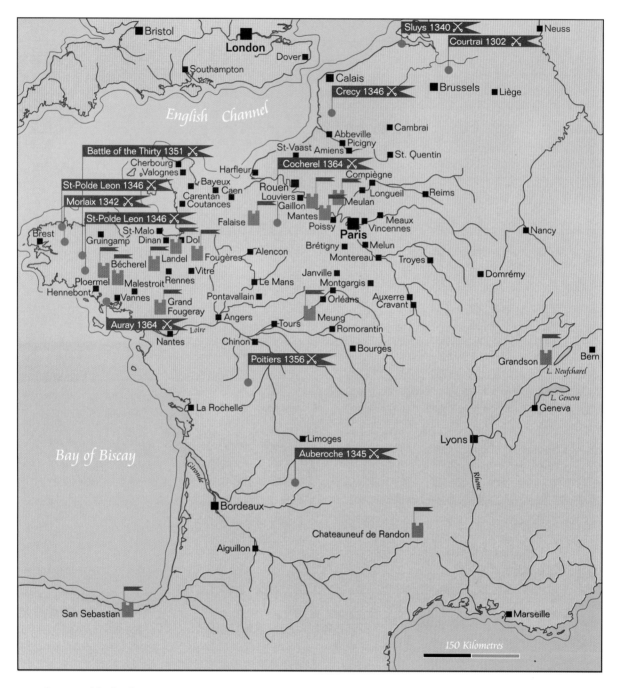

Gascony and the French
Wars of Edward III.

Yet government from a distance relied on the maintenance of lines of communication, particularly for the all-important wine trade. The overland route through Calais and Paris to Bordeaux could be travelled at some speed in almost three weeks. But war disrupted overland traffic, leaving the alternative of the possibly shorter, but always hazardous sea journey. With good winds and weather Plymouth to Bordeaux would take two weeks. If there were storms in the Bay of Biscay or marauding pirates it could take a lot longer, and to make matters worse one's starting dates could not be accurately forecast. For example, in 1355 the Black Prince voyaged to Gascony in eleven days, but he had already waited six weeks at Plymouth for a favourable wind.

It is not therefore surprising that the king/duke's administrator in the remote province (who was known as the Seneschal of Gascony) would often complain bitterly of the difficulty of his position. Nevertheless, this remnant of the Angevin Empire was always worth retaining. One statistic will suffice to illustrate the position. King Edward III obtained more revenue from the wine trade through Bordeaux than he did from the whole of domestic taxation in England. But there was a price to pay. Both diplomatically and militarily the French king was constantly nibbling at the Gascon frontier, so it is no wonder that at the time of the accession of Edward III older men looked back to a golden age when England called the tune over its distant but profitable colony. What irked the English more than anything else was the fact that to retain Gascony the King of England had to do homage to the King of France. The rights and wrongs of the arrangement had plagued relations between the countries since the time of John, and much ink had been spilt on the matter, but with the coming of the warrior King Edward III there was to be a fresh approach.

In 1328 legal disputes about control of the Aquitaine inheritance shrank into insignificance beside the great issue of the day: that of the succession to the throne of France. French law, which had recently declared that a woman could not inherit the throne, was now divided on the issue of whether the crown could pass via a woman to her male heir. What threw the matter into the forefront of international politics was that one of the closest male heirs to the late king was Edward III of England, at that time only fifteen, and firmly under the control of his ambitious mother who had scandalized the French court. As England itself was in a state of political turmoil, the claim that was advanced on his behalf must have seemed a formality made simply because it was expected of him as a grandson of a French king. Leaving the legal question wide open, the French chose Philip of Valois, a cousin of the last three kings, whose father had twice led attacks on Gascony.

With the accession of the new monarch homage for Gascony would be required, and to ensure that the young Edward complied with the duty, Philip seized the revenues of Gascony and hinted at a final confiscation, a threat which England was ill-prepared to challenge. Having been recently shamed at Weardale by a Scottish army, there was no military force with which Edward could threaten Philip, so on 6 June 1329 he paid homage to Philip of Valois at Amiens.

Effigy of Sir Oliver d'Ingham, in Ingham Church, Norfolk. Sir Oliver was Seneschal of Aquitaine from 1325 to 1327 and from 1331 to 1343, and Lieutenant of the Duchy of Aquitaine from 1338 to 1340. He died in 1344.

Since the beginning of his reign Edward had been reinforcing the English military presence in Gascony, a process that he accelerated once the formal homage had been given. At the same time Philip began to collect forces for its recapture. A document of 1329 contains an estimate of the force required as being 5,000 men-at-arms and 16,000 foot soldiers. These must have been acquired by May 1337, for in that month Philip ordered the confiscation of the duchy. Edward's response was dramatic. Referring to Philip of Valois not as King of France but as a usurper, he urged his rights in Aquitaine by claiming them through his own right to the throne of France.

It is difficult to say how seriously Edward's contemporaries took this statement. What is beyond dispute is that Edward himself took it very seriously indeed, and produced a speedy response. Leaving the defence of the duchy in the capable hands of his seneschal, Sir Oliver d'Ingham, Edward began hostilities with a brief and largely inconclusive campaign in Flanders, and when the raid produced no response from the French king, Edward was placed in a dilemma. Gascony was a huge distance to move his army, so how was he to obtain a toehold in France? Where was the door that would let him in? On 30 April 1341 that new door opened.

Funerary monument of Duke John III of Brittany. It was the death of this duke in 1341 which precipitated a succession dispute and the Breton Civil War, used by Edward III of England as a pretext for carrying out military operations on the French mainland.

Opposite: Charles de Blois was the French-supported claimant to the dukedom of Brittany during the Civil War which marked the entry of England into the Hundred Years' War. He was captured by the English at the siege of la Roche-Derrien in 1347, and killed at the Battle of Auray in 1364.

THE BRITTANY ADVENTURE

That day marked the death of John III, Duke of Brittany. Of all the great French feudatories none had maintained such an independence of mind and action as had the dukes of Brittany. They were peers of France by virtue of the duchy, but linked historically with the kings of England, the latter connection dating back to the time of William the Conqueror, who had presented the 'Honour of Richmond' to Alan Rufus of Brittany. The lands of the Honour of Richmond, which included large tracts of North Yorkshire and Richmond Castle and the title of Earl of Richmond, were thereafter held in the gift of the sovereign of England, and bestowed upon, or withheld from, successive dukes of Brittany depending upon the allegiance they were currently professing.

The resulting succession dispute for the duchy provided Edward III with a valuable opportunity to support one claimant (there was inevitably a pro-French and a pro-English faction) and thereby legitimately carry out operations on the French mainland. The English-supported claimant was John de Montfort, who enjoyed some early successes and then crossed to England to seek further support from Edward III, whom he eagerly acknowledged as King of France. Edward, in return, invested him as Earl of Richmond.

The French nominee Charles de Blois, the son-in-law of the King of France, then managed to capture John de Montfort after a siege of Nantes. It appeared that the War of Succession was over almost before it had begun, but there remained de Montfort's wife, Joan, Countess of Flanders, whom Charles de Blois had besieged in Hennebont on the west coast of Brittany.

The relief of Hennebont was the ideal expedition for Edward to begin his Brittany adventures, but because of the weather the voyage round

Charles de BLOIS

The fortified gateway of the town of Hennebont in Brittany, scene of one of the earliest engagements of the Hundred Years' War. Besieged in Hennebont by Charles de Blois, the Countess of Flanders appealed to Edward III for help, which was rendered in the form of a relieving force under Sir Walter Manny.

Cape Finistère took nearly two months, by which time Hennebont had almost surrendered after being pounded by a large trebuchet. The relieving force was led by a Hainault knight called Sir Walter Manny, whose ships ran the blockade, and after enjoying as generous a banquet as the beleaguered countess could provide, added to his reputation by sallying out and destroying the catapult.

THE FIRST BATTLE

Having gained a foothold in Brittany the English now had to maintain it against the French ability to provide rapid reinforcement, an uncomfortable fact of life illustrated the following year when the Earl of Northampton landed at Brest and laid siege to Morlaix. Immediately Charles de Blois set out to challenge him from his base at Guingamp. As he was outnumbered four to one Northampton abandoned the siege and advanced to meet the French in the first pitched battle of the Hundred Years' War.

The Battle of Morlaix was fought on 30 September 1342. Although little known by comparison with Crécy and Poitiers, Morlaix displayed many of their features including the use of archers, who broke the first French advance. When their arrows ran short, Northampton withdrew to the safety of a nearby wood. The battle was indecisive, but it certainly illustrated that even though these tactics could not guarantee victory, they were a good insurance policy against defeat.

The approach of winter made a withdrawal to winter quarters desirable for both sides, but Robert d'Artois, a renegade French knight in Edward's service, decided to sail from Hennebont to besiege Nantes. When the French fleet drove him away d'Artois changed his target to Vannes, and began a furious assault. When darkness fell a small detachment scaled the walls and caused such devastation that the garrison fled, including the commander Olivier de Clisson.

The disaster woke Charles de Blois to the inadvisability of taking to winter quarters while a hostile army was still at large. He therefore reinforced de Clisson's army, who returned to the fray and managed to dislodge d'Artois from his new conquest. When Edward III landed at Brest in October 1342 it was to hear that d'Artois was dead.

The city wall of Vannes.

Effigy of Sir John de Hardreshull, who held the office of Lieutenant of Brittany from 1343 to 1344, in the church at Ashton, Nottinghamshire.

In spite of this sad news, the confidence which Edward's previous victories and those of his commanders had given him was such that on his arrival he determined to attack all three of the major Breton cities simultaneously. Rennes, Vannes and Nantes were the targets, and it is worth noting that on the approach to them Edward forbade all burning and pillaging, in marked contrast to the later style of warfare that he was to develop. As an attempt to win support from the populace it is to be admired, and one must assume that feeding arrangements had been taken care of. The very boldness of the attempt, for it was now mid-November, was enough to make Charles withdraw from Nantes and appeal for help from the French king. Philip responded, and chose to command the army in person.

If Edward's companions had been expecting an early confrontation between the two monarchs they were to be disappointed. Edward was besieging Vannes but was threatened from the north by the combined armies of the King of France and Charles de Blois. As he was not yet ready to take on such a host, Edward sent urgent requests to England for reinforcements, and prepared to turn his siege lines into defensive ones facing in the opposite direction. Then fate took a hand. The French king's nerve must have failed him. Perhaps Charles de Blois had reminded him of what had happened at Morlaix. The Truce of Malestroit was drawn up, stating simply that each side should keep what it had except for Vannes, which would be neutral. The two parties withdrew for home and the first Brittany campaign was over. On the face of it little seemed to have been achieved, but the young Edward had been able to test himself and his armies on the mainland of Europe, and as a pilot project the results were encouraging. It had also been a very gentlemanly affair compared with what was to follow.

THE PRACTICE OF WAR

To the knights who fought in the Hundred Years' War the art of war was concerned with fighting battles against other knights, of doing brave deeds and seeing them recorded by the chroniclers whose role was not to produce candid, eyewitness accounts of their observations, but to be selective and produce that which the knightly classes wished to hear.

The picture that has come down to us from the pages of Froissart, with its brave challenges, its combat and its courtesy to captured nobles, therefore represents a very minor part of the activity that went on under the name of war. Battles, for that is basically what Froissart is concerned with, lasted a few hours, while war lasted weeks or months. Battles involved knights as fighters and leaders. War involved them as commanders, disciplinarians and, very frequently, self-seeking parasites as bad as the pardoned felons they led. Battles were fought by soldiers. War was fought by nations in arms, and included priests, civilians, women and children, as fighters and victims. In the 1340s and 1350s, when the names of Crécy and Poitiers passed into history, battles such as these provided a welcome relief from the day-to-day practice of war.

As to the personnel of war, Edward III commanded an army that consisted of much more than noble knights. Besides the indispensable archers were many labourers, servants and sailors taken along because of the particular talents they had to offer. Miners were much in demand when siege operations were contemplated. The ancient manner of recruiting men of lower rank was by 'commission of array'. The commissioners appointed by the king would confine themselves to their particular county and began by choosing, testing and arraying the available levies, then clothing, equipping and paying them. The orders for an array naturally specified that the commissioners choose the best men available, but this was not always done, and a particular levy of archers arrayed in 1341 were noted as being 'feeble'.

The second method of raising troops, and the one which Edward III was to refine into an efficient operation, was the raising of armies by 'contract'. A number of knights would act as recruiting agents, and would draw up a contract with the king for the number and type of soldiers they would provide. These contract captains would then subcontract with the soldiers they acquired. The details drawn up would include the number of men, their ranks, their rates of pay and period of service. The latter item was usually fixed as forty days initially, with extensions at given rates. The daily rates of pay from early in Edward III's reign were: earl 6s 8d; banneret 4s 0d; knight 2s; man-at-arms 1s; mounted archer 6d; foot archer 3d; Welsh spearman 2d. In 1341 the Earl of Warwick supplied under contract 3 bannerets, 26 knights, 71 men-at-arms, 40 armed men and 100 archers.

The third manner of recruiting an army was by inviting volunteers. Under certain circumstances, criminals could gain a pardon for service, and as many as one in ten of Edward's army may have been ex-outlaws. But from 1346 onwards it was not only criminals that were tempted to volunteer. Early successes brought back tales of plunder to be had, and certain commanders soon acquired a reputation for generosity with their troops. A leader skilled in war would have no trouble in recruiting, and Sir John Chandos, who began his career with very meagre lands, could by 1359 collect an army of willing followers which surpassed in size and quality the host of any of the nobility.

THE *CHEVAUCHÉE*

On 12 July 1346, Edward III landed at Saint-Vaast, at the tip of the Cotentin peninsula, to begin what has become known as the Crécy campaign. He arrived with the intention of making war upon the French king in a larger and more

Two civilians, c. 1380, depicted on brasses at King's Somborne in Hampshire. The life of the non-knightly classes formed the background against which knightly exploits were carried out.

thorough operation than either the Flanders or Brittany expeditions. The knights who fought for him were under no illusions about the nature of the tasks they were required to undertake, tasks which took them very far from their purely military use as heavy cavalry, and even further from their ideals of chivalrous conduct. It was total war.

The Hundred Years' War may be regarded as total war in one way because it was a conflict between two nations whose inhabitants were involved in paying for it through taxation and loans. So, whether they marched with the armies or not, those who financed it expected results, as shown by numerous parliaments that were decidedly cool about making further finance available. It is hardly surprising to see great developments in the use of propaganda to arouse consciousness in the involvement against the enemy. Through letters and dispatches, through pulpit and marketplace, those concerned with the preparations for war, the transport of troops and supplies, the voting of taxes and the prayers for the dead, were all made aware of their part in the great enterprise.

But total war has two sides. The foregoing records the need and ability of the population to give. The other side of the coin notes their suffering, and whereas the former were found in both countries during the Hundred Years' War, the latter was confined disproportionately to France. Scottish raids across the border (often timed to coincide with English involvement in France) and a succession of French raids across the Channel, which the naval battle of Sluys halted for twenty years, did little more than add to Edward's propaganda efforts against his enemies. But the bulk of English operations in France consisted of a long-term and systematic application of the means of destruction to the civilian population.

The most deadly weapon was fire. Destruction of an enemy's property by burning was not new in the practice of war, nor was it confined to the English operations in France, but the course of the movement of English armies was always marked by a wide swathe of burned ground, leaving no habitable building for men or beasts. The French historian Denifle wrote that 'fire was the constant ally of the English', and the chronicler Baker, more ready than many of his contemporaries to mention this aspect of warfare, described the scene near Cambrai one dark night in 1339, during one of Edward's first incursions into Europe. From the top of a church tower he could see the countryside lit up for miles in every direction from the fires of the English.

Destruction by fire was only the final stage of the process of devastation carried out during these expeditions, for which the French term '*chevauchée*' is commonly employed. The first stage consisted quite simply of obtaining food and drink for the army as it went on its way. Some food was brought from

The standard of Edward III, which proclaimed on a grand heraldic scale his claim to the French throne.

England, and lines of communication were maintained as best they might, but living off the land was imperative if the invading army was to survive.

The second stage of the destructive process, plunder, is best illustrated by the first major action fought by Edward III during the Crécy campaign. He had advanced down the Cotentin peninsula and a certain amount of pillaging had taken place to augment supplies, but there were other instances of pillaging that went far beyond the needs of the army. Various historians have suggested that these stemmed from lawless elements within the king's army, or revenge by those troops whose south-coast towns had to suffer marauding from the French.

Whatever the reason, on approaching the town of Caen the official policy was to be little different. From the military point of view the capture of Caen is an excellent example of the taking of a town by assault. As a means of conducting warfare such an approach had much to recommend it, because it spared both sides from the discomfort of a siege and forced a result comparatively quickly. The assaults on Caen were carried out simultaneously on various gates of the town, and Edward's fleet also played an important part. As he advanced eastwards the ships followed, conducting a *chevauchée* of their own along the Normandy coast. On reaching the mouth of the River Orne the fleet had sailed up to Caen about the same time as the army were attacking the town. This was probably more by luck than judgement, as such

The defence and supply of the town of Calais was always given top priority in any English strategic plan. For fourteen years following its capture in 1347 it was supplied totally from England.

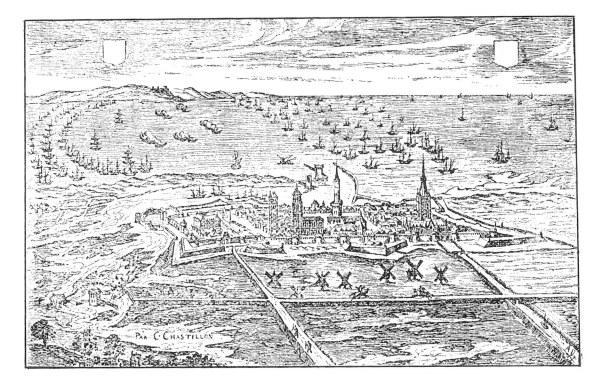

Par C. CHASTILLON

synchronization of land and sea forces was very difficult to organize. The arrival of the fleet enabled prisoners, wounded soldiers and booty to be sent back to England.

We are told by one chronicler that Edward had it proclaimed throughout his army that no one should imprison women, children, nuns or monks or harm their churches and houses, but his order appears to have been totally ineffective. According to Froissart, Sir Thomas Holland mounted his horse and rode into the streets and saved many lives of 'ladies, damsels, and cloisterers from defoiling, for the soldiers were without mercy'. Godfrey de Harcourt brought the situation to the king's notice, and then rode from street to street trying to enforce order.

Froissart blames the depredations upon the 'bad fellows and evildoers who must inevitably be found in a king's army', but the plunderers came from every social rank. One anonymous chronicler records that: 'The English desiring spoils brought back to the ships only jewelled clothing or very valuable ornaments.' The proximity of the fleet made it easier to get the loot home than on most campaigns. Froissart notes that the ships were 'charged with clothes, jewels, vessels of gold and silver . . .' By 1348 much of it had been dispersed throughout England, and Walsingham claims that 'there were few women who did not possess something from Caen, Calais or other overseas towns, such as clothing, furs, cushions. Tablecloths and linen were seen in everybody's houses. Married women were decked in the trimmings of French matrons, and if the latter sorrowed over their loss, the former rejoiced in their gain'.

Opposite: The savage sack of Caen in 1346. (Bibliothèque Nationale, Paris)

The strangest item of plunder from the sack of Caen was a document written at Vincennes in 1339 that apparently set out in detail the plans of the French king for invading England. It included military arrangements between the king and the Duke of Normandy, sources for finance and the maintenance of sea communications, and even the division of spoils. The document was immediately taken to London by the Earl of Huntingdon, where it was read publicly by the Archbishop of Canterbury at Saint Paul's churchyard. The details may have been several years out of date, but the find contributed greatly to the anti-French propaganda for Edward's war effort.

Such was the *chevauchée*, which, for the majority of the campaigns of the Hundred Years' War represented the practice of war. Its ultimate aim was political. France was too large a country for occupation to be considered. Garrisoning even parts of it, such as Brittany and Normandy, was expensive in terms of soldiers' wages and the inevitability of sieges. The *chevauchée* achieved rapidly what occupation took so long to do. It demonstrated the power of the English king and challenged the French king to react either by defence or counter-attack. If there were no reaction then loyalty to the king was seriously

Comment fix mille com
paignons partirent de la
ville de gand durant le
fiege et alerēt y affault
gaigner pillier z ardoir les
villes de Alcoft, tedremōde
z grantmont. Et puis
sen retournerent a gand.
Le fiege durant et
estant dēuāt gand
par la maniere q̄
le conte lauoit ap
fiege y eut fait plufieurs

efcarmouchx autour de la
ville. Car le p̄z dēghien et
le feneschal de haynau et le
suzle de flandres en trouuoiēt
a la fois a defcouuert dōt
ilz ne prenoient nulles rā
coes. Et aufauneffois ilz
estoient reboutez ſi dur q̄ſz
nauoient nulle loiſir de re
garder derriere eulx. Adōc
se recueillirent en la ville
de gand fix mille copaignōs
molt aidibles et eulx raffe

undermined, and it must be remembered that both monarchs were striving to retain the loyalty of their men, and loyalty depended upon success. The other argument for the *chevauchée* was that through inflicting devastation upon the non-combatant population, great political and financial pressure was brought upon the French king. Devastated areas could not pay taxes, and without taxes armies could not be paid. Thus war was continued steadily with every likelihood of success, in marked contrast to the ultimate sanction of a pitched battle.

We must also remember that at this stage in the war Edward had only limited experience from which to judge how his army might fare against a full French army. In the Brittany campaign the results of Morlaix had been encouraging but inconclusive, but a further victory in Gascony in 1345 added to his confidence. This was the Battle of Auberoche, fought on 21 October. Little is known of this engagement, which arose from a limited expedition to Gascony under Henry of Lancaster, accompanied by the formidable Sir Walter Manny. A French army was besieging Auberoche castle, which the English had recently taken, and were themselves surprised by another English army, who approached them through woods with the archers and men-at-arms advancing by different routes – a potentially hazardous operation.

THE BATTLE OF CRÉCY

Successful though these campaigns were, they were not enough to provoke the French king into committing his entire army to battle. Not that this would be entirely necessary to Edward's plans. The French king was being hounded enough without that particular gamble, but whatever the initial aims were, the current expedition was a campaign that ended in a battle so overwhelming in the victory gained that it was to become the best-known engagement of the entire Hundred Years' War: the Battle of Crécy.

Crécy was fought because Edward III was trying to avoid the army of the King of France until he could join forces with a Flemish army which had invaded France at the same time, but once Philip got on Edward's tail all notions of a conventional *chevauchée* were abandoned in favour of a rapid march north to link up with his allies. The Flemish army, accompanied by a small English contingent, set out at the beginning of August. At that time they were about 200 miles away, separated from Edward by two formidable rivers, the Seine and the Somme.

King Philip of France was at Rouen, thus forcing Edward to find a crossing farther upstream in the direction of Paris. For the next ten days the rival armies shadowed each other on opposite banks of the Seine. Louviers was sacked, and the castle of Gaillon captured, but not until Poissy was a bridge found. This was only partly destroyed and was weakly guarded. As Philip appeared to be

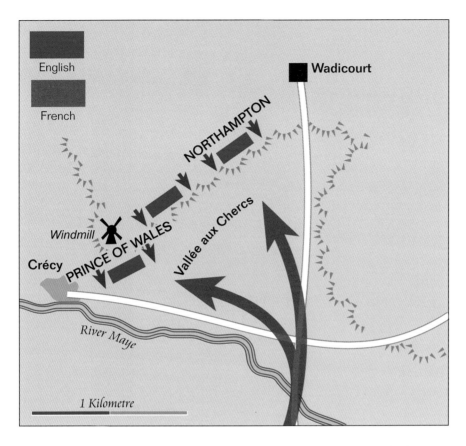

Map of the battle of Crécy.

continuing upstream Edward took his chance. Sending his son, the Black Prince, on towards Paris as a diversion to keep Philip guessing, the bridge was repaired and the army crossed on 16 August. Edward then headed due north, aiming for a point on the Somme about midway between Abbeville and Amiens, where he might expect to encounter the Flemings in about a week's time.

Having so successfully given Philip the slip, it must have been with some astonishment that Edward arrived on the Somme on 21 August to learn from his scouts that Philip's army had already crossed at Amiens and were ahead of him on the opposite bank. It may not have been his entire army, for they would have had to cover 24 miles a day to make up Edward's lead, but the fact remained that Philip had triumphed in the pursuit. Four miles lay between Philip and Edward. Fifty-five miles lay between Edward and the Flemings, and a reconnaissance force under the Earl of Warwick reported that all known crossings were heavily guarded.

The solution was provided by one Gobin Agache, a French prisoner. In return for the offer of a handsome reward, Agache disclosed the existence of a ford at Blanchetaque, where a man could cross at low tide in water at knee height. The army moved off before dawn to cover the six miles to Blanchetaque, and waited for the tide to fall as the army closed up behind its advance guard. But Philip had anticipated the move and had guarded Blanchetaque with a force of 500 knights and 3,000 infantry, including Genoese crossbowmen. The crossing was led by Hugh Despenser, and was uneventful until they came within range of the crossbows, but the English archers managed to scatter them and the crossing proceeded. This itself was quite an achievement and no doubt the element of surprise contributed a great deal, but the duel between longbow and crossbow was a foretaste of what was to come.

Edward had thus successfully surmounted the second of the two major physical obstacles in his path. All the omens were favourable. His army was in good shape. They had acquitted themselves well and morale was high. It was at this point that Edward made his fateful and historic decision not to wait for the Flemish army but to give battle, on ground of his choosing, to the French army that had pursued him. The ground he chose was on a ridge immediately to the north-east of the village of Crécy. The ridge is formed by a small valley, the Vallée des Clercs, the eastern end of which merges into a plateau immediately before the village of Wadicourt. On the highest point of the ridge stood a windmill which would make an ideal command post, while on the right flank any attack was discouraged by the village of Crécy and the river which runs through it. The English numbered between 12,000 and 13,000. Their right wing was commanded

The windmill at Crécy as it was before its demolition by a patriotic Frenchman in 1898. Edward III used it as his command post during the battle.

The Battle of Crécy, 1346, from Froissart's *Chronicles*. Note the English longbowmen in action against the French crossbowmen, one of whom is seen reloading his weapon.

by young Prince Edward, then only sixteen years old, with Godfrey Harcourt to assist him. The left wing was occupied by the Earl of Northampton, whose action at Morlaix had been carried out under similar circumstances. The lines of battle stretched between them with the archers deployed in wedge-shaped formations to enable them to provide fire that would force the French cavalry to concentrate in towards the part of the line held by the dismounted English knights. All afternoon they waited, and a brief storm forced the archers to disconnect their precious bowstrings, which they placed in their caps to keep dry.

The French army was composed of a number of different contingents. The regular troops consisted of the king's personal retinue of household troops, and the Genoese mercenaries, who always fought as one body under their own commander. Next came the foreign armies: the blind King of Bohemia with his son Charles, King of the Romans; John of Hainault, who was brother-in-law of Edward III's Queen Philippa; the Duke of Savoy, and James I, King of Majorca. There were also considerable numbers of levied French troops, indicating that the English were outnumbered, although by inferior soldiers.

The French advanced late in the afternoon of 26 August 1346, their unwieldy and uncoordinated movement being noted by the English on the ridge, and in particular by the English king high in the windmill. The Genoese crossbowmen led the way, to be met at a range of 150 yards by a tremendous volley of longbow arrows. The Genoese broke and fled, but coming up behind was the division of the Duke of Alençon. Accusing the Genoese of treachery, his knights rode them down and pressed on to engage the Prince of Wales's division. Soon the whole line was fighting, with any French casualties from the hail of arrows being quickly replaced from the rear.

It was at this point that the well-known incident concerning the Black Prince occurred. Fearing for the safety of his young charge, Godfrey Harcourt requested the Earl of Arundel to launch a flank attack to relieve the pressure on the prince, and at the same time asked the king for reinforcements. By the time the messenger reached Edward in the windmill, the king could see that the flank attack had already taken place, so there was no need to risk his precious reserve. 'Let the boy win his spurs' was his alleged comment. Baker says that a small force of knights, probably under the command of the Bishop of Durham, were sent, and found the Prince in good heart and with more than a thousand French dead before his troops. The Battle of Crécy continued until after dark, leaving dead on the field among others, King John of Bohemia and the elder brother of Charles de Blois. Monks from the nearby abbey listed the dead. The total of French lords and knights numbered 1,542, and of the lower ranks there were many more.

Crécy was the culmination of the process which had triumphed at Morlaix, Dupplin Moor and Halidon Hill. The knights had dismounted, and the two arms of archers and men-at-arms supported each other in a disciplined coordination of effort. The French, on the other hand, were an army of mixed nationalities, with vague leadership and no cooperation. Their missile troops – the Genoese – were concentrated in one body, and were directed against one portion of the line largely because they were mercenaries and would only fight that way. Crécy was the remarkable end to a remarkable campaign. The *chevauchée* would continue, but never again would Edward III be wary of engaging a French army on his own terms. It was not only the Black Prince who had won his spurs that day.

ARMS AND ARMOUR

It is appropriate to pause at this stage and look at the means of defence currently being employed by the knights, which seemed to be proving so ineffectual against the use of mass archery. During the fourteenth century the overall trend was the gradual transition from mail to plate armour, until by the end of the century their descendants rode into battle completely encased in plate.

Brass of Thomas Cheyne, Esq., from Drayton Beauchamp, Buckinghamshire. Note the close-fitting gipon worn over the armour, and the sword belt slung around the hips. His helmet, a bascinet, bears an aventail of mail. At this time, the mid-fourteenth century, plate armour was far from complete, and the leg defences are of brigadine.

The great lesson of the longbow was the extreme vulnerability of mail to a swift, sharp arrow. Crossbow missiles had a similar effect, but it was the sheer quantity of longbow arrows fired that made their deadliness so noticeable. In 1361 a Danish royal army slaughtered a levied army of Swedish peasants and townsmen at Wisby. The sole protection for the Swedes was mail, and after the battle their bodies were heaped into a mass grave. Excavations of the grave during the 1930s revealed that at least 125 men had suffered fatal head wounds from arrows and crossbow bolts which had struck their mail hoods. In many cases the arrowheads were found inside the skulls.

Mail performed better against sword strokes when there was no direct piercing action, but here again the results could be serious, for a strongly driven cutting stroke, though not parting the mail, could drive the unbroken links down into the flesh and produce a very nasty wound.

The first plate additions to armour took the form of roundels to protect the elbow joints and armpits, linked by plates along the outside of the arm called rerebraces for the upper arm and vambraces for the lower. Metal shinguards

Tomb of Hugh Despenser and his wife Elizabeth Montacute in Tewkesbury Abbey. Sir Hugh's effigy, dated about 1349, illustrates a style of armour which is probably typical of the time of the Crécy campaign.

47

One of the grave pits excavated at Wisby in Sweden, where a Danish army defeated a levied army of Swedes in 1361. Many of the bodies bear evidence of fatal head wounds caused by arrows piercing their mail hoods. Helmets of plate, the best defence against arrows, were still owned only by the better-off sections of society.

called schynbalds and plate shoes called sabatons provided defence for the leg. A knight who fought at Bannockburn would probably have worn this form of armour. By the time of Halidon Hill plate gauntlets were available instead of mail mittens, and an additional plate headpiece, attached to the mail hood, might be worn under the helmet.

The development of armour to protect the torso is more difficult to elucidate, largely because most monumental effigies of the period show a surcoat which almost completely covers what lies beneath. It seems clear, however, that as the long surcoats became shorter, some form of body armour was developed, either as a single breastplate, to which the sword, helmet or dagger could be attached by chains, or a series of plates, which we know eventually extended around the wearer's back as well.

THE YEAR OF VICTORIES

In his distress at the defeat of Crécy, Philip begged King David II of Scotland to invade England, whereupon the Scots crossed the border with quite a large army and advanced towards Durham, laying waste many places *en route*, including the abbey of Lanercost.

In the report from a commission set up later to look into the losses suffered from this raid, one landowner, a certain Robert Herle of Northumberland, reported that on 15 October, a Sunday, five villages were laid waste; the houses and crops were burned, and the tenants plundered of 70 oxen, 83 cows, 142 bullocks, 32 heifers, 316 sheep and other goods. What, the tenants might have asked, was a King of England going to do about it?

Before leaving for France Edward had guarded against the possibility of Scottish attack by deliberately excluding from recruitment any men from north of the Humber. As the Bishop of Durham was fighting beside the king in France, the task of organizing defensive measures fell upon the Archbishop of York. Assisted by the northern lords, notably Sir Ralph Neville and Sir Henry Percy, and probably Edward Balliol the ex-King of Scotland, he assembled an army of comparable size to the Scots, whom he found encamped near Durham.

It must have pleased the English commander, Sir Ralph Neville, to discover that the place at which they decided to make a stand against the Scots bore his name as Neville's Cross. It lies on a ridge of hilly ground to the west of Durham, a site comparable to that of Crécy, and Neville probably adopted similar dispositions. The presence of the Archbishop of York, and the threat to the holy relics of St Cuthbert preserved in Durham Cathedral, made the affair into something of a crusade. Perhaps remembering the stories they had been told about the Battle of the Standard in 1138, a group of monks left the city with the banner of St Cuthbert and proceeded into the area between the armies, where they knelt in prayer.

The battle started when two units on the Scottish right wing came down the hills in schiltron formation, but they became entangled with each other in a steep-sided depression, whereupon the English archers poured in their deadly fire on the disordered Scots. The English

The magnificent skyline of the city of Durham, showing the castle and the cathedral. This view is taken from the right of the English lines at the Battle of Neville's Cross, which was fought close to the centre of the city. In 1346 much of the castle had only recently been completed following extensive rebuilding.

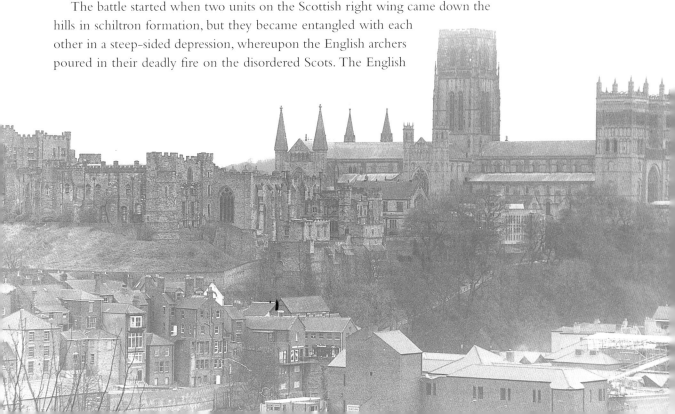

knights then swept down in as neat a combination of arms as would have distinguished the King of England himself. David of Scotland was captured, and languished in the Tower for some years.

While his countrymen were fighting the Scots, Edward was settling in to a year-long operation to capture the port of Calais. The town was well defended, so blockading and slow starvation were the only weapons suitable. The siege lasted until August 1347, by which time a relieving force under King Philip had arrived before the gates, only to withdraw shortly afterwards – perhaps the memory of Crécy was too fresh. The well-known story of how the surrender was accepted from six burgesses of Calais, bare-headed and with halters round their necks, was the dramatic and humiliating climax. The embellishment that Edward wished to have them executed, but was dissuaded by his queen, is probably apocryphal. His intention was to make Calais an English town, and he had no reason to alienate the population, though such an act was entirely in character, and we noted similar behaviour on his part at Berwick.

King David soon had company in the Tower. Another English army had been active in Brittany under Sir Thomas Dagworth, keeping up the nominal

The site of the Battle of Neville's Cross (1346), looking north towards the valley which divided the Scottish line in two. As they advanced across this broken ground the terrain naturally turned the wings in on each other, adding considerably to the effect of the English archery, which produced another notable victory in the year of Crécy.

cause of the house of de Montfort for the dukedom, even though the heir to the title was still a prisoner of his rival, Charles de Blois. On 9 June 1346, two months before Crécy, Sir Thomas Dagworth's army was attacked by a much larger force under Charles de Blois at Saint Pol de Léon, in the north-west of Brittany. Although he repulsed the first assault a second wave of cavalry charges followed, so that Dagworth's little force had to face attacks from three sides as the French army enveloped them. Once again an English army took a stand and poured in such a vicious flight of arrows that a virtual massacre ensued. Thus three times in one year three separate armies, fighting in widely different places, used broadly similar tactics to achieve notable victories.

Charles de Blois raised a fresh army in 1347 and laid siege to the English-held town of La Roche-Derrien. Sir Thomas Dagworth led a surprise night attack on the French camp. Resistance was stiff, inspired by Charles de Blois who emerged from his tent with no armour and plunged gallantly into the fray until he was captured and came to join the King of Scotland in his lonely sojourn. So the year that had begun as a ride of havoc ended as a procession of triumph. The combination of knights and archers, on and off the battlefield, had resulted in a year of victories.

A King's Ransom 3

In the last chapter it was argued that the practice of *chevauchée* raiding, which appears at first sight to be a regrettable and cruel addition to the practice of war, in fact formed a vital part of it, and that battles and combat between knights were the exception to this general pattern. It now remains to ask how the *chevauchée* idea fitted in with the knightly code of behaviour – the art of chivalry. Were such activities as burning, looting and ransom not contrary to the tenets of chivalry? If they were, and continued to be practised on such a large scale, was chivalry itself of any worth, or was it merely a cloak for excess?

Although looting was often blamed on undisciplined foot soldiers it was the prospect of loot and the desire to fight for a successful and open-handed commander that led many knights to war in the first place. The knightly class, as the leaders of men, must therefore bear their share of the responsibility for the excesses they created and the results from which they profited. There is a very strong impression given in the chronicles that real discipline was only enforced during a sack when the knights had had their share of the plunder. The discipline exerted by knights had a strong element of self-interest.

If the knights were partly to blame how did contemporary writers react to it? Froissart largely ignored it. But one writer tackled the subject head on. He was Honor Bonet, who wrote *The Tree of Battles*, a study of war illustrated by numerous incidents drawn from the struggle that was happening at the time. He deplores plunder and pillage, but in these words:

> The way of warfare does not follow the ordinances of worthy chivalry or of the ancient custom of noble warriors who upheld justice, the widow, the orphan, and the poor. And nowadays it is the opposite that they do everywhere, and the man who does not know how to set a place on fire, to rob churches and to usurp the rights and to imprison the priests, is not fit to carry on war. And for these reasons, the knights of today have not the glory and praise of the old champions of former times.

Opposite: Sir Lawrence de Hastings wears armour that would have been seen at Crécy and Poitiers. He died in 1348, and this effigy is in St Mary's Church, Abergavenny.

Previous page: A mêlée at a tournament, a miniature from a manuscript entitled: *Traite de la forme at devis comme on fait les tournois* by René of Anjou. (Bibliothéque Nationale, Paris)

A nineteenth-century engraving depicting a mêlée, the form of tournament that most resembled a mock battle. The knights wear heavy tilting helms on top of which are ornamental crests. In the right foreground a squire tends to a fallen knight.

This tendency to contrast unfavourably the knights' behaviour with their illustrious forebears is a common theme in the literature of the time. It is an easy statement to make, but it is perhaps significant that it was made at a time when the knight's prowess on the battlefield was also coming under scrutiny.

This brings us to the second question. If the evils of war were part of the art of war, what purpose did chivalry serve? Had its ideals become so divorced from the harsh realities of medieval warfare that it was no more than a charade, an empty spectacle more honoured in the breach than the observance? To answer this question we must examine chivalry in the context of the times. The mid-fourteenth century may have witnessed war on a large scale, but it was also the time when the concept of chivalry received its greatest impetus in the founding of a number of Orders of Chivalry, among which the most notable was the Order of the Garter. It is impossible to avoid the conclusion that the two were in some way connected. Chivalry in the fourteenth century was the code of behaviour of a military elite. Some of its values had changed and would change.

Others remained immutable, but chivalry largely came about not as a means of rejecting the reality of war, but rather as a way of accepting it. The concept of chivalry was not an artificial creation, but an expression of caste solidarity among the knightly class, without which they could not survive.

Let us consider what influences were being brought to bear upon the fourteenth-century knight. If he were French he had to suffer the horror of seeing his comrades killed around him in large numbers. If he were English he had to swallow his aristocratic pride and fight beside the archers. On *chevauchée* he had to overcome any feeling of revulsion at the work he was required to do. What more natural reaction could there be than for knights to seek solace among their companions and be inspired by the heroic tales of their ancestors, so that when courage was needed it could be found within the group. Chivalry was the glue which bound this society together. To express this in the form of an institution of knighthood for a super-elite such as the Order of the Garter, was a masterpiece of psychology, an achievement by Edward III that must rank beside his use of fighting men from the lower end of the social scale. It inherited from the religious orders of knighthood their notion of brotherhood, and provided support to the knights in the context of serving the king.

A fine example of a tilting helm. This form of helmet, produced for extra protection when taking part in tournaments, was very heavy and would not be used in battle. (Wallace Collection, London)

THE TENETS OF CHIVALRY

Two ideas were central to the notion of chivalry, both of which may be examined in social terms. The first regarded warfare as a positive experience, ennobling in itself. In the same way that the king was expected to be a leader in war, so were his knights expected to follow, and to lead in their turn. The knight was first and foremost a fighting man, and war was the natural state of his life.

If war was ennobling, the implication was also there that it was only the knightly classes who were ennobled by it. The belief among knights that they were as much a social as a military elite comes over very strongly in the passages quoted in the last chapter dealing with the attribution of atrocities to the lower classes of soldier. Real fighting was for knights. When the Gascon Jean de Grailly, Captal de Buch (the first foreign knight to be chosen for the Order of the Garter) was captured he demanded to know of his captor whether or not he was a man of gentle birth 'for he would sooner die than surrender to one who was not'. During a skirmish at Longeuil a group of English knights were cut to pieces by a force of peasants, and were mourned by their comrades particularly because they had been killed by such ignoble hands.

Knights at a tourney, from a fifteenth-century manuscript illustrating the life of Sir James Astley.

Another important characteristic of knighthood was its international outlook. The knights of rival countries were united by a caste solidarity that went far beyond seeking out a suitable opponent for combat. Their mental world was that of an international chivalric class, equally at home on the mainland of Europe as in England. Sir Walter Manny, a Hainaulter, and the above-mentioned Jean de Grailly, Captal de Buch, are excellent examples, but the royal families produced the most striking illustrations. Edward may have been after the throne of France, but his claim was that it was his by right of inheritance, as part of that great Anglo-French tradition of monarchy which, from his point of view, made the Hundred Years' War a civil war fought between rival houses, where national boundaries and languages counted for little. When the old, blind King of Bohemia was killed at Crécy both King Edward and his son were deeply saddened.

This international brotherhood was put on display at the numerous tournaments held during Edward's reign. At one set of jousts held at Windsor in 1358 safe conduct was granted for foreign knights to attend, and captive French knights then in England also took part. Worthy knights, whatever their origin, were genuinely honoured and admired for their own sake, irrespective of their allegiance. So the Marshal d'Audrehem might be praised by his enemies after Poitiers for being 'ever at all times right greatly to be esteemed, for he was a very goodly knight'.

All goodly knights also recognized the legitimacy of ransoming prisoners. Religious notions of chivalry may have made general condemnation of the pursuit of gain in battle, but to the knights themselves it had much to recommend it, and Bonet, after a lengthy discussion, decides in favour of ransom: 'All that a man can win from his enemy in lawful war he may of good right retain . . . good custom and usage are approved, and among Christians great and small there exists the custom of commonly taking ransom one from another.' Bonet, however, does insist that only a reasonable and knightly ransom' should be demanded. His criticism of the knights of his day, from which we quoted above, includes comments on ransom, saying that 'they cause them to pay great and excessive payments and ransoms without pity or mercy'.

THE BATTLE OF THE THIRTY

When war began again it was Brittany that felt its effects. Sir Thomas Dagworth, the victor of La Roche-Derrien, was killed in an ambush and was replaced as King's Lieutenant by Sir William Bentley, who proved to be a wise administrator and a strict disciplinarian of his garrison troops. Resentment against the English presence was growing high in Brittany by the 1350s, because while John de Montfort and Charles de Blois were absent Brittany became a battleground for rivalries. In 1351 this culminated in one of the strangest battles of the Hundred Years' War. Its circumstances were so bizarre that the Battle of the Thirty has often been confused with a tournament. Certainly Froissart's language is picturesque enough, but this encounter was in deadly earnest.

In the centre of Brittany were two strong castles: Josselin, commanded by Jean de Beaumanoir for the pro-Blois party and, seven miles away, Ploermel, under the English knight, Richard Bembro. For some time the two garrisons had skirmished as they ravaged the countryside on raids or foraging expeditions. In

Josselin Castle. From its courtyard, Josselin now bears the appearance of a decorative château, but a view such as this, from the river, retains its medieval flavour. Josselin was the major French stronghold in Central Brittany during the earlier part of the Hundred Years' War, and it was the garrison of Josselin which took part in the famous Battle of the Thirty in 1351.

This column between the town of Ploermel and Josselin commemorates the Battle of the Thirty in 1351 between two picked forces of knights from the French and English garrisons.

The site of the Battle of Mauron in 1352. This little-known battle destroyed the newly founded Order of the Star, despite a temporary reverse of the English archers at the hands of the French knights.

March 1351 the two leaders arranged an armed encounter between thirty knights from each side, to be fought at a spot midway between the two fortresses. The battle took place on 27 March 1351. From Josselin were 30 Breton knights under Jean de Beaumanoir, facing an international brigade of 20 English, 6 Germans and 4 Bretons. The battle became a series of duels to the death, which lasted for several hours, interrupted by a break for rest. At the end of the day the French were victorious. The English commander was killed, together with eight of his men, and the rest were taken prisoner, including two who were to become very famous knights, Sir Hugh Calveley and Sir Robert Knowles. Much courage was shown, as the chroniclers proudly tell us, of which one example will suffice. During the struggle de Beaumanoir, badly wounded, asked for a drink. 'Drink your blood, Beaumanoir,' replied his companion, 'your thirst will pass.'

So much for romance, but what a picture the Battle of the Thirty conjures up if we look beyond the immediate situation! Here we have two garrisons of proud, ruthless, highly trained knights, eager to make a name for themselves yet frustrated by the inactivity of garrison life. Raids and foraging, and the occasional encounter with their rivals, serve to break the monotony of their existence, as well as giving the opportunity to ride about the countryside in full armour. Then the opportunity arises of engaging their rivals in a genuine knightly battle, exactly like the scenes they have always cherished from the romances – a battle just like the good old days, without the presence of foot soldiers. The battle is fought and won in a limbo of knightly virtue. Its effect on the overall conduct of the war in Brittany and beyond was insignificant, but, win or lose, at the level of knightly conduct it was the creation of a legend. There is no better illustration than this of the constant paradox of chivalric life: the idealization of behaviour being given its impetus by the unpleasant reality of the warfare they were required to carry out. In chivalry the two extremes come together. Several years later, as the English knights were due to set out with the Black Prince on his Spanish expedition, the chronicler refers to their eagerness

for 'chivalric encounters without foot soldiers and bourgeois'.

There can be no greater contrast with the Battle of the Thirty than the encounter which took place the following year only a few miles distant: the Battle of Mauron. Mauron was the result of a French attempt to reconquer Brittany and oust the English garrisons once and for all, and as such was fought with the weapons of reality. France now had a new king. Philip VI had died in August 1350, to be succeeded by his son John (Jean le Bon). The appellation 'the Good' indicated no particular moral stance, but rather should be taken as a lover of mirth and display. Like his rival, King Edward of England, John the Good revelled in tournaments and the gaudy trappings of chivalry. One of his first acts on becoming king was to found a French order of knighthood, the Order of the Star, to rival and, he hoped, eclipse Edward's Garter. On a wider scale, by August he had assembled sufficient knights and foot soldiers to attack Brittany. He sent an army to besiege the fortress of Fougères which held the key to the Breton Norman frontier. The attack was beaten off by Sir William Bentley, who promptly put in order the defences of the rest of the duchy.

The ideal of knightly warfare: the delicate features of the funerary effigy of John II, Duke of Brittany.

King John set a French knight, Guy de Nesle, in charge of his army with the title of Governor-General of Brittany. Early in August, de Nesle led his army over the border and marched on Rennes, intending ultimately to cross Brittany to Brest. Leaving Fougères wide on his right flank, de Nesle easily took Rennes, as Bentley was wisely concentrating his forces near Ploermel. He had two alternatives: to fall back towards Brest; or to advance north, cut off the route west to Brest, and give battle to the French army. Bentley decided upon the latter course – and all the recent military experience suggested a good chance of victory. Thus it was that on 14 August 1352, the rival armies were approaching each other near the town of Mauron.

Bentley had an army of about 3,000, and wisely chose to remain on the defensive. He drew up his forces dismounted in a single line with no reserve, the knights in the centre, the archers on the flanks. The French army, according to Baker's *Chronicle*, 'under the Marshal's leadership, of set purpose set up their position with a steep mountain slope behind them, so that they could not fly; their purpose was to increase their zeal for fighting by knowledge of the impossibility of flight, as is usual with courageous men. There were also present many of the Order of the Knights of the Star, who in their profession had sworn never in fear to turn their backs on their foes . . .'

Guy de Nesle had dismounted his soldiers, except for a single body of 700 knights whom he deployed on his left flank. These were the first into action, and charged the English archers on Bentley's right flank. It was the same situation as at Crécy, but here the results were very different. The archers gave way, and about thirty of them fled to the rear. The immediate result was that the knights on the

The reality of knightly warfare: a skull excavated from the grave pits of Wisby which still bears the remains of a mail hood similar to that depicted on the Duke of Brittany's peaceful head.

attack, but also led a counter-offensive. Encouraged by this, the English knights followed suit and soon the French army was broken, and victory plucked from the jaws of defeat.

The Battle of Mauron brought a temporary halt to the Breton civil war. The French had been so crushed that they were not to interfere until 1364, when Edward III would be calling the tune. It also made a sad end to King John's new Order of the Star. No less than eighty-nine of its new members fell at Mauron. The little-known battle was an English victory, but it had nearly been a defeat. The temporary embarrassment of the archers on the right flank, scattered by a well-timed cavalry charge, serves to illustrate the fact that archers were not invincible. The point I have made throughout, of the need for a combination of arms, is well shown by what had happened subsequently: the archers and knights supported one another in the counter-attack, which the French had failed to do in the initial stages.

THE RELIEF OF AQUITAINE

Possession of the Duchy of Aquitaine had been a major factor in Edward's original claim to the throne of France, but since 1341 Aquitaine had become a secondary theatre of military operations. Compared to the turmoil of Brittany and the *chevauchée*s of northern France and Normandy, Gascony had witnessed border skirmishing and little more. But as French influence waned in the more northerly territories, pressure increased on Gascony, leading to a group of pro-English Gascon nobles, including the Knight of the Garter, Jean de Grailly, Captal de Buch, to call on the King of England for help to withstand new French aggression. In July 1355, Edward responded by appointing his eldest son, Edward, Prince of Wales, as his Lieutenant in Gascony. It was the beginning of an extraordinarily successful association between the Black Prince and the duchy.

The nobility of chivalry, that honour which finds its highest expression in its recognition by an enemy, soon came to be personified in this young man during his reign in Aquitaine. Many chroniclers praise his military skill, the splendour of his court and his generosity. Superlatives pour from their pens in describing the prince's accomplishments. He was indeed a noble knight, and like most others began military operations to defend Gascony by the now familiar but unglamorous and brutal *chevauchée*.

He was accompanied by about 2,600 men, who had been brought across from England in July 1355, including a large number of experienced military

The defence of a fortified town. The defenders appear to be throwing everything at the attackers! Note the gateway hinged at the top, designed to be closed quickly in an emergency.

leaders, many of whom had fought with him at Crécy: the Earls of Warwick, Oxford, Suffolk and Salisbury, and knights such as Sir John Chandos and Sir James Audley. The *chevauchée* was launched in October, the initial objective being the lands of the Count of Armagnac. Much booty was taken, and great devastation was wrought. The important towns of Carcassonne and Narbonne were burned, although their inner castles withstood attack. In effect, the Black Prince demonstrated the extent of his powers by burning his way to the Mediterranean coast and back, avoiding pitched battles and all but minor skirmishes with French troops. The Gascons were delighted, especially those whose lands had been similarly ravaged by the Armagnac troops, and Bordeaux enjoyed the presence of a successful military leader in its midst.

After a few more limited operations the Black Prince set out on another major *chevauchée* in August 1356. The spring had seen a great build-up of supplies, horses and weapons destined for Gascony, and such was the demand that at one stage even arrows were in short supply. Edward had sent an agent to England to obtain 1,000 bows, 400 gross of bowstrings and 2,000 sheaves of arrows, but because the king had so many armies active (the Earl of Lancaster

had carried out a *chevauchée* in Normandy that summer, coming to within 75 miles of Paris) no arrows could be obtained, and the prince had to order his agent to Cheshire to seize available arrows from the fletchers. Once sufficient supplies had been procured the *chevauchée* went ahead, advancing north through Périgord towards Bourges. There was a skirmish at Romorantin, and from there the march led to the Loire near Tours, which he could not cross because all the bridges had been broken. Frustrated in his hope of linking up with Lancaster's army, the prince turned south and headed homeward, until he found that his way was blocked by a large French army at Poitiers.

Opposite: Edward the Black Prince of Wales, as he would have appeared at the Battle of Crécy and Poitiers, represented in the magnificent equestrian statue of him at Leeds.

THE BATTLE OF POITIERS

The result was one of the most famous battles of the Hundred Years' War. The prince's army was about 6,000 strong, and the French numbered more than 20,000. Prince Edward drew up his men behind a hedge which ran perpendicular to the road out of Poitiers just beyond a fork. The Earl of Salisbury commanded the right wing, the Earl of Warwick the left, while the Black Prince headed the reserve in the rear. The French army was deployed in four divisions. Only the vanguard, under Marshal d'Audrehem and Marshal Clermont, were mounted. Next came the Duke of Normandy, then the Duke of Orléans, and finally King John. For convenience on the march from Poitiers, where they had left their horses, they had discarded their spurs and had shortened the length of their lances to 5 feet.

By the morning of Monday, 19 September the French had shown no signs of attacking, and the Black Prince was thinking of moving off again towards home and safety. As a first step he began to move the supply wagons back, and this caused the French vanguard to think that the army was retreating. They therefore advanced to the attack in two columns, following the two roads through the hedge. Many broke through, protected from the fire of the archers by their breastplates, a new advance in military technology that looked towards the complete plate armour which would be seen later. Mail was already becoming a second line of defence, filling the gaps where, at this stage, the plates did not quite overlap. Defensive plates could now be provided for the inside of the arms as well as the outer surfaces,

Map of the Battle of Poitiers.

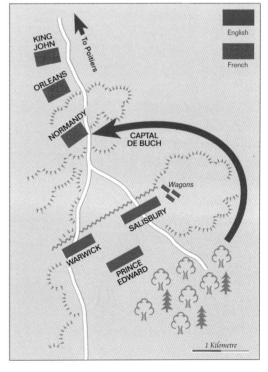

The Battle of Poitiers 1356, from Froissart's *Chronicles*. Once again, the English longbow was to be used to devastating effect. A stylized view of the castle of Poitiers, like Caerlaverock triangular in plan, is seen at the rear.

and for the rear of the legs. The aventail, which hung round the neck, was now the only mail part which showed, and in time this too would disappear from view. The Earl of Oxford took charge of the archers and ordered them to move sideways into the neighbouring marsh, which protected them from the over-zealous knights and allowed them to fire more obliquely at the unprotected horses rather than at the heavily armoured riders.

The second French column now arrived on foot. The hedge, which had offered some cover, was probably trampled flat and the masses of men-at-arms collided. Having exhausted the English troops, the French withdrew in good order, to leave room for a further assault by their comrades, but the following column, under the Duke of Orléans, had been so damaged by the archers that they had already fled the field without engaging. All that remained was the column of the King of France, still wending its way from Poitiers. This was a mighty force, however, and the English chroniclers are surprisingly frank about the effect its appearance had on the weary English. Baker tells us bluntly that 'the great number of the enemy frightened our men'. There may have been some desertions at this point, perhaps in the guise of escorting wounded to the rear, and there was certainly some grumbling about the number of men they had left behind to defend Gascony.

Sir Nele Loryng, one of the original Knights of the Garter, and a companion of the Black Prince during the Hundred Years' War. This illustration shows him in a robe ornamented by garters.

Statue of Edward le Despenser from his chantry in Tewkesbury Abbey. He was an early Knight of the Order of the Garter, and fought with distinction in Edward III's French Wars. He was present with Sir Nele Loryng at the skirmish near Romorantin and shortly afterwards took a prominent part in the Battle of Poitiers. This representation of a knight in a kneeling position is unique.

The Black Prince was faced with the most difficult decision of his career, but the result of his decision made him a hero. He could not have known about the disappearance of the Duke of Orléans's division, and must have thought that he was facing almost the entire French army, whose small vanguard had done so much to worst him. His army had been battered, but had maintained that defensive posture which had been the hallmark of the English since the beginning of the Hundred Years' War. The French were in the open, deficient in archers. It would be in the English tradition to let them come on. But Edward decided otherwise. With the decisiveness he had inherited from his father, the Black Prince ordered the English army to attack.

The knights mounted up and spurred their horses forward in a classic chivalric heavy cavalry charge. Two charges in fact took place – one frontally under Sir James Audley, the other, led by the Captal de Buch, into the French right flank. Following the mounted knights, the archers joined in. The great French column, assailed furiously on two sides, crumbled and broke. Geoffrey de Chargny, bearer of the sacred Oriflamme of France, was cut down and killed, and in the confusion a great prize came to hand. To capture a king? What honour, what glory awaited the man who could claim to have captured the King of France! And taken he was, by so many people that he was nearly crushed to death in the tumultuous fighting over his person. That night, among the field of the slain, the king sat down to supper with his captor – the Prince of Wales.

Poitiers was a major turning point in the Hundred Years' War. The King of France, the King of Scotland, and the Duke of Brittany were now all prisoners in England. It should have established Edward III as unquestioned conqueror of France. We will see in the next chapter why it did not quite do that, but Poitiers remains, tactically, one of the most perfect of medieval battles. It made the name of the Black Prince, and confirmed the ascendancy of English arms in the conventional warfare of the great pitched battle. During the next twenty years the French had to learn other ways of countering this tremendous challenge.

Poitiers is also the classic illustration of the combination of dismounted and mounted troops. It began as a repetition of Crécy, with the damage being done by the humble archers. It ended with as fine a cavalry action as any chivalric knight could have hoped for. If the knights had been bored by garrison work, disgusted by the *chevauchée*, and shamed by the archers, Poitiers was the perfect antidote to all these feelings which were so much a part of the cult of chivalry. Here a knight had commanded, and knights had led, as leaders of men and an elite in their own right. The Garter had gone to war, and returned victorious from a knights' battle.

John the Good, King of France, who was defeated at the Battle of Poitiers in 1356 and died in captivity in 1364.

Opposite: Caesar's Tower, Warwick Castle, as seen from across the River Avon. It is fourteenth-century work, and was finished early enough to house prisoners taken in 1356 at the Battle of Poitiers. The great tower, which rises 147 feet above its base, is built on solid rock and has never been mined.

The Ill-made Knight 4

As victories are better remembered than defeats, Jeanne d'Arc (Joan of Arc) is probably the one French name to be well known in England from the Hundred Years' War, but in this chapter I will examine how France performed a similar miracle of recovery in the third quarter of the fourteenth century. This revival stemmed from a number of factors, not the least of which was the service to the French king and the inspiration to the French armies, rendered by a Breton knight called Bertrand du Guesclin. Unlike the Maid of Orléans, he is practically unknown outside his own country, yet his unconventional style of warfare produced the counter to the terrible *chevauchée*, so that, although he was of lowly birth du Guesclin rose to the highest office that France could bestow.

The reason why du Guesclin's career is so little known outside France lies to some extent in the timing of his appearance on the military scene. While he was winning modest victories for France, his nobler, but less adaptable contemporaries were busy suffering catastrophic defeats, and the popular English chauvinism which tends to close the history books at Poitiers and reopen them at Agincourt dwells little on the years between. This chapter will perhaps make amends.

Bertrand du Guesclin was born in about the year 1320 near Dinan in Brittany. He was the eldest of ten children and apparently a bit of a handful, being boisterous to the point of brutality, his heavy features and incredible strength terrifying his younger brothers and sisters. Only the intervention of a nun, who foretold his future greatness, prevented his distraught parents from disowning him.

His adolescent years were spent, we are told, in organizing the local children in gangs to fight one another, the young Bertrand always playing the part of commander. In 1337, at the age of seventeen, he went to Rennes where a tournament was being held to honour the marriage of Charles de Blois with Jeanne de Penthièvre. He rode a carthorse belonging to his father, and was met by jeers from the well-to-do young knights assembled for the joust. His father, apparently, was there in an official capacity, which begs the question of why an impoverished Breton family had been invited to a tournament. In fact the whole incident is apocryphal, and comes from the pen of du Guesclin's first biographer, Cuvelier. His *Chronique de Bertrand du Guesclin* is a heroic poem composed shortly after du Guesclin's death in 1380, by which time he had already become a legend in his own lifetime. Cuvelier's work is one of the last flourishes of the *chanson de geste*, written by a man who was effectively one of the last minstrels, an admirer both of the knight who formed his subject, and the tradition of the heroic poets of the eleventh century. The *Chronique* is, therefore, a dramatic hagiography, embellished by some imagination, but, according to Cuvelier, based on eyewitness accounts by du Guesclin's contemporaries.

The tournament story finishes in suitable style. After his haughty dismissal we find our hero borrowing a horse and armour from one of his cousins who is just leaving, and with a closed visor concealing his identity this unknown knight enters the lists and proceeds to win every joust set against him. After a dozen combatants are unhorsed his own father presents a challenge. To the amazement of the crowd, Bertrand declines, but continues to joust with others, until a Norman knight opens his helmet with the point of his lance, displaying the stranger's identity to the admiring crowd and a delighted father.

The coat of arms of Bertrand de Guesclin is depicted here in stone relief work above the doorway of a house associated with du Guesclin in Dinan. The eagle is black, on a white field, with a red bend.

DU GUESCLIN GOES TO WAR

Little is known of du Guesclin's movements during the first years of the Breton civil war, except that he is mentioned as a man-at-arms in the Blois forces, and may have been present at the brief siege of Rennes by the Earl of Northampton in 1342. Such activities were the exception, because while English armies came and went du Guesclin began the form of warfare at which he was to make his name. For fifteen years he led a vigorous guerrilla campaign from the safety of the great, and to the Breton mind enchanted, forest of Paimpont, pouncing on isolated columns of English or de Montfort troops. He raided their castles and towns and harassed their communications. One of the earliest recorded exploits of du Guesclin, and one of the most dramatic, was the taking of the castle of Grand Fougeray. This incident probably happened late in 1350, if his nineteenth-century biographer, Luce, is to be believed in his statement that the Captain of Grand Fougeray was Robert Bembro, who was to meet his death at the Battle of the Thirty in May 1351.

Whoever the commander was, he was absent from the fortress when a band of woodcutters arrived at the gate bearing firewood. We may presume that du Guesclin's guerrilla operations had made the neighbouring forests hazardous for the English garrison, so the woodcutters and their faggots were welcomed into the castle. When the gate was opened the woodcutters revealed their true colours, flinging down the bundles of wood to prevent the gate from being closed, whereupon their companions joined them in the courtyard and attacked the garrison.

Glorious though such exploits were, du Guesclin was still little more than a self-employed brigand of lowly birth. His unconventional ways of fighting may have earned him the praise of the more far-sighted of his contemporaries, but guerrilla fighting was unglamorous work that found a place only in the practice of war and not in its code of conduct. Like *chevauchées*, partisan raiding was not a chivalric exercise. As a result du Guesclin did not receive the recognition he deserved, nor was he admitted to the honours of knighthood.

All this was to change within a few years by a simple but brilliant feat of arms rendered in person to a very senior French knight, the Marshal d'Audrehem. In March 1345 d'Audrehem had taken the castle of Landal in north-east Brittany, a useful strategic move as Landal was close to the major French coastal base of Pontorson. Encouraged by his success, d'Audrehem turned his attention towards one of the major English possessions in Brittany: the fortress of Bécherel, which lay midway between Rennes and Dinan. Scarcely 6 miles from Bécherel was Montmuran, a strong French-held castle, where lived the widow of Jean de Tinteniac, who had fallen at the Battle of Mauron. It being Holy Week she invited the Marshal and his reconnaissance party, which included du Guesclin, to join her in Montmuran on Maundy Thursday, 10 April 1354.

The Porte Saint-Pierre at Dinan, little changed from the time of the siege of Dinan by the Earl of Lancaster in 1357. The siege was an attempt to increase pressure on the already heavily invested city of Rennes, but guerrilla activity by du Guesclin and the resolution of the defenders led to the siege being abandoned.

King Charles V of France, who with his protégé, Bertrand du Guesclin, set in motion a series of military reforms that took advantage of the growing weakness of the English and led to the end of the first phase of the Hundred Years' War.

It is difficult to guess the social stance adopted by the guerrilla on this occasion, but his military mind was as active as usual, and whatever part he took in the festivities must have been a very brief one. The commander of Bécherel was Sir Hugh Calveley, a Cheshire knight of renown, whose reputation for surprise and ambuscade must have been near to that of du Guesclin's, for the latter warned d'Audrehem that it would be perfectly within the pattern of Calveley's operations for him to try a raid on Montmuran to seize the Marshal. (The humble du Guesclin would probably not have commanded a price.) To guard against a surprise attack du Guesclin concealed thirty archers along the road from Bécherel with orders to prevent any approach by Calveley and to warn the garrison of Montmuran.

His assumption proved correct, and on hearing the archers engaging with Calveley's troops both du Guesclin and d'Audrehem hurried to the scene of action and a fierce skirmish ensued. Sir Hugh Calveley, flung to the ground from his horse by a violent charge from a certain Enguerrand d'Hesdin, was captured as a prize. It was at this point, having fought fiercely and well, leaving few fugitive English to regain Bécherel and tell the tale, that du Guesclin was taken to one side by a knight of Caux called Eslatre des Mares, the Captain of the castle of Caen, and knighted on the field of battle, des Mares girding him with his own sword. According to a strong local tradition, the ceremony of knighthood was completed in the small chapel of Montmuran. Here du Guesclin received the white robe of knighthood, and from this time adopted his famous war cry 'Notre-Dame Guesclin!' which was soon to be heard on a wider stage.

Du Guesclin's achievement of knighthood was a major turning point in his life. Handicapped by his origins, and his very uncharacteristic willingness to lead a band of simple peasants in war, a prejudice had built up against him that only the good sense of someone like d'Audrehem could overcome. How unfortunate for France that the impetus given by his elevation could not have been properly exploited, that his ideas and style of warfare, so suited to the circumstances of the day, could not have been immediately adopted to counter the dreaded *chevauchée*. Instead, within two years France was to suffer the disaster of Poitiers, and from 1356 onwards the country was to reel like a ship without a helmsman under the pressure of English attacks.

While negotiations for King John's ransom continued, the Breton civil war came more into prominence. One month after Poitiers England's other notable prisoner was released. Upon payment of the bulk of his ransom, and following entreaties by Pope Innocent VI, Charles de Blois was given his liberty after nine long years. With what cynicism, one wonders, did Edward III agree to the deal? France lay prostrate at his feet, with only one outstanding matter to be settled – the question of Brittany. What better than to send back the cause of the trouble,

Opposite: The tower of the castle of Montmuran. It was in this tower that, according to tradition, Bertrand de Guesclin was admitted to the honours of knighthood in 1354. The building remains a superb example of medieval military architecture.

The ruins of Bécherel Castle in Brittany mark the site of a number of fierce and prolonged sieges during the fourteenth century. Bécherel was one of the strongest English bases in the peninsula, and withstood attacks by du Guesclin and de Clisson until it finally fell in 1373.

who would inevitably cause more disasters for France? Charles de Blois agreed to undertake no military action until the balance of his ransom was paid, and as a further precaution Edward also sent to France Charles's rival, John de Montfort. He, incidentally, was the son of the former John de Montfort, who had escaped from French custody in 1345 and died shortly afterwards. The young John was brought up in England. His valiant and strong-minded mother, Joan, Countess of Flanders, whose exploits fill so many pages of the beginning of the war, was now a virtual prisoner in Tickhill Castle, a royal fortress near Doncaster, where she had been confined on the grounds of suspected madness since coming to England.

THE SIEGE OF RENNES

In charge of the young de Montfort was Edward's trusted lieutenant, Henry of Lancaster, who was now given an official commission as Lieutenant of Brittany. Lancaster arrived in Brittany in August 1356, almost at the same time as Charles de Blois. He quickly assessed the military situation, and on 2 October began a siege of Rennes, which had remained stubbornly pro-Blois, in the name of John de Montfort, Duke of Brittany. It was likely to prove a difficult task for the small Anglo-Breton army. The line of the walls was long, and Lancaster had very little in the way of siege engines. On the other hand, the layout of the city was familiar from the brief attempt at siege in 1342, and the success at Calais had shown that almost anything was possible given time.

The French attempts to assemble a relieving force from among the post-Poitiers debris of their army were sincere, but limited in scope. The lord of Rochefort was appointed Captain, and established his headquarters at Vitre, nearly 20 miles due east, with 1,000 men-at-arms and 500 archers. It looked like being a time-consuming but ultimately successful operation for Lancaster – until Bertrand du Guesclin came on the scene and transformed a routine operation into a romantic drama.

Du Guesclin was not within Rennes when the siege began. He was born locally, and utterly familiar with the countryside, so Lancaster's patient blockade was the perfect target for his guerrilla operations. Avoiding pitched battle at all costs, du Guesclin led the French troops in raids on Lancaster's supply columns. These continued into the depths of winter, which was a particularly harsh one, suffered all the more uncomfortably by Lancaster's troops who were out in the open.

As the winter progressed du Guesclin's attacks became fiercer, and after each sortie he would retire to the comfort of Dinan, Fougères or Pontorson, living the life of a knight and fighting like a bandit. Never had the combination been so happily realized. So firm was his grip on the English troops that in January 1357 the dauphin Charles, who reigned as Regent of France during his father's captivity, was able to bring a relieving army as close as Dinan, where he established his headquarters. The presence of this more conventional army forced Lancaster to take upon himself the additional task of besieging Dinan, which would be difficult to accomplish if he were not to loosen his grip upon Rennes.

Although it is du Guesclin's name that has passed most prominently into history concerning the defence of Rennes, we must record the ingenuity of his companions within the city, which was under the command of Bertrand de Saint-Pern, captain of the city, and the Lord of Penhoet, keeper of the castle. Lancaster attempted to mine the walls, but by excellent organization of the populace, who were set to watch and listen for any signs of underground disturbance, the mine was discovered and skilfully countermined.

Lancaster thereupon tried a little psychological warfare. Knowing that the inhabitants were running short of food, and perhaps hoping to demonstrate that du Guesclin's raids were not a total success, the English drove a herd of 4,000 pigs before the walls of hungry Rennes. Naturally enough there was considerable pressure on Penhoet to make a sally and capture the pigs, but he was too astute to fall for such a trick. Instead, he ordered that the gate nearest the herd be opened, and suspended a piglet by its hind legs above the drawbridge. Its squeals soon drew the attention of the herd, which rapidly headed for the gate. The drawbridge was lowered, the piglet was released and as it scuttled back in, still squealing loudly, the herd obligingly followed, pursued by the angry English.

This stained glass window in the chapel at Montmuran Castle represents the surrender of Sir Hugh Calveley to Bertrand du Guesclin after his unsuccessful raid on the castle in April 1354. Calveley's aim had been to capture and hold to ransom the Marshal d'Audrehem, but du Guesclin frustrated the attempt, an achievement which gained him wide recognition.

Despite the hardships suffered by both sides, time seems to have been found for the chivalric niceties of war. Lancaster's operations against Dinan appear to have been quite successful, for a forty-day truce was negotiated, the garrison promising to surrender if they had not been relieved at the end of that period. As one of the supposedly relieving armies was presently shut up in Rennes, Lancaster must have thought the risk to be a reasonable one. Among the garrison in Dinan was one of du Guesclin's younger brothers. One morning the young man took it into his head to go riding outside the walls. Even this was a violation of the truce conditions, and it was with great embarrassment that Bertrand du Guesclin heard that his brother had been captured, and was being held by an English knight with an eye to business. Ransom was always worth a try, and it must have been with some glee that the Englishman discovered that his prisoner was the brother of one of the leading French commanders, which probably accounted for the price of 1,000 florins that he demanded. Du Guesclin, according to Cuvelier, turned red with rage and challenged the knight to single combat. The challenge was accepted, and the resulting duel took place in the centre of Dinan.

The pigs incident at the Porte Mordelaise, one of the few moments of light relief during the siege of Rennes.

The Englishman's name is something of a mystery. He is referred to as Thomas of Canterbury, and du Guesclin's biographer adds the tantalizing information that he was the brother of the then Archbishop of Canterbury. However, having briefly entered history this Thomas was soon abruptly to leave it. In the presence of the Duke of Lancaster, who had been permitted to enter the city as witness with twenty knights as escort, the two adversaries charged at each other with such force that both lances shattered on the other's shield. After a long spell of fighting with swords, Thomas struck downwards at du Guesclin's head. He missed and his sword skidded out of his hand. Du Guesclin got down from his horse, retrieved the sword and flung it across the square. Armed only with his dagger, the Englishman refused to continue on foot as du Guesclin invited him repeatedly to do. Instead he reared his horse at his dismounted rival, trying to trample du Guesclin beneath its feet. But du Guesclin had swiftly removed his leg armour and was able to dodge to one side. Forcing his sword upwards he struck deeply into the flanks of the horse. The animal reared out of control, depositing Thomas of Canterbury on the ground. Du Guesclin flung himself on his adversary, dragged off his helmet and punched him in the face. Blinded by his own blood, Thomas surrendered. The ransom was liquidated with no charge, the brother was set free, and the impetuous Thomas of Canterbury was dismissed from the English army.

Incidents such as this did far more than relieve the boredom of a siege operation. They provided the opportunity for 'sample warfare' to be carried out

Opposite: The Porte Mordelaise in Rennes, which is all that remains of the medieval walls of the city that withstood a siege from 1356 to 1357.

A figure of an archer, carved in wood, on the front of the house in Rennes where Bertrand du Guesclin is said to have stayed during the siege of the city from 1356 to 1357.

under carefully controlled conditions of truce and safe conduct, which were universally respected. To a successful side it meant an increase in morale with the death or disgrace of a vital member of the opposing side. To the loser it meant a loss in confidence without the total catastrophe of a failed assault.

Rennes was shortly to receive a further fillip to its morale. Tiring of his hit and run raids, du Guesclin was chafing to take a more active part in the defence of the city. His chance came when Penhoet decided to get a message out to Charles de Blois. One of the garrison passed through the lines and gave himself up as a deserter. On being admitted into Lancaster's presence, he stated that a relieving army was expected to arrive from the east the following night. His story was believed, and with the man acting as a guide a large detachment of English set out to intercept it. In the darkness the deserter slipped away to join du Guesclin for an ambush. The French immediately launched a raid on the lightly defended English camp, setting fire to the tents and looting their provisions. Laden with useful spoil, du Guesclin led a triumphant entry into the city.

The siege then continued lethargically, but on 23 March 1357 a treaty was signed at Bordeaux between England and France, and one of its clauses called for the immediate raising of the siege of Rennes. Despite orders from Edward III, Lancaster refused to comply until early July. His honour was at stake. He had with him in camp the young de Montfort, Duke of Brittany, in whose name the business had dragged on for nine long months, and Lancaster had sworn at the outset not to leave Rennes before he had placed his flag on the battlements. By late spring 1357 the city was suffering greatly from hunger, which not even the indomitable spirit of du Guesclin could do much about, and the garrison consented to surrender on payment of 100,000 crowns. At last Lancaster was satisfied. He entered Rennes ceremoniously and with much ostentation placed his banner on the wall. Du Guesclin came forward and offered him wine. The duke drank it and left the town. As soon as he had gone the banner was torn down and flung into the ditch.

Naturally enough, both sides claimed the siege of Rennes as a victory. To the French it was to become much more. As Orléans was to be fifty years later, the raising of the siege of Rennes, and its association with a charismatic hero figure, became a symbol of hope for France. Within a year of the shame of Poitiers, Rennes had provided an example of what could be achieved.

THE ABSENCE OF PEACE

Du Guesclin's tactics had been shown to be effective in French eyes, and there may be some echo of this in the subsequent request by the Duke of Lancaster to be allowed to return to England. To this the king consented, but only after the

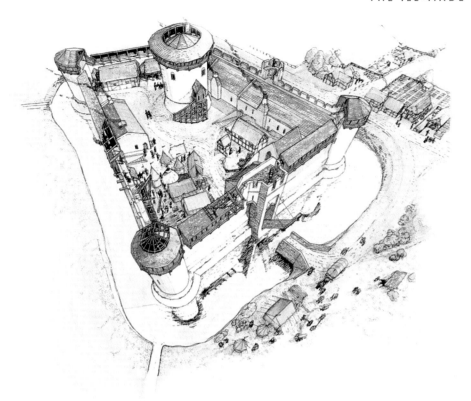

Skenfrith Castle, a fortress on the border between Wales and England, as it may have appeared during the fourteenth century. The curtain walls and towers are all shown with projecting wooden hourds, or fighting platforms. (Illustration by Chris Jones-Jenkins 1991, Cadw: *Welsh Historic Monuments* Crown Copyright)

duke had carried out a thorough review of the financial and administrative arrangements of the duchy of Brittany. Finance presented the greatest problem. It was comparatively simple to raise money for short-term expeditionary forces and *chevauchée*s, and once the troops had returned home victorious and laden with booty they were taken off the pay-roll. But garrison life was different. Local taxes were difficult to gather, and had the added disadvantage of alienating pro-de Montfort Bretons, many of whom changed sides during the 1350s. Large garrisons with time on their hands and suffering irregular payment of wages made matters much worse by what is politely known as 'irregular foraging', the situation that had led to the Battle of the Thirty. Such points were recorded in a memorandum by Sir William Bentley, who served as Lieutenant of Brittany in 1350–53 and was given extensive powers of inspection and supervision. Discipline within the Anglo-Breton army was to be tightened. Wages were to be paid according to orders. Soldiers were to be ready for action when required, and would not be allowed to leave Brittany without Sir William Bentley's permission.

Against this background of rebellious subjects, weak loyalties towards the English nominee, and the presence of large numbers of under-employed English soldiers irregularly paid, du Guesclin continued his tireless work of wearing down English resistance. Between the years 1358 and 1363 he was twice captured and subsequently ransomed.

The round keep of Skenfrith Castle as it may have appeared during the fourteenth century. The keep is shown without the later doorway cut into the basement level. (Illustration by Chris Jones-Jenkins 1991, Cadw: *Welsh Historic Monuments* Crown Copyright)

Opposite: The tower of Skenfrith Castle as it is today. The earthen mound was heaped round the base of the tower after its construction.

Officially, of course, the country was at peace. The Truce of Bordeaux lasted for two years, and was then extended in the confusion of negotiation over the payment of the French king's ransom. But somehow the talks never reached a satisfactory conclusion, and the English demands continued to rise. Their garrisons were now well established in Brittany, Anjou, Maine, Touraine and Burgundy. Foreign armies crossed France with impunity, and lawless bands of unemployed, former mercenaries carried out their own private raids and feuds.

On the grand scale of things, Edward III was preparing the *coup de grâce* of a triumphal march across France with a huge army, the culmination being a coronation ceremony for himself at Reims. The result was not quite so spectacular, but ended in the Treaty of Brétigny, sealed by both monarchs in 1360, which guaranteed the English possession of Gascony. It also bought France a breathing space, although King John had not long to live. He died on 8 April 1364, and his body was conveyed from its exile in England with great pomp and solemnity, to be received with sadness by the new monarch, Charles V.

So far as the reconstruction of France's military power was concerned, the truce was real enough, and in three particular instances the new king, and his trusted champion, Bertrand du Guesclin, began to rebuild a force and a reputation. The first challenge concerned the inheritance of Charles V's younger brother, Philip.

The dukedom of Burgundy became vacant in 1361, and the late king had promised it to his young son, who, at the age of fourteen, had fought valiantly beside his father at Poitiers. But there was one other claimant, by an argument every bit as complicated as the Breton succession, on behalf of Charles the Bad, King of Navarre. The military threat from Charles the Bad was a very real one, because such was the state of France that a few determined mercenaries could easily besiege Paris. Furthermore, Charles the Bad had extensive possessions in Normandy, including the castles of Meulan and Mantes. The new king, whose coronation had not yet taken place, entrusted the handling of events to du Guesclin, who took the role of regular soldier to present the king, by way of a gift on his accession, with a brilliant victory in the pitched battle of Cocherel, on 16 May 1364.

At Cocherel, which is in Normandy, the forces of the King of Navarre were augmented by a large Anglo-Gascon contingent, the whole being under the command of Jean de Grailly, Captal de Buch, the same renowned Knight of the Garter who had fought at Poitiers. His army took up a defensive position on the small hill of Cocherel, planting their banner in the centre as a rallying-point. The Captal, in the English tradition, gave orders that the army was to maintain height and let the French come to them. At the request of the Count of Auxerre, the senior French knight present, du Guesclin took command of the French forces and detached thirty brave knights for an assault on the Captal's command post. This provoked little response so, holding most of his troops in reserve, du Guesclin launched a larger frontal attack followed by a feigned retreat. Such manoeuvres are always difficult to execute effectively, but du Guesclin seems to have got it right, and some at least of the Captal's army followed in pursuit. The Captal had little alternative but to follow, at which point du Guesclin delivered a flank attack from his reserves which assured a French victory.

Cocherel brought du Guesclin great renown. He had shown his new monarch that he was able to win conventional battles as well as raids and skirmishes. Admittedly Cocherel was not fought against a full English army, but it augured well for the new partnership that was being formed between the king and his lieutenant.

THE BATTLE OF AURAY

The second great problem of Charles V's reign was also solved with the assistance of du Guesclin, but with less happy results. In 1362 Edward III had again played the Breton card, once more returning John de Montfort, now grown to manhood, to his troubled duchy. For the English garrisons in Brittany the proposed renewal of the conflict was welcome relief from the boredom of occupation, and the French resources to oppose them were stretched to the limit. Bertrand du

Guesclin could not be in two places at once, and the campaign against Charles the Bad kept him from taking a full part in Brittany until 1363, when he conducted a siege against the English hornet's nest of Bécherel. The castle held out (it was to provide a challenge for many years to come), so du Guesclin rejoined the army of Charles de Blois for a march to relieve the castle of Auray.

Auray is a picturesque town situated on the southern coast of Brittany, some 10 miles from Vannes. It is built on the bank of the River Loch, crossed at the town by a beautifully preserved medieval bridge. In 1364 its castle, of which nothing now remains, was under siege from the de Montfort party and their English allies. The defenders of Auray had made an agreement with the besiegers that they would surrender if they were not relieved by a certain day.

The Battle of Auray, 1364. John de Montfort (on right) with his English allies, defeated Charles de Blois in this decisive battle.

By the evening of the day before the expiry date, a relieving army was encamped across the river, waiting the chance to settle the issue.

John de Montfort wished to attack the French, but was dissuaded by two of his captains, Sir Robert Knowles and Olivier de Clisson, du Guesclin's great Breton rival, who pointed out that the river was deep and the ground marshy, as it is to this day, and that the French camp was well defended by a palisade. An attempt at settlement was summarily rejected by Charles de Blois, so John de Montfort passed the complete control of his army into the capable hands of Sir John Chandos, who posted scouts along the river to watch for French movement, and forbade any nocturnal raiding.

On St Michael's Day, 29 September 1364, the Franco-Breton army, led by du Guesclin, began to cross the River Loch to line up north of the Anglo-Breton positions. Today there is a small bridge where the river narrows at the north of the Kerzo marsh, which may well mark the actual crossing point. The movement went without incident, for an afternoon's truce had been arranged by Jean de Beaumanoir on the Blois side. It seems incredible that such gentlemanly negotiations could take place and allow the French to form order of battle unmolested, but from Chandos's point of view it was a sensible decision.

The site of the Battle of Auray in 1364, which settled decisively the question of the Breton succession. Charles de Blois was killed at Auray and Bertrand du Guesclin was captured. This photograph is taken from the bridge at the north of the Kerzo marsh, which probably marks the spot where the French army crossed the river prior to engaging the English.

It fulfilled the requirements of the deal made about the siege. It drew the French out of their fortified camp and the protection of the marsh, and above all it made a decisive battle that much more likely. The Breton civil war had dragged on for twenty-five years, and now the two claimants were present with every hope of a conclusive result. Let them cross in peace, reasoned Chandos, and settle the matter by battle. Chilling confirmation of this is indicated by the similar orders from the commanders of both sides before the battle began: no ransom for either de Montfort or de Blois. Auray was to be to the death.

The Franco-Breton army crossed the river in the four 'battles' it would deploy for the ensuing struggle. The first, under du Guesclin, consisted of knights and squires of Brittany. The Earl of Auxerre, who had fought beside him at Cocherel, took the second, which was composed mainly of French troops, while Charles de Blois had personal command of the third. The rearguard was under various French knights, including de Raix, de Rieux and du Pont. Each division consisted of about 1,000 men.

The Anglo-Breton army opposed them with a similar disposition. Olivier de Clisson and his pro-de Montfort Bretons faced the Count of Auxerre. Sir Robert Knowles, Sir Walter Huet and Sir Richard Burley opposed du Guesclin's division, while John de Montfort faced his rival Charles de Blois. Sir Hugh Calveley, after some protest, took charge of the rearguard. In Froissart's picturesque description of the scene 'the troops of the Lord Charles were in their best and most handsomest order, and drawn up in the most brilliant manner . . . they marched in such close order that one could not throw a tennis ball among them'.

The battle began with skirmishing between the forward spearmen and an exchange of archery fire, which did little harm because both sides were dismounted. As the archers shouldered their bows and fought hand to hand, Charles de Blois launched a vigorous charge against de Montfort which entered deep into his ranks, forcing Sir Hugh Calveley to bring up the rearguard in support. Sir John Chandos fought a commander's battle, moving from one part of the field to another advising and calling up fresh troops. Olivier de Clisson wielded his battleaxe to great effect against Auxerre, until a French battleaxe struck off the visor from his helmet and the point destroyed his eye. The Count of Auxerre was captured, and, seizing the advantage, Chandos launched a major advance supported by Calveley, and headed straight for du Guesclin's division. Some of the French had already begun to retreat. Du Guesclin fought like a desperate man. Having broken all his weapons he was striking out with his iron gauntlets when Chandos pushed through the mêlée and persuaded him to surrender. The words the chronicler puts into Chandos's mouth are so natural they must be near the actual words spoken: 'The day is not yours, Messire Bertrand: you will be luckier another time.' He was luckier indeed than Charles de Blois.

The funerary effigy of Olivier de Clisson, nicknamed 'The Butcher'. De Clisson began his military career fighting on the side of the English, and lost an eye at the Battle of Auray in 1364. He then joined his fellow Breton Bertrand de Guesclin as a loyal soldier for King Charles V. He became Constable of France after du Guesclin's death, and is buried at the Cathedral of Notre Dame des Ronciers in Josselin.

There are two versions of Charles de Blois's death: the inevitable propaganda one of later times, that he was captured and then foully murdered, and the more likely version that he died in the thick of the battle, fighting bravely. Elsewhere in the field another debt of vengeance was paid. Olivier de Clisson had been only a boy in 1343 when his father, suspected of treason, had been executed by order of the King of France. No prisoners were taken by his division, leading to the nickname of 'the Butcher', which he was to bear for the rest of his life. The most reliable figures indicate that French casualties at Auray numbered about 1,000 dead and 1,500 prisoners. Charles de Blois was dead, so John de Montfort became indisputably Duke John IV of Brittany. The strange sequel to the story is that for some reason best known to himself he then paid homage to the French king! As du Guesclin was speedily ransomed the Battle of Auray began to look like a French victory.

The keep of the castle of Dinan is one of the finest examples of the revival of castle building in France at the end of the fourteenth and beginning of the fifteenth century, the result of the defensive policy of King Charles V.

THE BATTLE OF NÁJERA

The next we hear of du Guesclin is of him fighting in Spain as a mercenary against Pedro the Cruel, King of Aragon. Among his motley band were Sir Hugh Calveley and Matthew Gournay. Calveley's presence is particularly ironic. He and du Guesclin had fought each other for the past twelve years since the affair at Montmuran, and in that time each had separately captured the other and held him to ransom! But the whole situation was bizarre. The presence of the mercenary companies disguised the fact that it was an official French campaign, and anyone who asked awkward questions was told they were going on a crusade against the Moors of Granada.

The initial campaign proved an easy one. Pedro the Cruel fled and Henry of Trastamare was crowned King of Castile in Burgos Cathedral, but when Pedro returned to the fray he was accompanied not only by mercenaries, but by the mighty Black Prince. Approximately half his expeditionary force were English troops and soldiers from the Gascony garrisons. The rest were made up from English 'Free Companies' (the mercenaries who are described in detail in Chapter 6), Pedro the Cruel's own soldiers, and an international band recruited by Sir Robert Knowles. In all, the force totalled about 10,000 men. They began to cross the Pyrenees in mid-February 1367, ascending the Pass of Roncesvalles through deep snow.

The Marshal d'Audrehem supported du Guesclin's suggestion that their best tactics would be to avoid a pitched battle at all costs and bottle up the English in the northern mountains, but Henry of Trastamare wanted to fight for his throne. When the Black Prince eventually came down from the mountains to the easier terrain, Henry followed a parallel course, and established himself between the Black Prince and Burgos at a little hamlet called Nájera, the River Najarilla separating him from the prince's force.

On Friday, 2 April 1367, the English scouts reported to the Black Prince the astonishing news that Henry had abandoned his position behind the Najarilla and had advanced down the road towards them. His former position would

Map of the Spanish Campaigns.

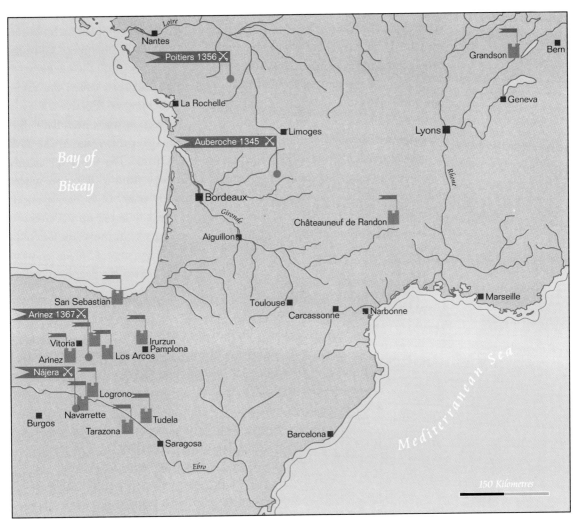

An English Great Helm c.1370. (Board of the Trustees of the Royal Armouries IV 600)

His first moves were political, with a little dabbling in the affairs of the duchy of Aquitaine, which was in complete contravention of the Treaty of Brétigny. When the English response came it served only to demonstrate what Charles had suspected and hoped for – that the ailing Edward III was no longer capable of original military thought. Once again it was the same pattern of *chevauchée* raiding. In 1369 John of Gaunt marched from Calais to Harfleur and back without achieving anything. The following year Sir Robert Knowles landed at Calais and marched straight on the Ile de France, burning the Parisian countryside and defying the king in his own capital. It was a daring raid, made more remarkable in that it was led by a knight who was a mere commoner instead of a noble, an almost unique event.

The French king's riposte to a commoner's incursion was to set his own great commoner against him, and du Guesclin was raised to the highest military office that France could bestow – that of Constable, giving him full command of the entire French military effort. It was the summit of du Guesclin's achievements. Perhaps moved by the promotion of his fellow Breton, Olivier de Clisson, who had fought du Guesclin at Auray and Nájera, and then sworn loyalty to the French king, joined du Guesclin in a military alliance of tremendous potential.

Charles V knew what his father and grandfather had suffered at the hands of the English *chevauchée*s, but he also knew how du Guesclin had countered them. Twenty years of experience were now brought to bear against the latest *chevauchée* and the English garrisons. To complement these operations Charles V entrusted the more aristocratic and conventional Duke of Anjou with the task of taking the war to the English in Gascony, which he proceeded to do with a subtle combination of siegework and political persuasion.

Opposite: The main gateway tower of the castle of Vitre. Together with Fougères, Vitre was a major fortress on the borders between Brittany and the rest of France. This tower has been carefully restored and provides a characteristic example of French military architecture of the period.

Meanwhile du Guesclin and de Clisson harried Knowles's columns remorselessly, picking off stragglers, launching night attacks, and reducing the hard commander to a state of indecision. Knowles began to retreat towards Brittany, where he hoped to find some refuge among the remaining garrisons with local, pro-English, support. But 'the Butcher' had sealed his fate. On 4 December 1370, de Clisson and du Guesclin fell upon Knowles's rearguard at Pontvallain, near Le Mans, and annihilated it. The victory, the nearest thing to a pitched battle the French had dared attempt, became the first French success against an entirely English army since Poitiers. Knowles's remnant struggled home to tell the tale. That is what comes, said his aristocratic superiors, of entrusting the command of an English expeditionary force to a mere commoner. But their criticism was misdirected. Knowles's failure came about because of lack of discipline in an army accustomed to brave adventuring. Frustrated by delay and French attack, his army had fragmented, the rearguard choosing to go its own way, and paying the price. Nonetheless, Knowles had to suffer considerable mortification before he was readmitted to the king's pleasure.

One by one the great English knights were coming to the end of their careers. Late in 1369 Sir John Chandos, gallantly defending Aquitaine, attempted an ambush of a party of French soldiers. The morning was cold, and the ground was frozen solid. Since losing an eye in a hunting accident five years previously Chandos had never worn a visor. Descending from his horse to assist a fallen esquire who was being attacked by a group of Frenchmen, his foot caught in the long white armour robe that he was wearing against the cold. When he slipped on the icy ground he was recognized and swiftly seized. The point of a spear was thrust into the open helmet, ending the life of the architect of Poitiers and Auray.

The Prince of Wales, whose life was also rapidly slipping to an end, completed a ruthless career by an act of strange brutality. In Gascony defections were occurring right, left and centre, but when the supposedly loyal Limoges rebelled it was too much to bear. That the gates of the city had been opened to the French forces by the Bishop of Limoges, the godfather of the prince's son Richard, added insult to injury. The Black Prince, a sick man, overreacted totally. He supervised a fierce siege from the litter in which he was forced to be carried, and when the town fell allowed a brutal sack and massacre. Historians have argued long about the rights and wrongs of the prince's action. It has even been pointed out that the sack of Limoges was fully within the rules of war as they were accepted at the time. So it may have been. The important point about Limoges is that the prince's action was totally unnecessary. It could never have achieved anything. If it were meant to terrorize other towns into confirming English rule, the Black Prince showed a deplorable lack of appreciation of the psychology of a populace who know they are winning. The following year he returned to England for the last time. In a brutal age he had controlled his savagery with wisdom and good sense, until this final, pointless massacre.

In 1372 the Earl of Pembroke, newly named Lieutenant of Aquitaine, sailed for the troubled province with an urgently needed relieving army. As his ships approached La Rochelle they were attacked by a dozen Castilian galleys. The battle lasted two days, and resulted in the total destruction of the English ships and the capture of the earl. With the lines of communication cut on the direct sea route, the Gascon strongholds began to topple before the combined efforts of the Duke of Anjou, du Guesclin, and de Clisson. Poitiers (August 1372) and La Rochelle (September 1372) opened their gates to the French without resistance. In a battle at Soubise in that same August, the English suffered a further blow in the capture of Jean de Grailly, the Captal de Buch. For the first time in the Hundred Years' War, military sense took precedence over the profit motive, and ransom was refused. This new policy of Charles V was highly unpopular among the French knights, and particularly so with the esquire who had actually captured him, but the decision was a sign of the times, and the unfortunate Captal remained in captivity in Paris until his death in 1376.

Ironically, du Guesclin's native Brittany remained the one place in the west where an English army could land relatively safely and where a raiding party could seek sanctuary. The continued existence of English garrisons in the duchy resulted almost entirely from the duke's less than total loyalty to the pledge he had made to Charles V. In 1372 he finally threw off his mask, repudiated his homage to the French king, and fled to England from where, in 1373, a 4,000-strong English army came to Saint-Malo, though the duke was not with them. A rapid advance by du Guesclin from Rennes forced them to re-embark and sail round the peninsula to Brest, where they provided a welcome supplement to the garrison. Du Guesclin, however, had demonstrated to Edward III that the north coast of Brittany could not be relied upon as a staging post for Aquitaine. He reinforced the point by taking Bécherel, which still dominated the peninsula, and in spite of attacks had resisted him since 1363. As a further gesture he used Saint-Malo as a base for a raid on Jersey.

While Olivier de Clisson laid siege to Brest, du Guesclin hurried back to Paris in August 1373. John of Gaunt had landed at Calais, and was leading the largest and most destructive *chevauchée* that France had seen for many years. Gaunt appears initially to have had no great aim apart from the usual one of causing havoc, but it soon became evident that he planned to march right across France to relieve Gascony. He actually reached his target, and the arrival of his bedraggled army, depleted and harassed by du Guesclin, must have put heart into the defenders of Bordeaux. But the state of Gaunt's troops, weakened and weary of the war, only showed in microcosm the general feeling on both sides. Charles V had restarted the war and was winning, but he feared that he had not the resources to finish it. In

Sunset over Saint-Malo. In 1373 Bertrand du Guesclin used Saint-Malo as a base for a raid on Jersey. In 1378 he negotiated with Sir Hugh Calveley the withdrawal of an English expeditionary force which used Saint-Malo as a landing stage.

January 1374 du Guesclin concluded a local peace with John of Gaunt, which eventually spread to a general truce. In 1376 the Black Prince died, followed within a year by his father, the mighty King Edward III. On every hand men were tired of war.

For Charles V there remained a little local difficulty concerning the Duke of Brittany. In December 1378 the duke was accused of treachery and Brittany was annexed to the French Crown. Even though du Guesclin and de Clisson supported the king, the act proved to be an immense miscalculation. The population rose as one in support of the de Montfort duke, giving du Guesclin the unsavoury task of going to war against his own countrymen. The Constable demonstrated an acute political skill which he had never before had the opportunity to employ. In a rare example of a negotiated settlement, du Guesclin managed to persuade an English army to return home without a fight. The commander, incidentally, was none other than Sir Hugh Calveley. What conversation, what reminiscences, must have been exchanged by these two men – now the elder statesmen of their respective armies?

Following this temporary solution du Guesclin settled in Brittany, perhaps hoping for a well-earned retirement. He was, after all, nearly sixty years old, and had been fighting throughout his entire life, but a final call came from his king. The people of Languedoc had rebelled against the Duke of Anjou and threatened the newly found stability of the area. It was to be du Guesclin's last campaign. Bidding farewell to Brittany at the cathedral of Dol de Bretagne, where he reviewed his troops, he drove the brigands from Auvergne, and laid siege to a fortress called Châteauneuf de Randon. Here he was taken suddenly ill, and rapidly slowed down from the furious pace at which he had habitually lived his life. Forced to command the siege from his bed, he died there on 13 July 1380. The captain of the besieged castle, moved by the unexpectedness with which he had become part of a moment of history, brought the keys of the castle and laid them on du Guesclin's body.

So died the great, tough little Breton. His life was unique in its military style, breaking all the social conventions of the day, and even in death he aspired to a certain renown, for such were the demands for the honour of providing his last resting-place that his body literally had to be shared. Whereas it was customary for the remains of Kings of France to be separated into heart, skeleton and entrails for burial in three places, the great Constable's were laid to rest in four. His entrails were interred in the Church of the Jacobins at Puy and his flesh at Montferrand. It had been his wish to be buried at Dinan, in his native Brittany, but his heart was all that the king would allow. What was left of him was placed in Saint-Denis, beside the tomb which Charles V had prepared for himself, and which he was to occupy only two months later. Du Guesclin's heavy features and stocky build are well represented in the alabaster effigy of him, which is not that of the romantic, stylized knight, but of a sincere man of the people. At his feet, in place of the customary lion, is a dog, the symbol of fidelity.

Alabaster effigy of Sir Hugh Calveley, who died in 1393. Sir Hugh was one of the most famous captains of the Free Companies in the Hundred Years' War. He served in Spain during the invasion by mercenary companies, and later joined the army of the Black Prince. In 1380 he took part in an unsuccessful expedition to France led by the Duke of Gloucester.

Unlike Jeanne d'Arc, Bertrand du Guesclin gave out no prophecies and suffered no martyr's death. But as she was to do half a century later, he seized the moment when France could reassert herself after black despair. He rejoiced, quite naturally, in the honours and titles heaped upon him: Count of Longueville, Duke of Molina, Earl of Trastamare, Constable of France, but always retained that common touch which enabled him to understand the mind of the ordinary soldier he had once been, whether to lead him or to oppose him. Had his patient strategy been heeded by those who came after him, Henry V's army would never have reached Agincourt in one piece, and the Hundred Years' War would have been known by another name.

The funerary effigy of Bertrand du Guesclin is far from the traditional stylized monument. Here is the simple man of the people, who rose from obscurity to the highest military honours that France could bestow. This cast of the original statue, which is in Saint-Denis, is preserved in the castle of Dinan.

The Last Crusaders 5

As wars had now temporarily ceased between France and England the knightly virtues had to find expression in other ways, and of all the possible expressions of chivalry, none encompassed its ideals better than a crusade. Edward III, however, was not an enthusiast for crusading. It suited his plans better to let the idea of a crusade slowly die away so that the notion of a chivalric brotherhood, which the crusades had previously represented, could be harnessed as a means of national politics and expressed as service to the monarch, a notion that found its consummation in the Order of the Garter.

In spite of Edward III's lack of support, the idea of taking the Cross and making war against 'the innumerable throng of Satan's satellites' remained the epitome of everything in which the knight professed to believe. When one monkish chronicler heard of the awful casualties at Crécy he lamented that the combatants had merely been killed 'for the sake of an earthly kingdom', at which unhappy state of affairs there would be 'rejoicing at the event among the citizens of Hell'. How much better, he argued, if they had been 'stained in waves of their own blood by infidels, on behalf of the celestial kingdom and for the defence of the Catholic Faith'.

During the first phase of the Hundred Years' War a crusade could also provide an honourable solution to any problem of conflicting loyalties. A certain Gascon knight, Sir Aymenion de Pommiers, was torn between his duty to France and to England, and resolved that instead of joining either party he would 'take the Cross and go as a pilgrim to Jerusalem and many other fair places'. As Jerusalem was now unattainable, the growing power of the Turks provided a new challenge, and in 1365 a number of Gascon and English knights took advantage of the lull in the fighting occasioned by the peace of Brétigny to join King Peter of Cyprus in his expedition to Alexandria. The Turks, however, were an enemy that required an essentially large-scale response. For a knight who wished to see personal action, collect some booty and receive remission for his sins while doing so, there was one outstanding theatre of operations – the long crusade against pagan Lithuania that was being conducted by the Teutonic Knights.

Opposite: Henry IV, the most illustrious of Lithuanian crusaders from England, depicted in a stained glass window in Canterbury Cathedral

THE TEUTONIC ORDER

Throughout their stormy history, and long after their eventual disappearance in 1525, the Teutonic Knights of Germany have provoked strong emotions. Lauded as the Christian conquerors of pagan Prussia, pitied as the Mongols' victims at Liegnitz, and reviled for their methods and mythologies as proto-Nazis, they have always been the most controversial brotherhood ever to have called themselves 'Knights of Christ'.

The Teutonic Order had its origins in about 1190 as a makeshift field hospital at Acre, where its brethren were committed to caring for the sick and assisting in the defence or recovery of the holy places in a similar fashion to the more numerous members of the Knights Templar and the Knights Hospitaller. By 1197 they had received a charter of incorporation from the pope, and when the German emperor Frederick II took the Cross in 1215 the Order's fortunes improved by leaps and bounds.

The conquest of heathen lands now became the brothers' new *raison d'être*, but, unlike the other military orders, the Teutonic Knights, who were over-whelmingly German in their recruitment and composition, were often able to campaign far nearer to home. In place of the heat and the barren wilderness of Palestine, these northern crusaders pursued the pagan foe among the cold and gloom of the forests and rivers of the Baltic, until by 1283, according to the Order's chronicler, the conquest of heathen Prussia was complete. Their next target was Lithuania.

A knight of the Teutonic Order during the late thirteenth century, wearing mail armour and a long white surcoat.

THE LITHUANIAN CRUSADES

The Lithuanians were the last pagan people in Europe, and fought fiercely under the protection of Perkun, the god of the thunderbolt, the greatest among many other benevolent deities. The extent of the Lithuanian conquests had meant that most of their new subjects were Orthodox Christians, and their geographical situation also ensured that they were hemmed in on two sides by Catholic states: the Teutonic Knights, who barred their access to the Baltic Sea, and the kingdom of Poland.

Both were enemies of Lithuania. Raids into Poland had long been a feature of Lithuanian military life, but of the two the Teutonic Knights were the more dangerous. They first came into conflict with the Lithuanians when both sought to exploit the same peoples whose lands they coveted, and by the end of the thirteenth century it was obvious that the territory owned by the Teutonic Order lay under serious threat from the aggression of these pagan warriors. The loss of Acre in 1291 had ensured that the Order had no future in the Holy Land, so the campaign against the Lithuanians quickly took on all the hallmarks

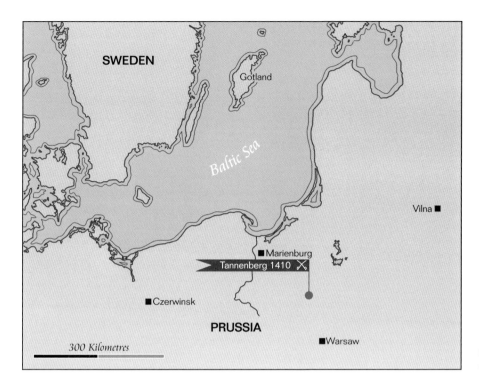

Map of the Lithuanian crusades.

of a true crusade, where the enemy were heathens, the fighting was bloody, and the plunder was enormous. It eventually became a hundred years' war conducted with great brutality on both sides. Captured Teutonic commanders could find themselves being burned alive or suffocated by smoke as they were sacrificed to the heathen gods, and doomed Lithuanian garrisons often preferred death at their own hands to a crusaders' massacre.

Yet midway through this bitter war of attrition and brutality the Order also faced a severe challenge from another direction, because the whole concept of knightly Orders and their conduct was being questioned at the highest ecclesiastical level. In 1307 Pope Clement V authorized the arrest and dispossession of the Knights Templars. Many of the charges were evident nonsense, but the ease with which they were pursued alarmed the Teutonic Order, who would have to face accusations that were more serious and much better substantiated.

Seeking to distance himself physically from the scandal that daily threatened to erupt, the then Grand Master left Venice in 1309 and established his headquarters within his own Prussian territory at Marienburg castle, which is now Malbork in Poland. He was not a moment too soon, because the following June Clement V issued a Bull which authorized a full investigation of the charges that had been made against the Order, who had been 'waging war on such people against Christ, and with various cunning ruses'.

With such a threat hanging over them the Teutonic Knights decided that their best course of action was to demonstrate to the pope that they were carrying out their crusading role with efficiency and success, so the war against Lithuania was stepped up. It was therefore politics rather than proselytism that sealed the destinies of the Teutonic Knights and their Lithuanian enemies.

CRUSADER TOURISM

One remarkable feature of the Lithuanian crusades was the ease with which the Teutonic Order recruited noble supporters from outside its own ranks to join in the endeavours. Such ventures were always temporary and often of short duration, and some attempts at 'crusader tourism' were simply cancelled because of bad weather even after the distinguished guest crusader had arrived in Marienburg. In 1394 the Duke of Burgundy wrote to the Grand Master asking if there would be a crusade the following year, and received the reply that it was impossible to guarantee any action, because so much depended on 'God's will and disposition, and also on the weather'. When the Duke of Austria arrived one year having made a vow to go on crusade before Christmas the Grand Master put on a token crusade in case the weather did not improve.

Many of the temporary crusaders genuinely cherished the ideals of an earlier age. King John of Bohemia, who was to meet his death at Poitiers in 1356, summed up this attitude when he wrote of the Teutonic Knights as 'an unbreakable wall to defend the faith against the Lithuanians and their partisans, whoever they may be – pestilential enemies of Christ'. To join such a noble undertaking was fully in keeping with chivalric principles, and was an opportunity that was too good to be missed. In addition there was the prospect of the joyful rediscovery of the companionship of the international brotherhood of knighthood that the Hundred Years' War had sundered, a feeling of group solidarity expressed in the drinking song:

The knight in this engraving, which is based on the tomb of Count Gunther von Schwarzburg, wears a full-skirted surcoat gathered at the waist.

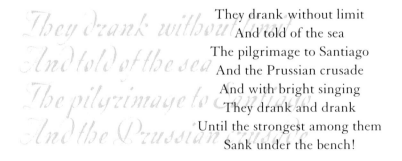

They drank without limit
And told of the sea
The pilgrimage to Santiago
And the Prussian crusade
And with bright singing
They drank and drank
Until the strongest among them
Sank under the bench!

Henry Bolingbroke, Earl of Derby and later King Henry IV, became the Order's most illustrious English visitor when he served with them in 1390, even if his fame as a northern crusader was to become eclipsed by an entirely fictional character in the person of Chaucer's knight. Bolingbroke took part in the siege of Vilnius, where the chronicler noted that 'he had many fine archers, who did much good', and his second expedition of 1392 also illustrated the financial benefit to the Teutonic Order of encouraging foreign nobles to go on safari with them. His retinue consisted of over 100 men, including six minstrels, at a total cost to the Lancastrian purse of £4,360, and much of this sum passed into the local economy through the purchase of silverware and the hiring of boats and equipment.

It is not hard to identify the reasons for such enthusiasm. By the end of the fourteenth century the opportunities for crusading against the Muslim world

Chaucer's knight, whom the author of *The Canterbury Tales* sent off on a crusade to Lithuania. Crusades conducted on behalf of the Teutonic Order against Lithuania provided military experience for a generation of knights.

had become few and far between. The battle of Nicopolis against Beyazid's Turks in 1395 was such a disaster that it well deserved the appellation commonly given to it of the 'Last Crusade'. But if opportunities were few, the doctrine still flourished of how the crusading vow ensured the remission of sins. As early as the 1260s German knights who did not belong to the Order went along as a penance, grateful for the local opportunity to discharge their obligation to God. There were collecting boxes for financing crusades in every parish, where regular reminders were issued from the pulpit, and after Nicopolis it was Lithuania alone that permitted penitential fervour to be expressed as a military campaign.

Conflicts such as the Hundred Years' War also meant that there were more professional fighting men about than ever before, and whenever there was a truce or a treaty hundreds of knights were left wondering how best to utilize their skills. Marshal Boucicault of France went to fight beside the Teutonic Knights on three occasions 'because there seemed to him that there was a great lack of warfare in France at that time'. Service as a mercenary in Spain or Italy did not have the same cachet, nor did any papal commission to fight Pisa ever promise the forgiveness of sins.

Whatever the motives of the visiting crusaders, there is no doubt that the Teutonic Knights took the whole business very seriously indeed, and even though they indulged the whims of some of their guests, their overall attitude towards such men as Henry Bolingbroke was to look upon them dispassionately and unemotionally as mercenaries who actually paid for themselves. The thirty-one-year rule of Grand Master Winrich von Kniprode from 1352 to 1382 was marked by a ruthless and pragmatic approach to the Lithuanian problem, of which the presence of the 'International brigade' drawn from European chivalry was but a detail in the equation of supply.

DANGEROUS TERRITORY

The overall strategy adopted by von Kniprode and his successors was one of raids, havoc and gradual conquest, a decision which owed much to the wild terrain over which the Lithuanian crusades were fought. Their opponents also showed a remarkable capacity to copy any innovation in warfare introduced by the Order and to use it against the knights themselves, so the construction of brick castles and the use of heavy siege weapons and gunpowder artillery gave the Order the upper hand for only a short time in each case.

Another important factor was the location of the Lithuanian castles upriver from the Teutonic strongpoints. As river transport was the only practical means of moving heavy cannon from place to place across the forested and swampy terrain, this meant that Lithuanian artillery could more easily bombard the knights' castles than the reverse. The first appearance of cannon on crusade was in 1381, and in 1384 the newly built fortress of Marienwerder fell after a six-week bombardment from Lithuanian guns, in spite of 'counter-battery' fire that put a Lithuanian trebuchet out of action by smashing its counterweight.

Such abrupt conclusions to military activities, however, were the exception to a general rule of long marches, trailblazing, wading through swamps led by local guides and general misery. Knights who set out on their own, or left the track, were more than likely to die of starvation or be drowned in a marsh. As noted above, river transport was a better alternative to trailblazing, and most of the fortified places on both sides followed the lines of the rivers. But even this was not without its problems, and the meandering nature of many rivers

How to topple the captured tower of an enemy using props that will be burned through.

slowed an army's progress considerably. A fifteenth century source described how the Niemen river was so winding that boatmen could spend a day going round one of its bends and then light their evening fire by walking a short distance over to the embers left in yesterday's camp. Heavy rain and snowfalls added to the difficulties. During the winter of 1323 common soldiers fell dead from the cold as they marched along, and armies often trudged through snowdrifts. Snow and ice melting into seas of mud made movement equally impossible. A hard frost, with little snow, made a winter campaign feasible, as did hot sun for summer activities, but sudden changes in the weather could be as devastating as a surprise attack by human enemies. In 1332 a Polish army was caught between two swollen lakes, and in 1348 the thawing of a river cut off the retreat of the fleeing Lithuanians.

Caught up in the middle of the long conflict were the ordinary peasants, whose fate may have been no more terrible than any of their contemporaries in Brittany or Normandy, but whose deaths were to give the Teutonic

Nowhere is the notion of 'fall' of a castle better illustrated than at Montecastrese, near Lucca in Tuscany. Here the victor toppled the castle's central tower, and it has lain on its side ever since. The base may be seen to the left.

Effigy of Heinrich Ulrech, 1397, from a sepulchral slab in Nordhausen.

Knights their dreadful reputation for violence. In 1372, we read of a Teutonic raider that 'he goes into the wilderness with a hundred picked men to plunder and harass the pagans . . . entering four villages that were not warned of their coming and putting to the sword whoever they find beginning their night's sleep: men, women and children'.

High-ranking Lithuanian knights fared much better when the great tradition of ransom became more universally applied. In part this was due to the influence of the visiting crusaders, but the Order was not slow to realize the profit that could be made from ransoming a prisoner. Eventually, any Lithuanian over the rank of knight who was captured had to be handed over to the Order for a fixed sum assessed on a sliding scale of nobility, and the Grand Master would then negotiate his release at a handsome sum.

THE CONVERSION OF LITHUANIA

These bizarre international expeditions continued into the fifteenth century in spite of an event that changed forever the balance of power between the Teutonic Knights and Lithuania. In 1386 Jogaila (1351–1434) ascended to the Lithuanian throne at the age of twenty-six. Although he was a renowned warrior Jogaila soon realized that he could not hope to hold off the two mighty powers of Poland and the Order at once. Conversion to Christianity, and the military alliance that would come with it, was only a matter of time. As conversion via the Teutonic route usually involved the point of a sword, Poland was by far the more attractive option, and the promise of a pretty young princess was an added inducement. So in February 1386 Jogaila accepted both baptism and a crown to become King Wladyslaw Jagiello of Poland, and for nearly two centuries afterwards the united Kingdom of Poland and the Grand Duchy of Lithuania would work to a common purpose, the first aim of which was the coordination of operations against the Teutonic Knights.

Wladyslaw Jagiello took his new role as a Christian monarch very seriously, and proceeded to convert Lithuania with a fervour that the Teutonic Order would have both recognized and admired. From his wedding in Cracow Wladyslaw went straight to his old capital of Vilnius and decreed the abolition of the ancient gods. The groves of sacred oaks were felled and a cathedral founded in their place. Mass baptismal ceremonies followed, with everyone receiving the same white robe and the same Christian name.

The reader may be forgiven for asking how the notion of a crusade could now be sustained when the intended victim had not only accepted baptism for himself and all his subjects, but had also allied himself through marriage with one of the staunchest Catholic countries in Europe. To the Teutonic Knights the answer was simple. Their problem was primarily a strategic one, because the military threat to their Order had not been diminished by the events of 1386. Indeed, the alliance between Poland and Lithuania meant that the challenge had greatly increased, and as for the Christian bit, the Order followed a policy of pretending that their enemies were actually Saracens. It was a comforting assurance that was given some minor semblance of truth by the presence of some genuine pagan survivors at the geographical extremities of the Poland/Lithuanian alliance, and it sufficed for the Henry Bolingbrokes of this world, who continued to go on crusade with the knights. The chronicler Monstrelet echoes this illusion when he notes in his commentary on Tannenberg that the King of Poland 'had just recently pretended to become a Christian in order to win the Polish crown'.

An alternative view looks at a different element in the situation, because among the most valuable booty taken by both sides throughout the long conflict were

A knight of the Teutonic Order dressed in the style of armour of the late fourteenth/early fifteenth century which would have been seen at Tannenberg. He wears the traditional white mantle bearing the black cross.

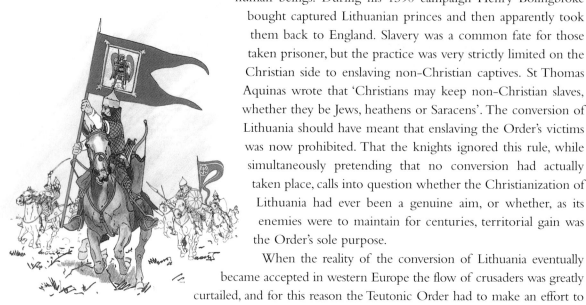

The banner of the Smolensk contingent of the Lithuanian army at the Battle of Tannenberg/Grunwald. (Reproduced with kind permission from Banderia apud Grunwald [Banners at Grunwald] by Andrzej Klein.)

human beings. During his 1390 campaign Henry Bolingbroke bought captured Lithuanian princes and then apparently took them back to England. Slavery was a common fate for those taken prisoner, but the practice was very strictly limited on the Christian side to enslaving non-Christian captives. St Thomas Aquinas wrote that 'Christians may keep non-Christian slaves, whether they be Jews, heathens or Saracens'. The conversion of Lithuania should have meant that enslaving the Order's victims was now prohibited. That the knights ignored this rule, while simultaneously pretending that no conversion had actually taken place, calls into question whether the Christianization of Lithuania had ever been a genuine aim, or whether, as its enemies were to maintain for centuries, territorial gain was the Order's sole purpose.

When the reality of the conversion of Lithuania eventually became accepted in western Europe the flow of crusaders was greatly curtailed, and for this reason the Teutonic Order had to make an effort to recruit the service of mercenaries. In 1394 Philip the Bold, Duke of Burgundy, acted as intermediary for the recruitment of 150 Genoese crossbowmen. A letter of thanks from the Grand Master mentions his gratitude to Philip both for the cross-bowmen and for a gift of wine. In 1409, the year before Tannenberg, a letter from the Grand Master Ulrich von Jungingen stated that the Order has sent for 'guests', which probably means crusaders, and for Genoese crossbowmen.

SHOWDOWN AT TANNENBERG

In 1407 Conrad von Jungingen, Grand Master of the Teutonic Knights, died. According to the Order's chronicler he was both a martyr and a prophet, his martyrdom arising from his refusal to have sexual intercourse, the remedy his doctor had prescribed to cure his gallstones. He was a prophet because he recommended that the Order should not appoint his brother Ulrich as Grand Master, whose extreme hatred of the Poles would lead the knights into disaster.

Conrad's prediction came true within months of Ulrich's accession. The firm alliance between King Wladyslaw of Poland and his cousin Grand Duke Witold of Lithuania could only be prevented from moving against the Order if the Polish/Lithuanian Union feared an attack in its rear from Emperor Sigismund of Hungary. But the emperor's neutrality had been bought with gold, and on 1 July 1410 Wladyslaw crossed the Vistula (Wisla) at Czerwinsk on a bridge of pontoons to link up with Witold and a Bohemian detachment under Jan Zyzka. There was also a Tartar contingent from the Golden Horde, whose stubborn paganism provided a godsend to the Teutonic propagandists who would later describe Tannenberg as a defeat of crusaders by pagan hordes.

The advancing Poles and Lithuanians wreaked a terrible revenge as they swept through Prussia. Depending on one's personal bias the reports of their atrocities mean either that they equalled the Teutonic Knights in their brutality, or that the Order's propaganda machine equalled that of the Poles. So frequent are the references to the looting and desecration of churches that there must be some factual basis, but even this is nothing remarkable compared to the havoc that was already common in France.

The Grand Master expected an attack downriver on the district of Dobrzyn, but when this did not materialize he realized that the allied army were heading almost due north for a direct attack on Marienburg. It was likely that they would cross their last barrier, the River Drewenz (Drweca), a tributary of the Vistula, at the fords of Kauernick. The Order's army accordingly hurried there and drove stakes into the river and fortified the western bank. Their army was about 27,000 strong, and included several guest crusaders, who were about to get far more than they had expected on this particular trip.

Seeing the force drawn up against them the Polish/Lithuanian army decided to move round to the east in order to bypass the Drewenz at its source. The Teutonic Knights marched along parallel to them, and since the river makes a sharp bend towards the north, they crossed it themselves and assumed a defensive position near the crossroads in the village of Tannenberg. Curiously, the Order's army based itself around the village of Grunwald (Zalgiris in Lithuanian), the name chosen by the Poles to designate the battle, while the Polish/Lithuanian army encamped near Tannenberg, the German choice, a village now known as Stebark. Of the two armies the Teutonic Knights had the longer march (16 miles) compared to the Poles' 5 miles, but the terrain, which was crossed by awkward ravines, gave them some advantages in their defensive position. The allied army, however, were able to conceal many of their troops in the woods.

While both armies were still ordering their ranks two messengers from the Grand Master came up to King Wladyslaw and handed him two swords as a challenge to fight. They did not have long to wait for a response, and the Lithuanians on the allied right were the first to move. They were met

The attack on the Grand Master Ulrich von Jungingen by Dobieslaw of Olesnica at the Battle of Tannenberg /Grunwald. (Reproduced with kind permission from Banderia apud Grunwald [Banners at Grunwald] by Andrzej Klein.)

by a hail of bolts and arrows from the crossbowmen and archers, but as a sudden thunderstorm had wet the Teutonic powder their field artillery was ineffective.

We may never be able to reconstruct with certainty the events which followed the initial Lithuanian charge because the Order's leaders did not survive to give their version of the battle that ensued, but after an hour of bitter hand to hand fighting the Lithuanians gave ground, and the Order's knights pursued them for many miles. Among them were many of the visiting crusaders, elated at what they thought was an early and easy victory. The different interpretations of this initial action vary from a genuine Lithuanian retreat to a planned false withdrawal perfectly carried out in accordance with the Tartar contingent's traditional Mongol tactics. The result in either case was that many of the Order's knights were either dispersed across a wide area, or simply busied themselves with looting the allied baggage train, no doubt recovering much of their own stolen property.

Meanwhile the rest of the allied army advanced, undaunted by any apparent defeat on their flank. There was a worrying moment when the Polish royal

The Battle of Grunwald, from an engraving of 1597 where the participants are shown using sixteenth-century pike techniques rather than depicting them in authentic early fifteenth-century weapons and armour.

ensign fell from the grasp of its bearer, but it soon rose again and the fighting continued with great intensity. At this stage the Grand Master committed his fresh units to the battle with the primary target of King Wladyslaw himself. The field of Tannenberg/Grunwald now became one huge mêlée, the advantage going to neither side until the remnants of the Lithuanian right wing regrouped and came back into the fray. At this stage someone engaged the Grand Master in single combat and he was cut down.

As the Order's army began to give way the Polish foot soldiers moved against the enemy baggage train, killing and looting. There they found wagons laden with shackles and chains for the expected prisoners, but the outcome was the exact opposite. Hundreds of Teutonic Knights, almost half their strength, lay dead, and 14,000 prisoners were taken.

THE PRICE OF DEFEAT

The disaster would have been much greater if the allied army had then been able to take the fortress of Marienburg, but the great citadel was stubbornly and heroically defended for fifty-seven days, and at the end of September Wladyslaw lifted the siege. His army, already depleted from the battle, was being steadily weakened by dysentery, and an acute cash-flow problem meant that he was unable to pay his Bohemian mercenaries.

Tannenberg therefore did not mean the extinction of the Teutonic Order, but it severely tested it in many ways, including its finances. The reparations demanded by the victors following the Treaty of Thorn (Torun) in 1411 almost bankrupted it, and led to silver crosses and other church furnishings being melted down to raise an indemnity of £850,000 – ten times the average income of the King of England. But the Order was also faced with expenditure of a different kind, because the loss of 200 knights and thousands of foot soldiers had severely weakened their fighting strength, so in the face of continuing Polish aggression the recruitment of mercenaries was the only quick solution. The supply of visiting crusaders, needless to say, abruptly dried up after Tannenberg. To fight Christians whom one pretended to be Saracens was one thing. To be defeated by them was quite another.

By December 1410 no less than 7,500 mercenaries had arrived in Prussia to strengthen the Order's forces but, as was the way of mercenaries, they only fought when they felt like it, and not at all while they remained unpaid. In 1411 one group of mercenaries in Danzig (Gdansk) seized a ship on the Vistula and became pirates. The point was not lost upon King Wladyslaw Jagiello of Poland, who kept only the important prisoners for ransom after Tannenberg. Most of the mercenaries were immediately set free, because the king reasoned that they would cause

An effigy of a Polish knight bearing the arms of Krystyn of Kozieglowy, the Castellan of Sacz. A member of this family fought at Tannenberg /Grunwald.

Detail from the famous painting in Warsaw by Matejko of the Battle of Grunwald where the artist has patriotically but incorrectly included a Polish winged hussar of the early seventeenth century.

more trouble for the Order by their pay claims from a defeated employer.

The Order was therefore gravely weakened, and in the decades which followed the knights were flung more and more on to their own resources. The last so-called crusaders to fight with them in Prussia left in 1422, and they were all native Germans. From then on the Teutonic Knights fought alone, and after a war lasting thirteen years from 1454 to 1466 Prussia was torn in half. West Prussia became part of the lands of the Polish crown, leaving only the poorer East Prussia in the Order's hands. What role did the Order now have? They could move eastwards to counter the growing Turkish threat in the same way that the Knights Hospitallers of St John of Jerusalem had become the Knights of Rhodes, but that would have meant abandoning Prussia. Although one or two brave contingents made the jump their efforts were disastrous, and most of the brothers stayed on German soil, where their secularization at the Reformation eventually achieved what Wladyslaw Jagiello had not managed at Tannenberg.

THE GHOSTS OF TANNENBERG

As the reality of the Teutonic Order faded into history, so the myths of its nobility, its cruelties and the crucial experience at Tannenberg began to grow. Chroniclers from both sides told the tales with the added nationalist coloration that their readers expected. The *Lübeck Chronicle*, for example, numbered the Order's opponents at 5.1 million men, and so the stories grew until Hitler and Stalin, the most notorious abusers of the Tannenberg myth, finally transformed a battle between a predominately German yet always international brotherhood and Poland/Lithuania into a straightforward conflict between Germans and Slavs. To Hitler the Teutonic Order served as a model for the SS, who put aside their own free will and performed deeds that may have been regarded as immoral in a personal sense, but were justified in driving back the 'Slavic inundation'.

In an odd parallel, official Communist historiography claimed that Tannenberg 1410 had been fought by 'Soviet peoples' who won the battle by applying Stalinist principles in complete accordance with the teachings of Marx and Lenin. A mythical 'Red Army' of 1410, in which the Smolensk contingent (who were actually Lithuanian) played a major role, was therefore invoked to reinforce the supposed homogeneity of the Soviet Union and to discredit nationalist feelings in Poland and Lithuania.

Stalin's appropriation of the myth of the fascist Teutonic Knights therefore complemented Hitler's own approach, and in 1945 the retreating German army blew up their own monument at Tannenberg so that it would not be desecrated by any Russian or Pole who happened to agree with both their leaders that on this battlefield a curse of centuries had been born.

Opposite: Effigy of the Margrave Rudolph IV of Baden-Durlach (died 1348) in Lichtental, Germany. (From the archive of Sir James Mann. By courtesy of the Board of Trustees of the Royal Armouries.)

The Italian Job   6

War has always provided opportunities for adventurers and mercenaries, as the story of the Nájera campaign and the Lithuanian crusades illustrates so well, and the early decades of the Hundred Years' War saw many other examples of men fighting in armies for the personal gain that could come either from loot or from an agreed fee. In many cases, however, mercenary companies or individual 'soldiers of fortune' are indistinguishable from the rest of an army in the overall operations of siege and battle, and it is only during times of truce that real mercenary activity can be identified.

The Peace of Brétigny in 1360 provided just such an opportunity. Large bodies of troops were suddenly disbanded, and instead of returning home, sold their skills to the highest bidder, and even, when no bidder was available, started wars of their own. It is with a sense of shame that one records the name of Sir Hugh Calveley and Sir Robert Knowles as leaders of these despicable bands. Profit had once been made from the capture and ransom of the rich. Now it was to be scraped from the bottom of war's empty barrel. A stable government, such as that exercised by the Black Prince in Aquitaine, could close its borders to them, but this only put the pressure on to neighbours in turn. As a result the so-called 'Free Companies' flourished where the populace was weakest to withstand them, and where relatively unspoiled lands promised rich pickings. All that was necessary was for them to take a few castles and hold the populace to ransom. Local defence against them was almost non-existent, although the towns built as fortified *bastides* fared better than others. As for getting rid of these brigands there seemed little alternative to paying them to go away and attack someone else – a scarcely satisfactory arrangement, unless the alternative place were a distant country. As Lithuania, which provided working holidays for the nobility, was hardly a convenient dumping ground for unwanted plunderers, a much more promising location was to be found in Italy.

CONDOTTIERI WARFARE

Service in Italian wars was not a new phenomenon, and in fact the curse of the mercenary was to afflict the peninsula for a further century and a half. When the French king Charles VIII invaded Italy in 1494 and captured Naples within six

Opposite: A view of the walls of Montagnana showing the fortified gateway and the Rocca della Alberi.

months, his rapid success was blamed on the predilection of the Italians for employing mercenaries. According to influential commentators such as Machiavelli, the Italian states were crushed so easily because for centuries they had hired others to fight on their behalf rather than relying on their own militias. To name names, Italy owed its latest disaster to the long and disreputable history of the condottieri.

The condottieri were the captains who represented the supply side of the mercenary equation. They owed their title and their continued livelihood to the granting of a *condotta* or contract between an employer, usually a prince, a baron or a city, and the captain who would supply soldiers to fight on the commissioner's behalf. Machiavelli's sense of outrage was given additional colouring from a long humanist tradition that cherished the notion of free citizens rallying to the flag to defend their homes, and despised and vilified the very notion of the mercenary. He was not alone. Another Florentine politician wrote of a contemporary condottieri captain that 'in general all men of his occupation disgust me, because they are our natural enemies, and despoil all of us, and their only thought is to keep the upper hand and to drain our wealth'.

Effigy of Can Signorio della Scala (died 1375) in Verona, showing a fourteenth-century gipon with the family's heraldic charge of a ladder.

These were perceptive comments, because, although mercenaries clearly had their uses, they were a highly volatile and extremely dangerous commodity. Stories abounded of mercenaries coming to a halt within sight of an advancing enemy and refusing to engage in battle until they were paid in advance, and of condottieri captains changing sides so frequently that even their own men were unsure whom they were expected to fight. In 1441 the condottiere Piccinino insisted on a guarantee that he would be given the fief of Piacenza before he would agree to attack the Venetian army, which provoked an explosive outburst from the man who had hired him to do just that.

Most employers of condottieri no doubt appreciated that any contract to provide such an unpredictable service as mercenary warfare, where the signatory faced his own possible extinction, was naturally prone to ambiguity and wide open to exploitation. But to Machiavelli condottieri warfare was an inferior product compared to the heroic deeds that could be expected from a national militia. Indeed, he claimed, the wars waged by condottieri had not been real wars at all, but bloodless mock battles contested by rival mercenaries who were concerned only to give the show of conflict for the benefit of their respective paymasters, who could then each be threatened with real force if the cash was not forthcoming. 'Wars were commenced without fear,' he wrote in a famous passage, 'continued without danger and concluded without loss.'

In fact Machiavelli was sorely mistaken about the true nature of condottieri warfare. At the Battle of Anghiari in 1440, according to Machiavelli, 'one man was killed, and he fell off his horse and was trampled to death', but according to reliable eyewitnesses the list of dead topped 900. At Molinella in 1467, where 'some horses were wounded and some prisoners taken but no death occurred', the actual losses were 600. The one justification for Machiavelli's exaggerated comments may lie in the fact that in these battles, as in similar encounters throughout contemporary Europe, the bulk of the casualties tended to be lower-class troops who were both more numerous and less well protected than their betters, and out of 170 named condottieri captains only a dozen actually died fighting, and some of these deaths may have been as a result of assassinations carried out under the convenient cloak of anonymity that a battle provided.

Montpazier, one of the finest examples of a fortified town, or *bastide*, the best defence against uncontrolled and unemployed mercenaries. (Photograph by Daphne Clark)

This fresco in the church of St Fermo Maggiore in Verona shows a knight of the fourteenth century in an allegorical scene probably intended to illustrate the Last Judgement, but provides also a chilling reminder of the reality of contemporary warfare against civilians carried out by mercenary bands.

THE FIRST CONDOTTIERI

The condottieri had their origins in thirteenth-century Italy, when a handful of mercenaries were employed by the Lombard and the Tuscan Leagues to counter the aggression of the German emperors. These mercenaries, who were primarily foreigners (although to a Florentine the term applied equally well to an inhabitant of Genoa) were hired as individuals, not as companies. As external threats diminished so the hostility between neighbouring cities increased, and political factions within a city made it more difficult to recruit militiamen from among the citizens. In addition, an exile from one city might well be tempted to enrol as a mercenary in a neighbouring place to fight against the men who had expelled him. The increased sophistication of weaponry such as the crossbow also led to the emergence of men who could offer skills in these specialities surpassing any that could be expected from part-time militia soldiers, and it was only natural that such skills would be offered at a price.

Opposite: The d'Este castle in Ferrara, built by the Ferrara lord in 1385 for defence against his own citizens. It is no wonder that such men frequently recruited mercenaries.

One other factor that encouraged the recruitment of mercenaries was the mistrust that existed between certain rulers and their subjects. The classic example is the d'Este family of Ferrara. Having seen his unpopular tax collector torn in pieces by the mob and fed to the dogs, the ruler of the family built a castle next to his palace in 1385 as a defence against his own subjects. It was therefore clear that to raise an army from them when an enemy threatened was not likely to yield much enthusiasm.

Yet at no time were the condottieri and their men more dangerous than when they had just finished fighting a battle. For them to accept their pay and then go home proved to be an exceptional occurrence, and a more likely scenario was for them to stay on and seek employment with someone else, possibly even the lord against whom they had just fought. Alternatively, they

The Torre Guinini in Lucca (Tuscany), the city that was sacked and sold by a Free Company. The tower has a tree growing out of it!

preferred to engage in little private wars of their own where payment was obtained in the form of loot, often by robbing the very lord who had recently employed them. In 1329, for example, 800 German cavalrymen deserted the imperial army of Louis of Bavaria at Pisa and made a spontaneous attack on nearby Lucca. The assault failed, largely because the mercenaries lacked siege equipment, but they looted the suburbs thoroughly and then took to winter quarters. Much alarmed, the emperor sent an envoy to negotiate with them, but he promptly joined the mercenary band and became their leader. The company returned to Lucca the following spring to make a surprise attack. This was completely successful, and to add to the huge amount of loot they turned in an extra profit by selling the entire city of Lucca to the Genoese for 30,000 florins! The company then decided to quit while it was still winning, so they divided up their spoils and disbanded, leaving an alarming precedent behind them.

Paradoxically, such activities by these apparently uncontrolled bands served to endear them to potential employers, and their contracts increased in number. A Swabian knight called Werner von Urslingen provides an excellent example. He and his men were first employed in Italy by the della Scala family of Verona. When the renowned Cangrande della Scala died in 1329 Werner continued to serve his nephew Mastino II, who then disgusted his mercenary troops by making a humiliating peace settlement with his enemies. Having no need of mercenaries now, Werner and his men were paid off, but instead of disbanding and returning home they immediately offered their services to Pisa, which was then under threat from Florence. This provided another three years' work, at the end of which Werner forced Pisa to give his men redundancy money. But still they did not disband, and the year 1342 was to see this newly named 'Great Company' of 3,000 men roaming all over central Italy, fighting campaigns for anyone who would employ them and blackmailing any who would not. Only the Bolognese resisted them sufficiently to order a truce over their territories, a peaceful passage that was instantly abandoned once another area was entered, and in the end the Great Company was literally paid by the Lombard cities to go home. Five years later, however, Werner was back, and this time he was in the pay of the Hungarians, who had hired his company to help them invade Italy!

THE WHITE COMPANY

In 1361 a new force appeared on the Italian scene in the persons of the famous White Company, so-called because they kept their armour so brightly burnished. They were also known as the 'Inglesi', because they were mostly men who had taken part in the Hundred Years' War, but they were not all Englishmen, and their first leader was in fact a German. Nevertheless it was under an Englishman, Sir John Hawkwood, that the company achieved its greatest renown. The knights of the White Company preferred to fight on foot

Cangrande della Scala, lord of Verona, who was one of the earliest employers of mercenaries. This statue of him is in the Castello Vecchio, Verona.

in units of three: two men at arms and a page who kept their horses in readiness. One very 'English' characteristic about them was the use of the longbow, but they were also equipped with siege weapons, and provided a well-disciplined and ready-made army for anyone who wished to employ them. So formidable was their reputation that on one occasion when they were late turning up to fight for Pisa against Florence, the Pisans dressed their own men up to look like the White Company, and the Florentines withdrew.

Sir John Hawkwood was born in about 1320, and is described by Froissart as being 'a poor knight having gained nothing but his spurs'. He is believed to have fought at Crécy, but it was as a condottiere in Italy that he achieved renown, serving several masters, but each in turn, because treachery during a campaign was not acceptable to the condottieri code, even if extortion may have been. In 1368, for example, he defended Borgoforte, a castle that commanded a vital river crossing of the Po, against the German emperor Charles IV. The action included flooding the emperor's camp by breaking an embankment holding back the fierce winter river. In this Hawkwood was providing a service to the whole of Italy, but it was Bernabo Visconti, Duke of Milan, who had employed him on loan from Pisa and, being the paymaster, Visconti's own reputation was enhanced as much as that of the Englishman who did the actual fighting.

In such ways did Sir John Hawkwood and his White Company provide a high-quality service for their Italian employers. There were many grumbles, because being a soldier of fortune meant having to make a fortune out of being a soldier. To put it bluntly, mercenaries murdered for money, and any mercy that a condottiere might display through declining to slit the throat of a captive had more to do with the greater value of the man ransomed than with Christian charity. Looting, too, could be regarded as an economic necessity, either to provide goods for one's employer from which he could cover the agreed fee, or to make up any shortfall should payment be delayed. In this the Church was Hawkwood's worst employer, and on one occasion the pope, who no doubt felt personally safe from the White Company, simply terminated Hawkwood's contract while it was still in financial arrears.

It was about this time that St Catherine of Siena addressed a letter to Hawkwood beseeching him to give up the life of a condottiere and lead a crusade. In a very perceptive sentence she urged that Sir John, 'from being the servant and soldier of the Devil, should become a manly and true knight'. This belief, that a mercenary was not a 'true knight' and indeed an inferior being, summed up the feelings that many people already had about these companies upon whom too many people were coming to rely too much. Hawkwood was equally dependant on receiving a succession of contracts, and in 1375 he had little choice but to accept a new contract from the pope when the alternative was unemployment.

The job given to the White Company was to invade Tuscany, and in May 1375 Hawkwood set out in that direction with an army that included the latest versions of bombards for demolishing Florence's walls. He was not surprised when Florentine envoys met him at the borders of their territory. While not wishing to persuade him to change sides, they assured him, what would be a reasonable sum for them to pay him to cross Florence off the list of cities to be captured? Sir John named his price, and when the Florentines had picked themselves up off the floor they negotiated an indemnity for their city for five years at the price Hawkwood demanded. News of the deal quickly spread, and before long Hawkwood had negotiated similar non-aggression pacts with Siena, Arezzo, Pisa and Lucca. It was the most profitable and least warlike campaign that bold Sir John had ever engaged in, and confirmed a true side for the caricature of 'mock battles' that Machiavelli was later to paint, except that these were not mock battles, but rather no battles at all. Not surprisingly, the pope soon got to hear that the bombards remained unfired and that the walls of Tuscany were still upright, and quite understandably withheld Hawkwood's pay, a situation that lasted until the noble Sir John kidnapped a cardinal and held him to ransom.

Mastino II della Scala, nephew of Cangrande, whose actions disgusted the mercenaries who fought for him. They soon left his service, and transformed themselves into the 'Great Company' that ravaged much of central Italy. This statue is on top of his tomb in Verona.

Sir John Hawkwood, the English knight who was one of the greatest condottieri, from the commemorative fresco in the cathedral in Florence.

Yet within a year of this romping farcical tale of 'mercenary as mobster', the story of Sir John Hawkwood took a sickening turn. A certain Cardinal Robert of Geneva had occupied the town of Cesena with his own mercenary troops, who were mainly Bretons. They began looting the town as mercenaries regularly did, at which point the citizens put up a fierce resistance. Being unable to defeat them, the

123

cardinal tricked the people into surrendering their weapons in return for a guarantee of safety. But the affair was not to end there, because Cardinal Robert wanted revenge, and knew that his small force were insufficient to provide it. Sir John Hawkwood's White Company were not far away, and as they were in the employ of the Church, they could be required to 'administer justice', as the cardinal put it. After initially protesting that he could persuade the citizens to lay down their arms by peaceful negotiation, Hawkwood succumbed to the cardinal's evident intentions, and joined the Bretons in a brutal and thorough massacre. The piazzas of Cesena were heaped with bodies, and the moats were full of dead people who had drowned rather than face the swords waiting for them at the gates.

Well might later chroniclers record that Hawkwood 'let many escape', and historians argue that he was only obeying orders. Where was the negotiator, the profit-hungry but shrewd mobster who had bought off half-a-dozen Tuscan cities? Where, indeed was the chivalrous knight, the bold tactician of Borgoforte? Sir John Hawkwood now stood exposed as the servant and soldier of the Devil, just as St Catherine of Siena had anathematized him. Here was the essential weakness of the whole condottieri system. No contract could ever give an employer total control over a mercenary band. There was always this huge grey area of unpredictability which went far beyond the simple fighting of battles, and could manifest itself either as farce or as tragedy, as rape or racketeering.

The tower and bridge of the Scaligeri's castle in Verona, the object of Sir John Hawkwood's siege of 1385. From here he led a false retreat and won a great victory at Castagnaro.

The year 1385 was to find Sir John fighting much more honourably for Padua against Verona, and pulling off a stunning victory at the Battle of Castagnaro, where he abandoned the siege of Verona in a false retreat and lured the Veronese army to its destruction beside the River Adige. With the Battle of Castagnaro the reputation of Hawkwood as a commander and a military hero were dramatically enhanced. More campaigns followed, and on his death in 1394 a personal request from King Richard II, no less, was received asking that the body of 'the late brave soldier' be brought back to England for honoured burial. No absentee mercenary could have asked for more.

THE SFORZAS OF MILAN

With the death of Hawkwood the time of the foreign condottieri in Italian service began to fade, and from this time on the most prominent names in the annals of Italian wars were no longer English or German but Italian. The pattern of employment also changed, producing in one outstanding case, that of Francesco Sforza, an example of a man who started off as a mercenary captain and became a lord in his own right.

Francesco Sforza was the son of a certain Muzio Attendolo (1369–1424), a rough and illiterate soldier

who earned himself the nickname of 'Sforza' ('the Force') through his prowess as a mercenary captain. On the death of his father Francesco inherited his command and his long tradition of service to the Visconti dukes of Milan. Sforza was one of two condottieri whom Visconti employed. The other was a certain Piccinino, and an understandable rivalry grew up between them, a jealousy probably fostered by Visconti, who saw it as a way of keeping them from revolting against him. Piccinino had overall command of the Visconti forces, while to Sforza had long been promised the hand of Visconti's daughter. In the early 1430s Sforza was sent south with an open brief to take the sides of the hill towns against the new and unpopular pope. So successful was he in this that Visconti became alarmed by the following and the lands that his employee was amassing and, in breach of his contract, was also retaining for himself. Meanwhile Piccinino had been sent elsewhere on a similar expedition and had obediently handed over all his conquests to Visconti.

As his relations with Visconti deteriorated and the prospects of marrying his daughter receded, the opportunistic Sforza, a condottiere if ever there was one, threw in his lot with Milan's great rival, Venice. A full-scale war with Milan erupted in 1438, but Sforza kept prudently in the shadows, allowing the famous condottieri Gattemalata and Colleoni to take the lead in Venice's battles against his old colleague and rival Piccinino. He finally took the field against Piccinino at the Battle of Anghiari in 1440, the bloody encounter later to be dismissed by Machiavelli as having only one casualty. The greatest

The Battle of Anghiari, 1440, was dismissed by Machiavelli as 'a bloodless battle where only one man was killed, and he fell off his horse'. (National Gallery of Ireland, Dublin)

The beautifully restored Fenis castle in the Aosta Valley of Italy, and a view of the richly decorated interior.

casualty at Anghiari, however, was Piccinino's reputation. Defeated by Sforza, he asked Visconti to retire him, at which the duke realized that the time was ripe to negotiate. The terms were quite straightforward. If Francesco Sforza would arrange a peace between Venice and Milan then he would receive the long-promised Visconti daughter and a large dowry. Victory was indeed sweet.

Francesco's marriage to Bianca Visconti proved to be both happy and highly profitable. Bianca was also a redoubtable woman in her own right. On one occasion when Francesco was off campaigning some rebels seized one of his castles. Not wishing to have her husband distracted from his contractual duties Bianca led an army herself and recaptured the fortress.

The summer of 1447 found the Venetian army dangerously close to Milan. Sick and near to death, the old Visconti duke summoned Sforza's army to his aid, and while on the march Sforza received further news that the duke had died. Through his marriage and his unquestioned military skills Francesco Sforza had every chance of succeeding to the dukedom, but the citizens of Milan had other ideas. Suddenly they had the opportunity to throw off the old regime of dukes and their hired condottieri, and unilaterally declared the birth of the 'Golden Ambrosian Republic'. But even a republic needed an army, and being stuck fast in the Italian mercenary tradition, Milan chose Francesco Sforza to be its captain general! Realizing the amazing opportunity he had been given, Sforza persuaded Milan to recruit the great condottieri Colleoni as well, and began a series of campaigns on the republic's behalf that promised nothing but personal success for the Sforza fortunes.

By 1448 Milan was running short of money, so Colleoni changed sides and went back to Venice. Sforza stayed on, thus demonstrating his great personal loyalty to the Milanese. A few months later his army was surprised early one morning by the Venetians at Caravaggio between Brescia and Milan. Keeping totally calm, Sforza sent a cavalry detachment round to the enemy rear while he held on against the frontal assault. The result was one of the most convincing condottieri victories of all time. Thousands of Venetian prisoners were taken, and so devastating was the defeat that Venice was forced to sue for peace. Negotiations, however, were conducted with Francesco Sforza himself, and not with the leaders

The greatest success story in the history of the condottieri is surely Francesco Sforza, the condottiere who served the Visconti family of Milan, inherited their domains and became a prince of the Renaissance.

The drawbridge and gate of the formidable Sforza castle in Milan.

of the Golden Ambrosian Republic, and a deal was struck whereby Sforza would receive Venetian support for his eventual takeover of Milan in return for a pledge on certain disputed territories. It was the sort of private arrangement that only a condottiere could make, and, like many a condottieri arrangement, it was as easily broken, because when Sforza did not deliver within almost a year Venice struck its own peace deal with Milan, leaving Francesco Sforza completely isolated. Swift action was needed, so Sforza rapidly laid siege to Milan, and as the citizens grew hungry for bread, pro-Sforza sympathizers in the city stirred up a popular feeling for an honourable surrender. In February 1450, therefore, Francesco Sforza rode in triumph through Milan's open gates.

Thus did the son of an illiterate soldier rise to become one of the princes of the Renaissance through the greatest example of personal gain from mercenary service. Yet it was not to the glory of the Sforzas that Machiavelli and his contemporaries were to look when they searched their souls for the reasons for Italy's collapse in 1494. To them it was the earlier condottieri such as Hawkwood who had planted the seeds of Italy's humiliation through a form of warfare that men like Sforza had done nothing to control, and which was to leave such a bitter legacy behind it.

Bartolomeo Colleoni, who fought as a condottiere for Venice and is commemorated by the fine statue in the city he served so well.

Swords and Prophecies

Richard II came to the throne of England in 1377 as a boy of ten, the heir to the glorious military reputation of his father and grandfather, and heir also to the troubles that had arisen when that fearsome reputation had begun to decline. The Hundred Years' War may have begun with the semblance of a civil war, a family struggle between Valois and Plantagenet, but by the 1370s it had become a war between nations, engendering a hatred between the two countries which in the years to come would so easily be rekindled into a renewed war. The very triumphs that Richard inherited made it difficult for him to obtain a peaceful settlement when peace was needed. The knights had returned with prisoners and booty. They expected success, and their honour demanded it.

THE MARCHER LORDS

Wars in distant lands for God or for king brought their own problems. The maintenance of peace in one's own country provided a different challenge. Since the victory over the Scots at Neville's Cross in 1346, England did not greatly fear a large-scale war with its northern neighbour. The need in the late fourteenth century was for what was basically a policing operation that was large enough to cope with a raid and had sufficient local knowledge to prevent excesses from the English side during times of truce. As the English sovereign could not afford to maintain a direct military presence in these distant parts, the local soldiery had to be recruited and led by leaders whom they would respect and follow. There was, therefore, little alternative to entrusting the guardianship of the Scottish border to the so-called Marcher lords.

From the king's point of view the great disadvantage was that he had so few Marcher lords to choose from. Richard II's choice was effectively between only two families: the house of Percy and the house of Neville, a fact of northern life which was to extend until Tudor times. The Nevilles acquired their title during Richard's reign, Ralph Neville becoming the Earl of Westmorland in 1397.

As for the Percys, John Harding wrote in the fifteenth century that they 'have the hearts of the people by north and ever have'. The Percys provided personal

Opposite: King Henry IV, victor of the Battle of Shrewsbury in 1403, immortalized in stone on the east gable of the church built on the site of the conflict.

Richard II, from his tomb
in Westminster Abbey.

service and large armies for battles from Crécy to Barnet, and in five generations
no less than eight Percys met violent deaths. They became Earls of
Northumberland in 1377, and owned large estates and manors in Yorkshire,
where their castle at Spofforth, the birthplace of the famous Henry Hotspur,
was the only one of their residences that was not first and foremost a fortress.

To fulfil his military duties a Warden of the Marches acted like a contract
captain under Edward III. For an annual payment from the king he undertook
to raise troops as and when necessary, and to safeguard against either the Percys
or the Nevilles becoming too powerful the border command was divided
between them with their periods of responsibility alternating. This system lasted
until 1489, during which time there were Nevilles in the West March for 59
years, and Percy Wardens of the East March for eighty-one years in total.

Beyond his duty to the king, the Warden was given virtually a free hand, and
in 1388 this resulted in a curious little encounter called the Battle of Otterburn.
Like the Battle of the Thirty, it was almost literally fought for the sake of
fighting, and arose from a raid across the border led by James, the second Earl of
Douglas, who was the grandson of Archibald Douglas, the regent of Scotland
killed at Halidon Hill. Two armies crossed the border. The larger headed for
Carlisle while the smaller, Douglas's host, poured down Redesdale, crossed the
Tyne, and ravaged County Durham. Laden with booty, and perhaps a little over-
confident, they advanced on Newcastle where they were met by Henry
Hotspur. The Percys and the Douglases were old rivals, and this encounter was
nothing new. A skirmish ensued, from which the Scots managed to escape after
some fighting. They did not, however, escape empty-handed, but took with

them the pennon from the end of Hotspur's lance, torn off during the mêlée. Henry Hotspur swore that he would recapture the pennon before the Scots crossed the border, and having made that vow, honour now entered very much into the situation. We can envisage this young man with the adrenalin pumping through his body, the impetuous nature that gave him his nickname forcing him to respond dramatically to the challenge. The race was on!

There was equal determination on the other side to see the matter through. Douglas had returned the way he had come, and, having failed to take Otterburn Castle, was advised by his companions to make good the lead they had on Percy and retire over the border with their booty. Douglas rejected the suggestion. He had been told of Percy's vow and was determined to give him the opportunity of trying to fulfil it.

Percy's army was probably all mounted and consisted of about 2,000 men-at-arms and 5,000 hobilars (mounted infantry). They came upon the Scottish camp as it was getting dark on 19 August 1388. The surprise was total. Douglas and his men were unarmed and ready for feasting when the attack came, so there was little time to prepare. Henry Hotspur launched two attacks, one to the front and one, under Sir Thomas Umfraville, round the flanks from where he assaulted the camp which had now been vacated. But Douglas rallied sufficiently to lead a counter-attack. The English had not expected this, and in the dark and at such close quarters their longbows were useless. In time the fact that the Scots had enjoyed food and rest began to tell in their favour. Henry Hotspur and his brother Ralph were captured for ransom and the English army drew away. Dawn found the Scots in undisputed possession of the battlefield, their

Spofforth Castle, near Wetherby, was the birthplace of Henry Hotspur. Although associated with Northumberland, the Percys held many lands in Yorkshire, and Spofforth was one of the their least well-defended castles because of its position so far south of the Scottish border.

The standard of Henry IV when he was merely Henry Bolingbroke, Duke of Hereford. Note the red rose of the House of Lancaster, one badge among several, but the one that was to capture the imagination of a generation of later historians.

victory made less than happy by the loss of James, Earl of Douglas, slain by an unknown hand and whose body was trampled by a thousand hooves – and all for the sake of a knight's banner!

THE TRIUMPH OF LANCASTER

The Percys reached the zenith of their powers during the 1390s. Between 1391 and 1396 Henry Percy, Earl of Northumberland, was Warden of the East March while his son Hotspur was Warden of the West March. They ruled their territory like autonomous princes, until Richard II, wary of their independence, tried to curtail their power by giving the Penrith Estates to Ralph Neville, but soon this threat was overtaken by the Percys playing their part in a much larger drama: the deposition of the rightful king.

The coup which placed the erstwhile Lithuanian crusader Henry Bolingbroke on the throne of England as Henry IV, the first of the Lancastrian dynasty, occurred while Richard II was in Ireland. As Richard had no heir he had named his successor before he left on a previous campaign, and it was not unexpected that he should choose the second most senior surviving line of Edward III to provide his heir – that from Lionel, Duke of Clarence. But Clarence had been survived by a daughter who had married into the family of Mortimer – a Marcher lord dynasty as formidable on the Welsh border as the Percys were on the Scottish one.

The Mortimer heir was a young boy, Edmund, but his line to the throne lay through female descent, and the next senior line was all male. This was the House of Lancaster, whose heir was Henry Bolingbroke, the son of John of Gaunt. Having been banished from the realm by Richard II, Bolingbroke took advantage of the king's absence to return in force to claim all the titles and lands of which Richard had deprived him. This may have been all he originally desired – but the

The lion rampant of the Percys, beautifully captured in stone on the wall of the keep of Warkworth Castle.

support of the Marcher lords, in particular the Percys, made him play for higher stakes. Richard was arrested, and Henry was proclaimed King Henry IV.

The actual coup was bloodless, so the main problem facing Henry IV was now what to do with the rightful, anointed king and the heir whom he had named. Young Mortimer was the easier to deal with, and he was kept securely in a place of safety. Richard II, who naturally had a much higher profile, had to suffer the horrors of the gloomy Pontefract Castle, where he was placed under the care of Thomas Waterton, a staunch Lancastrian official. The precedent of what had happened to Edward II must have terrified Richard, but in that sorry case there had been a son to put in his place whom the people would accept. This time there was no son, so there seemed little alternative to keeping Richard in Pontefract and waiting for him to die.

Rarely has a king's reign begun so inauspiciously as that of Henry IV. With the rightful king incarcerated the new monarch was mistrusted even by his allies. Yet throughout a succession of rebellions and revolts, the one sure support Henry had during his short reign was his son Henry, Prince of Wales. The popular tradition which has Prince Hal's younger days spent brawling and carousing comes from a very early source, because the *Brut Chronicle* tells us that when he was Prince of Wales, 'he fell and inclined greatly to riot, and drew to wild company'. But his military exploits do not seem to have suffered from any excesses, and he took service on his father's behalf at an early age, when the first threat came from Wales.

Sir Robert Waterton, depicted here on his tomb at Methley, Yorkshire, was a staunch Lancastrian who had charge of the deposed sovereign, Richard II, during the latter's captivity and death at Pontefract Castle.

The remains of the keep of the great castle of Pontefract, for centuries the most important royal castle in the north of England. It was the place of imprisonment and death of Richard II.

THE REVOLT OF OWAIN GLYNDWR

In about 1359 there was born a man called Owain Glyndwr, whose name is often anglicized as Owen Glendower. He had been both a law student and a knight during the latter half of the fourteenth century, and took up arms against Lord Reginald Grey of Ruthin in 1400, ostensibly over disputed lands on the Welsh border. This local quarrel soon took on the elements of a Welsh revolt, and in September his followers proclaimed Glyndwr as Prince of Wales. During that month he attacked Denbigh, Ruthin, Rhuddlan, Flint, Hawarden, Holt, Oswestry and Welshpool, only to be temporarily halted by an army somewhere along the River Severn.

The situation was sufficiently serious to demand direct intervention at the very highest level, so Prince Henry and Henry Hotspur took charge, and controlled operations from the old Edwardian castles of North Wales. One of these, Conwy, was attacked by Welsh rebels in 1401, and while they were thus occupied Glyndwr carried his operations to South Wales, where he defeated an English army at Hyddgen, and in 1402 scored another victory at the Battle of Bryn Glas when the Welsh archers in the English army turned against their leaders. Edmund Mortimer (the uncle of the boy of the same name who was the rightful heir to the throne) was captured by Glyndwr along with many others.

The Welsh border was now in a higher state of tension than even the Scottish border had been for many a year. In September Henry IV advanced from Shrewsbury in search of Glyndwr, and was caught in a terrific rainstorm which collapsed the tent in which he was sleeping. He would probably have suffocated had it not been for the fact that he was sleeping in his armour. Glyndwr's continuing success, and in particular his uncanny ability to disappear after a battle, quickly gave him the reputation of being a magician. In complete contrast, Henry's reputation had reached rock bottom. The only thing that saved him from total disgrace was a victory against the Scots at Homildon Hill in Northumberland, where the Percys destroyed another Scottish raiding army. The Scots were led by another Douglas, in this case Archibald, the fourth earl, and the grandson of James the Good, and victory was secured when the Scottish knights charged the English archers.

The Battle of Homildon Hill was undistinguished, but was very important politically, because Douglas was captured by the Percys, who naturally wished to ransom him in revenge for Otterburn. But Henry wanted Douglas kept as a lever for future negotiation with the Scots, which infuriated the Percys and turned them against him for the first time. Henry was also in no hurry to ransom Edmund Mortimer the Elder, judging wisely that any Mortimer was safer in captivity, but it turned out that no ransom would be demanded, because Edmund Mortimer stayed

This martingale, bearing the arms of Owain Glyndwr, was discovered during excavations at Harlech Castle.

Opposite: Map showing the campaigns of Owain Glyndwr and Henry IV.

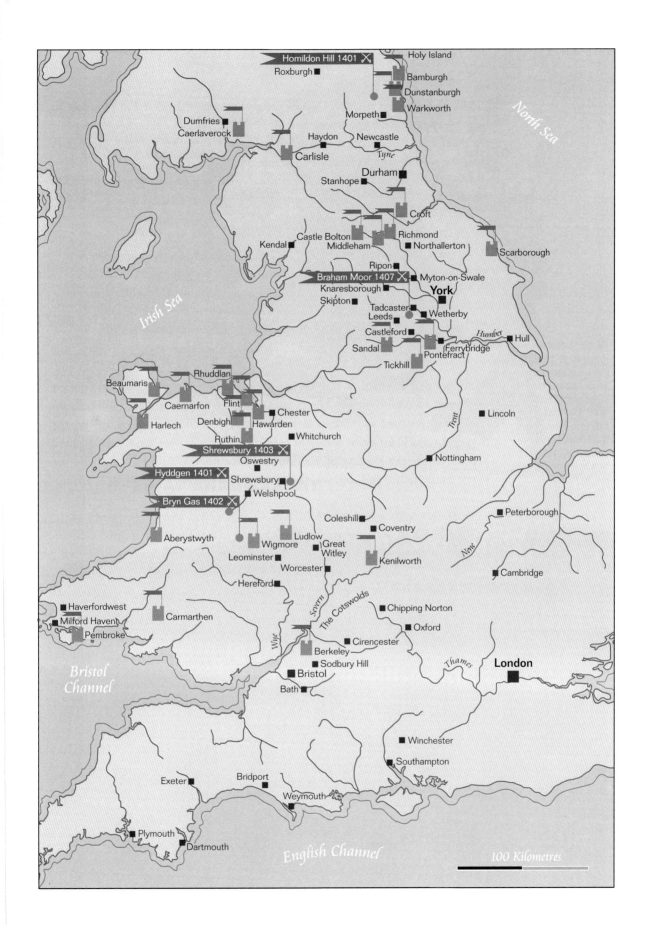

Homildon Hill 1401

Holy Island
Roxburgh
Bamburgh
Dunstanburgh
Warkworth

Morpeth

Dumfries
Caerlaverock

Haydon
Newcastle

Tyne

Carlisle

North Sea

Durham
Stanhope

Croft

Castle Bolton
Middleham
Kendal

Richmond
Northallerton

Scarborough

Ripon
Myton-on-Swale

Braham Moor 1407

Knaresborough
Skipton

York

Tadcaster
Leeds
Wetherby

Humber

Castleford
Sandal

Ferrybridge
Pontefract
Tickhill

Hull

Irish Sea

Rhuddlan

Beaumaris

Caernarfon

Flint

Chester

Denbigh
Hawarden

Harlech

Ruthin

Whitchurch

Shrewsbury 1403

Oswestry

Hyddgen 1401

Shrewsbury

Trent

Lincoln

Nottingham

Welshpool

Bryn Gas 1402

Coleshill

Coventry

Peterborough

Aberystwyth

Wigmore
Leominster

Ludlow
Great
Witley

Kenilworth

Nene

Cambridge

Worcester

Hereford

Severn

The Cotswolds

Chipping Norton

Oxford

Haverfordwest
Milford Haven
Pembroke

Carmarthen

Wye

Cirencester
Berkeley
Sodbury Hill

Bristol

Thames

London

Bath

Bristol Channel

Winchester

Southampton

Exeter

Bridport

Weymouth

Plymouth
Dartmouth

English Channel

100 Kilometres

impetuous youth, even though Shakespeare would have us believe that Hotspur and Prince Hal were of the same age. In fact, Henry Hotspur was thirty-nine, and the wild days of his youth at Otterburn were distant memories. His stand at Shrewsbury was a calculated risk, not another gamble for chivalric honour.

The Battle of Shrewsbury, which its chronicler called a 'sorry battle between Englishmen and Englishmen', was fought on 21 July 1403. It had one unique feature for the time – a contest between rival armies, both of which had long-bows. It must have been a strange experience for the archers, and accounts of the battle give the impression of the two front ranks nervously approaching each other before letting fly at their counterparts.

Hotspur's army had the better of the initial encounter. The archers whom he had recruited in Chester, the prime breeding ground for bowmen, overcame their rivals and allowed Hotspur to lead an advance on the king's centre division with the aim of capturing the monarch alive. But Prince Hal on the left wing had not suffered from the archers' fire, and was able to lead his wing in a flank attack on Hotspur. An arrow fired by an unknown hand transfixed Henry Hotspur, and with their leader dead, the rebellion collapsed.

The castle of Chepstow, the most dramatic of the border castles, looking across the River Wye from England.

The site of the Battle of Shrewsbury is today marked by a church which was raised by Henry IV as a chantry chapel. An effigy of the victorious king crowns the gable end, while all around are gargoyles whose faces are supposed to represent the rebels. Shrewsbury deprived Glyndwr of two allies, for Thomas Percy, Earl of Worcester, was captured and beheaded shortly afterwards. The old Earl of Northumberland remained an ally, biding his time in the Marches, while his son's and brother's places were taken by armies of a very different kind: the French.

THE FORGOTTEN INVASION

The story of French support for Glyndwr's revolt is a little-known episode in English history. It began with a number of raids on the south coast in 1403 and 1404. The targets included Plymouth, Dartmouth and the Isle of Wight, and achieved little, one Breton leader, the Sieur de Castellis, being killed by local people during the Dartmouth raid. In November 1403 the Welsh, perhaps accompanied by a small

A gargoyle on the wall of Battlefield Church, Shrewsbury, depicting a knight loading a cannon.

French expeditionary force, attacked Edward I's mighty castle at Caernarfon, which led to the following pathetic letter being received by Henry IV from the Constable of Chester:

> . . . Robert Parys, the Deputy Constable of Caernarvon Castle, has informed us through a woman, for neither man nor woman dare carry letters on account of the rebels of Wales, whom Owen Glyndwr, with the French and all his other power, is raising up to assault the town and castle of Caernarvon . . . And in the castle there are not in all more than twenty-eight fighting men which is too small a force, for eleven of the abler men who were there at the last siege of the place are dead . . .

The Welsh castles were all meagrely garrisoned. An extant document refers to the numbers at Conwy being just fifteen men-at-arms and sixty archers. Harlech and Aberystwyth fell early in 1404, giving Glyndwr sufficient confidence to call a parliament and undertake a further conference with the French. So dramatic were his successes that the County of Shropshire arranged a three-month truce with him and recognized Wales as an independent state.

In 1405 the Percy/Mortimer/Glyndwr alliance was given a strange legitimacy by a statement which combined in one grandiose scheme the prophecies of the Welsh bards, the share of the spoils, and a very complicated division of territory. It arose from a meeting between Glyndwr and one Hopkin ap

Thomas, whom Glyndwr held to be 'Master of Brut', meaning one skilled in the prophecies of Merlin. According to Hopkin ap Thomas the present combatants were all to be found in references contained within these prophecies. Henry IV was 'the mouldewarp accursed of God'; Glyndwr was the dragon, Percy was the lion, and Mortimer was the wolf, the three beasts who would divide up the mouldewarp's kingdom between them.

In practical terms, Mortimer's nephew was to be placed upon the throne as planned by Richard II, and then the kingdom was to be divided up very precisely among the conspirators, at which point Hopkin ap Thomas seems to have taken a back seat. Owain Glyndwr was to rule a notional 'Greater Wales', Percy would have the north of England, and Mortimer would retain the rest. They even agreed the boundaries between their respective territories. 'The North' was to consist of all of England north of the Trent, plus Leicestershire, Northamptonshire, Warwickshire and even Norfolk. 'Greater Wales' was to stretch along the Severn to the north gate of Worcester, thence to 'the ash trees

The Welsh Marches are so peaceful now, yet during the Middle Ages they were disputed lands fought over as fiercely as the Scottish borders. This particular area around the keep of Wigmore Castle was also the scene of much fighting during the Wars of the Roses.

on the main road from Bridgnorth to Kinver, thence by highway to the source of the Trent, then to the source of the Mersey and along to the sea'.

In fact the loss of Henry Hotspur at Shrewsbury had probably sealed the fate of any such scheme, and although Glyndwr controlled several of the major Welsh castles, he began to suffer defeat in field battles. Henry IV found further encouragement in the swift crushing of a northern revolt led by no less a person than the Archbishop of York. Seeking to make an example Henry had the archbishop beheaded outside the city of York. His tomb is in the Minster, and was the scene of many miracles from that day on. As if in heavenly judgement, Henry IV fell ill.

Meanwhile the French responded wholeheartedly to Glyndwr's call, setting sail on 22 July 1405 for Milford Haven, where they landed early in August. The army consisted of 2,600 men, including 800 knights and 600 crossbowmen. They joined Glyndwr's 2,000 Welshmen, captured Haverfordwest and Carmarthen and advanced across the border and through

Woodbury Hill is the little-known site of the furthest penetration on to English soil of a French army. An army including 600 crossbowmen had landed at Milford Haven in August 1405 in support of the revolt of Owain Glyndwr. Henry IV marched to Worcester to oppose them, and after some minor skirmishing the French withdrew and Glyndwr's support began to ebb away.

Herefordshire. The place where they made a stand was Woodbury Hill, near Great Witley in Worcestershire. This quiet wooded hill in the heart of England thus has the distinction of being the site of the farthest penetration by an invading force in the whole of English history since 1066.

Henry IV entered nearby Worcester on 22 August. There was some skirmishing between English and French/Welsh troops, then Glyndwr, taking the French with him, withdrew prudently to his mountains. It was a tactic which the French could not understand, and their support began to wane. By Lent 1406 the French army had left England, and Henry IV and his son fought back. Aberystwyth Castle was attacked in 1407, an action notable for the first appearance on the scene of a knight who was later to make a great name for himself in France – Sir John Talbot.

Further encouragement came with the defeat of another Percy revolt because, in a last attempt at overthrowing Henry IV, the Earl of Northum-

Bramham Moor, between Tadcaster and Leeds, was the scene of the defeat of Sir Henry Percy, the first Earl of Northumberland. As his son, Hotspur, had already been killed at Shrewsbury in 1403, the defeat of Bramham Moor marked the final eclipse of a Percy-inspired challenge to Henry IV. The earl was captured and beheaded at York.

'This worm-eaten hold of ragged stone' are the words Shakespeare used to describe Warkworth Castle, battered into surrender by Henry IV following the death of Hotspur at the Battle of Shrewsbury.

berland marched south with a Scottish army. Sir Thomas Rokeby, High Sheriff of Yorkshire, held the bridge at Knaresborough against them, and pursued Percy when he headed off to cross the Wharfe at Wetherby. He caught up with him at Bramham Moor, between Leeds and Tadcaster, and in a 'sharp, furious and bloody' battle the old earl was captured, and afterwards beheaded in York. In 1409 Aberystwyth and Harlech castles were recaptured, and at Harlech Edmund Mortimer the Elder was killed.

The following year Owain Glyndwr led his last raid into England with an attack on Shrewsbury. He then vanished from history, to live on in legend. With his disappearance the House of Lancaster seemed secure. Young Edmund Mortimer, in whose name so much had been attempted, was a prisoner, so the Mortimer line seemed almost certain to die out. He only had one legitimate sibling, a sister, Anne. She married the Earl of Cambridge and in 1411 gave birth to a son, but by a strange combination of fate and fortune this young man was to inherit both the Mortimer claim to the throne and another through his father. For this baby was Richard Plantagenet, the future Duke of York.

The white rose had begun to flower.

The Agincourt War 8

Henry V's invasion of France, the unexpected and crushing victory of Agincourt, and the diplomatic success of the Treaty of Troyes which effectively gave him what had been denied to his great-grandfather Edward III, are among the best-known events of the Hundred Years' War. In this chapter I intend to examine more closely how all this was achieved. What factors enabled Henry V to gain such a sweeping victory? What had happened to the reforms of Charles V and du Guesclin, and the lessons supposedly learned in the 1370s?

The France which Henry V invaded in 1415 was a very different place from the proud yet tired nation whose guerrillas had harried the last manifestation of *chevauchée* raiding in the fourteenth century. Charles V's successor, his son Charles VI, was subject to periodic bouts of insanity throughout his long reign. Lacking a firm ruler, the French court became a battleground for personal rivalries, particularly between two men: Charles's uncle, Philip the Bold, Duke of Burgundy and Charles's brother, Louis, Duke of Orléans.

The seniority of years which Burgundy possessed controlled the balance of power in his favour until his death in 1404, when he was succeeded by his son, John the Fearless. The new Duke of Burgundy needed all the bravery of his nickname to counteract his rival. For three years the quarrel continued until the Duke of Orléans was murdered by Burgundian agents in 1407. As the new duke was of tender years, command of the Orléanist faction was taken by Bernard of Armagnac, whose daughter married the young duke in 1410, and a civil war began between the Burgundians and the Armagnacs. John the Fearless was driven out of Paris and, in a fateful step, appealed to England for help.

Henry IV's policy had been to play off one French faction against the other. Under Henry V this attitude took on the more cynical aim of delaying the start of the inevitable war until he had fully completed his preparations for it. The English threat was so unmistakable that the Burgundians and Armagnacs in fact concluded an uneasy peace, neither side daring to suppose which way Henry would incline. But civil war had taken its toll. The Armagnac bands had caused even greater havoc and fear among their own countrymen than had the Free Companies of the previous century, so it was a stricken France which awaited Henry's incursions. England, by comparison, was a country blessed with unity. Opposition to the Lancastrian takeover had continued, but with little effect. An

Henry V, from the tomb in his chantry at Westminster Abbey. The head is a modern reconstruction recently restored to the wooden effigy.

attempt by Richard, Earl of Cambridge to put Edmund Mortimer on the throne was nipped in the bud while Henry's troops were preparing to embark, and did nothing to deflect the warrior king from his aims.

But what were his aims? Possibly his principal one was war itself. He had made his name as a war leader, and was determined to show his subjects that the traditional view of the king as a leader in battle, which Edward III had been, was alive and flourishing in his great-grandson. In the discussion earlier about du Guesclin's reconquests in the 1370s it was noted how the ailing king and the Black Prince had not been able to fulfil this role, and this perhaps offers a clue to Henry V's subsequent behaviour. He invaded France simply because it was expected of him.

HENRY'S NORMANDY INVASION

Henry V certainly seems to have been utterly convinced of the rightness of his claim to the French throne, and any consideration of the damage the pursuit of that claim might do to the country he purported to rule never entered his medieval mind. Throughout the negotiations which preceded his invasion he was talking in terms of recovering his just inheritance, and if any preference was made as to what that inheritance consisted of it seems to have concentrated on

The much ruined castle of Monmouth, birthplace of Henry V, from a Victorian engraving.

Normandy and Aquitaine. It may be that the latter was considered as a possible military objective early in 1415, but Aquitaine was a long distance to travel with the large army he was assembling, and there was always the threat from Brittany which could cut his lines of communication. Normandy was nearer. It had many castles and fortified towns which could be used as bases, so his original plan appears to have been a march to Bordeaux capturing Rouen and Paris on the way. Perhaps the story of his grandfather John of Gaunt's 'Grand *Chevauchée'* was taunting him to achieve great things.

Henry's army landed at Harfleur, a port on the Normandy coast now swallowed up in the modern complex of Le Havre. It was the key to Normandy, and Henry must have totally underestimated the resistance that would be brought against him when he attempted to reduce it. The resulting siege took five long, hard weeks which proved as expensive in casualties as it was in time. The vigour and determination of the French defenders was of the highest order as they repaired by night the damage Henry's guns wrought by day. Meanwhile the English soldiers, encamped in the unhealthy salt marshes, were debilitated by an epidemic of dysentery so severe that many had to be ferried home to recover.

The eventual fall of Harfleur looked like a disaster, a far cry from Shakespeare's glorious setting for Henry's 'Once more unto the breach . . .' The garrison surrendered by negotiation, having set a date for relief, but with so many of his army dead, sick or deserted Henry was forced to consider his next move very carefully. He could have garrisoned Harfleur and gone home, but that was not what was expected of a hero king, nor would it persuade parliament to make further monies available if that were all he had to show for his efforts, but a march to Paris, let alone Bordeaux, was now completely out of the question.

The French army, he understood, had concentrated in the capital, and Henry now had only 900 men-at-arms and 5,000 archers available. The resulting action was in a sense a compromise, but a compromise on such a daring scale that the majority of his council recommended strongly against it. Henry V would carry out a *chevauchée*, the manoeuvre which Edward III had always found

Sir Simon Felbrygge, on a monumental brass dated 1416, wears armour typical of that worn during the Agincourt campaign. It is 'alwite' armour, i.e., complete plate armour without the heraldic gipon or surcoat. The rigid helmet, although affording considerable protection to the neck, had the disadvantage that the knight could not turn his head independently of his body.

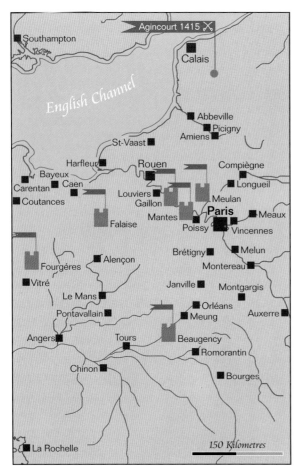

Map of the Agincourt campaign.

most useful for demonstrating his mastery of conquered territory. In Henry's case it must have been the bravado aspect of a *chevauchée* which attracted him, rather than the devastation it could cause. He had taken a long time to reduce a fortress in a country he claimed as his own. A different gesture was required, and to march with impunity through France to Calais would be appropriate. This view of Henry's *chevauchée* as a 'march of pride' is supported by the fact that his troops were kept under very tight discipline, and looting, burning and rape were forbidden. It was very different from Edward III's day, when such activities were the *raison d'être* of the *chevauchée*, and astonished the French, who had recently suffered all three at the hands of their own countrymen, the Armagnacs.

It does not look as though Henry was trying to provoke the French king into attacking him. Instead the whole course of the march suggests that he was trying to avoid the French army, rather than to bait it. Henry was very well informed of the potential of the French leadership. The older men, in particular the Duke of Berry, had personal memories of the later *chevauchée*s of the 1370s, and first-hand experience of the success of du Guesclin's tactics of avoiding pitched battles and harrying a column from a distance. Such men would be unlikely to be drawn into a pitched battle. Henry's force, isolated and weakened, would be a prime target for harassing tactics. Besides, whatever Henry's personal view of his own capabilities or those of his army, the fact remained that they were heavily outnumbered.

The long march which eventually ended at Agincourt was a military feat that brought credit to both sides. Credit went to Henry because, even if Agincourt had not taken place, it would have been quite an achievement to have established on French soil an alternative base to Calais, and linked the two by a well-disciplined march. To the French goes the credit for having responded so decisively to the challenge, and of having reacted so intelligently to Henry's movements. Marshal Boucicault, who had been disgraced at the Battle of Nicopolis, now showed himself as a good commander, and when Henry reached the Somme he found all the crossing places heavily defended for miles upstream from Blanchetaque, the place where Edward III had crossed before Crécy. So Henry turned right, and headed upstream while the French army, which had crossed at Abbeville, shadowed his every move on the far bank.

Amazingly, Henry managed to give them the slip. Either he had a rudimentary map of the area or a reliable source of local knowledge, but having approached the bridge at Corbie the English army turned sharp right to gain advantage of a similarly orientated bend in the river. The gamble paid off. The French army hurried round the course of the Somme, the English set off across country, and used a ford upstream from Peronne.

Henry may have crossed in safety, but he soon found that his way to Calais was now barred by the French advanced guard, who were prepared to resist him without the support of their main body. This is indicated by the battle plan drawn up, probably by Boucicault himself, to oppose Henry should he attempt to cross the Somme. It is interesting to note that it imitates the usual arrangement of the English army by placing dismounted men in the centre, archers in the front and mounted knights on the flanks. So determined was Boucicault to oppose Henry at Peronne that he proposed mounting servants and grooms on the unused horses of the dismounted knights. However, his total force was only slightly more numerous than Henry's, and only about a fifth of what could be assembled by joining the French main body, and it was this consideration that led the French to withdraw northwards.

The French must also have made the observation that the English army appeared to be in a very weak state. They had now marched for a fortnight, and there must have been considerable numbers of stragglers. The discovery of the bodies of dysentery victims on the way, and reports of continuing desertions, must have led to the inevitable conclusion that the time was ripe to strike in force. In this light the decision to fight what was to be known as the Battle of Agincourt can only be seen as an eminently sensible one.

THE BATTLE OF AGINCOURT

The great Battle of Agincourt might so easily have been fought elsewhere. The French had the opportunity of choosing their ground and, as we noted above, they abandoned it in favour of uniting their forces. Nonetheless the French still had the advantage in numbers and morale. The English army had marched for seventeen days with only one day's rest. The French had covered 180 miles in ten days, but they were nearly all mounted. Above all, the odds of four to one against them were appreciated by the English troops, and it was Lord Hungerford who actually voiced the opinion of needing more men, to which Shakespeare, in his Henry V, puts the words, 'We few, we happy few, we band of brothers' into the king's mouth for reply.

Sir William ap Thomas, known as the Blue Knight of Gwent, who fought at Agincourt. His effigy is in St Mary's Church, Abergavenny.

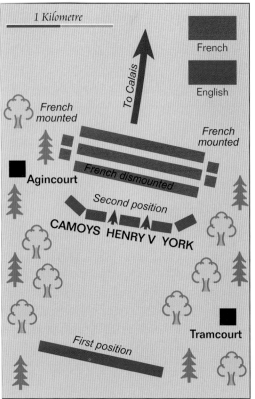

Map of the Battle of Agincourt.

Such heroic sentiments were far from the king's thoughts on the actual day, because we know that prior to the battle he offered terms to the French, stating that he would return Harfleur in exchange for a safe conduct to Calais. It was perhaps only after these proposals had been summarily rejected that the 'do or die' attitude, which is the best-remembered legend of Agincourt, really came into being. To the French a victory would be more than revenge for Poitiers. It could also be just recompense for the years of captivity suffered by their King John – for here was an English king for the taking.

The French had worked out a plan of battle which was based upon the successful English model that had been previously used against them, and it was a tragedy for them that the narrowness of the front they were compelled to take did not allow for the correct deployment. In fact, so totally were Boucicault's original ideas overruled and effectively abandoned that the archers and crossbowmen were placed at the rear of the wings and took little part in the subsequent action.

The English army drew up in a 1,000-yard front straddling the Calais road between two woods. The knights stood four deep, shoulder to shoulder with the archers, and there was no reserve except for a small baggage guard. For four hours there was no movement by either side, then the English advanced, planted stakes, and fired arrows to provoke the French into attacking. At last a response came from the French knights on the flanks who funnelled in towards the English lines, ignoring the archers and concentrating on the dismounted knights. At once they were hit by volleys of arrows, which forced them to turn in on the ranks of their own advance guard, causing great confusion as their charge got under way. But this charge also was halted by the archers, and amidst the confusion of dead and dying horses and men a huge mêlée developed on the muddy ground in the centre.

The archers left their bows and joined in with knives and swords. Within half an hour a wall of French dead had begun to build up across the field, a phenomenon that had not been seen since the Battle of Dupplin Moor, where the field had been much more restricted. So fierce was the crush that men could not move to fight. As one chronicler later commented, 'Great people of them were slain without any stroke.' One such victim was the Duke of York, who was suffocated in the press, and was found later without a mark on his body.

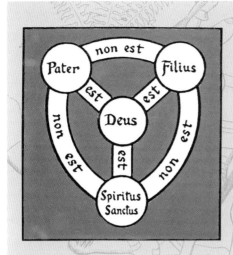

Left: The banner of the Holy Trinity, carried for Henry V at Agincourt. It illustrates the doctrine of the Trinity in a neat pictorial form.

Right: The arms of John de Wodehouse, an English knight who distinguished himself at Agincourt, and was thereupon allowed to change his ermine chevron to the blood-spattered golden one shown here.

The more nimble archers now began to take prisoners and escort them back to the baggage train. But one part of Boucicault's original plan remained – a separate attack on the baggage train. The sight of the French third line preparing to carry out such an attack instead of joining the mêlée in the centre led to Henry's order that all the prisoners be killed, a decision for which he is always heavily criticized as the proof of his bloodthirsty nature. In the circumstances he probably had no choice, nor did he have much time to make a careful decision about anything. During the battle he fought off attacks from eighteen individual French knights, and at one time stood guard over his fallen brother, Humphrey, Duke of Gloucester. Killing the prisoners was no mere act of vindictiveness such as had motivated Edward III after Halidon Hill.

That such a complete victory should be won once again by archers overcoming armoured knights is particularly ironic in view of the great strides made in defensive armour since the last disaster. Monumental effigies of the early fifteenth century show complete plate armour. The flexible aventail of mail which hung down from the edge of the bascinet was now replaced by one or more solid plates that rested on the shoulders, in a combination of helmet and neck guard known as the great bascinet. It was the most complete protection yet devised, but had the disadvantage that the knight could not move his head independently of his body, a hindrance which must have been very acutely felt at Agincourt, when the dismounted knights were set upon by the lighter-footed archers. It was the essential clumsiness of such armour, rather than any considerations of weight, that was its drawback.

Thus was accomplished the Battle of Agincourt, which resulted in 10,000 French casualties and numerous high-ranking prisoners, among whom was the

King Charles VI of France, whose army was defeated by Henry V at the Battle of Agincourt.

The bestowing of knighthood upon a man was sometimes carried out on the field of battle. Here the senior knight dubs the newcomer with his sword.

Duke of Orléans. The victory enhanced Henry's reputation in England and made his name abroad. It also served to consolidate his political position at home, and through him that of the Lancastrian dynasty. But in military terms it was the unexpected outcome of a modest raid, a welcome bonus to an otherwise pointless campaign whose only tangible gain was Harfleur, a potential drain on the English finance and manpower which would be needed to keep it defended. There were no long-term military consequences, except perhaps the most important of all: the fact that after the exhaustion of the 1370s, the English were back in France.

HENRY'S RETURN

In 1417 Henry returned to France to continue where he had left off, but his second campaign was conducted in a very different vein. The invasion of 1415 had been a raid, a gesture and a gambler's adventure. His new strategy shows greater deliberation, more long-term goals, and perhaps even a certain maturity. His army landed at Tonques, on the opposite side of the Seine from Harfleur, and headed for Caen as its first target. In an action not dissimilar to that of Edward III's siege Henry launched two simultaneous assaults from the new town onto the old, and soon after the town had capitulated the castle followed suit. To consolidate his position he decided to establish a line of fortified towns from Verneuil to Alençon, which he carried out town by town, siege by siege. Falaise fell to a bombardment from 20-inch diameter cannonballs, and with lower Normandy firmly in his grasp the next major prize was the Norman capital: Rouen.

In Chapter 1 the siege of Berwick by Edward III was studied in detail for the unparalleled illustration it gives of the chivalric aspect of military life as shown by the gentlemanly courtesies of agreement and negotiation. Henry V's siege of Rouen between 1418 and 1419 gives further insights into the conditions suffered by people at the opposite end of the social spectrum. From the military point of view the siege of Rouen is no different from scores of others. It lacks the strange complexity of Berwick, and the dash of the defenders of Rennes. What it has instead is a pitiable humanity, which brings the whole notion of knightly warfare down to an understandable scale.

Rouen was thoroughly blockaded by the English, who had surrounded it with the conventional palisade but with the addition of a ditch in which traps and pitfalls were concealed. By October the tightness of the English grip, and the constant bombardment, had brought the townspeople to the verge of starvation. John Page, a gentleman of London, was an eyewitness, and recorded his touching observations in the form of a long poem. In one section he dwells particularly upon the shortage of food:

> They ate up dogs, they ate up cats
> They ate up mice, horses and rats
> For a horse's quarter, lean or fat,
> One hundred shillings it was at.
> A horse's head for half a pound,
> A dog for the same money round.
> For 30 pennies went a rat
> For two nobles went a cat.
> For sixpence went a mouse,
> They left but few in any house.

Soon even these commodities became scarce, and the poem continues:

> Then to die they did begin
> All that rich city within
> They died so fast on every day
> That men could not all them in the earth lay
> Even if a child should otherwise be dead
> The mother would not give it bread
> Nor would a child to its mother give
> Everyone tried to live
> As long as he could last
> Love and kindness both were past.

The English army had other considerations concerning its own supplies, and Henry V wrote to the Lord Mayor of London asking, 'And pray you effectually

The fortress and monastery of Mont Saint-Michel, the only fortified place never to be taken by the English during Henry V's campaigns in Normandy. (Photograph by Daphne Clark)

A tower on the outer defence works of Mont Saint-Michel, whose walls are among the best-preserved and most evocative of medieval military architecture in France.

that, in all the haste that ye may, ye wille do arme as many small vessels, as ye may goodly, with vitaille and namely with drink . . . for the refreshing of us and our said host.' The mayor responded with 'Tritty botes of swete wyne, ten of Tyre, ten of Romeney, ten of Malvesey, and a thousand pipes of ale and bere, with thus thousand and five coppes for your host to drink.'

Meanwhile the inhabitants of Rouen starved, and were eventually driven out of the gates by the French garrison who had no means for their relief.

Henry regarded them as the garrison's responsibility, and with the stubbornness that was one of his chief characteristics would not let them through the English lines. Other examples in history had indicated that no honour was lost by allowing refugees out through one's siege lines, but Henry insisted. If the garrison would not take them back, then in the ditch they would stay. And there they did stay, to perish from cold and hunger. They may have been in the ditch when John Page saw them for the first time, and some English soldiers took them food and drink at Christmas time with the king's generous permission.

Eventually a conference was held between besiegers and besieged, and a deal was struck. There were no complex clauses as at Berwick, simply that Rouen must be given up if no relief arrived within eight days. As Agincourt had effectively robbed France of its army, no relief could come, and the city fell, thus ending a long and bitter year for both sides. One chronicler relates that a joust took place between an English and a French knight, but even this diversion sounds less than chivalrous. The Frenchman ran the other through with his lance, and the English had to buy his body back for 400 gold nobles.

Aerial view of Rouen, the capital of Normandy, and the site of one of the bitterest sieges in the Hundred Years' War. Henry V besieged the city in 1418, and the subsequent suffering of the inhabitants earned him a reputation for ruthlessness.

The seal of John the Fearless, the most skilled in military matters of all the Valois Dukes of Burgundy. His murder at the hands of followers of the Dauphin effectively neutralized any opposition to the English occupation of France.

All that could now stop Henry in his tracks would be an accommodation between the Armagnac and Burgundian factions whose rivalries had continued to hinder any serious resistance against him. In 1419 a meeting was arranged between the dauphin Charles, son of the king, who now represented the Armagnacs, and John the Fearless, Duke of Burgundy. The suspicion that the two men had of each other is shown by the choice of meeting-place: the centre of the bridge at Montereau, which had been barricaded at both ends. The suspicion was justified. The dauphin's attendants turned on the Duke of Burgundy and smashed open his skull with their battleaxes.

Henry could have asked for nothing more than this disastrous piece of vengeance which was to keep the French ruling classes divided for years. Well has it been said that the English entered France through the hole in the Duke of Burgundy's skull. A formal Anglo-Burgundian alliance soon followed, and in 1420 a treaty was agreed at Troyes, which provided for Henry's marriage to Catherine, daughter of the King of France, and the establishment of a dual monarchy. Charles VI was to remain King of France until his death, so at a stroke of a pen the dauphin was punished for the action of his followers on the bridge of Montereau by being effectively disinherited.

THE 'AULD ALLIANCE'

Following the Treaty of Troyes the victorious king went home with his French bride, leaving his brother, Thomas, Duke of Clarence, and his able general the Earl of Salisbury in charge of the French campaign against the dauphin, Henry's deadliest enemy. But where was the dauphin to look for help, when ranged against him were the joint forces of England and Burgundy? He turned to Scotland, England's old enemy and a constant source of irritation. But this time his plans were not for a Scottish raid across the border to coincide with a French advance. Instead he welcomed into France a large Scottish army.

It was also to the dauphin's great advantage that the absence of Henry V provided the opportunity for his lieutenants to indulge in the advancement of their own interests. Whereas Henry had been content to control and advance his lines of communication, of which the successful siege of Melun in 1420 was a good example, Clarence endeared himself to his troops by conducting *chevauchée*s to the south and south-west, which brought back large hauls of loot. But mobile raiding forces did not usually take large numbers of English archers with them, and Clarence was to pay the price of this omission. In one such raid into dauphinist territory just north of the Loire he was tracked by a Scottish army under the Earls of Buchan and Wigtown, and a French contingent under the Constable de Lafayette. An English foraging party captured some Scots and, as if this were a signal for a general pursuit, set off under Clarence's leadership for the village of Bauge, where they fought the Scots for possession of the bridge. As John Hardyng's chronicle puts it, the Duke of Clarence '. . . arranged his troops in fear and hurried to Bauge, and would not rest even though it was Easter Eve . . .' As the victorious English began to ford the river, more Scots appeared on the brow of a nearby ridge, and the dismounted Clarence led his men in an impetuous charge uphill. What can have been his motives? Unsupported by archers and isolated from his comrades, Thomas, Duke of Clarence broke every precedent of English arms in France, and paid for it with his life.

Thomas, Duke of Clarence, killed at the Battle of Bauge in 1421 when his force was defeated by a Franco-Scottish army. His death was a blow to his brother, Henry V.

The victory at Bauge put new heart into Dauphin Charles. The Earl of Buchan was created Constable of France, and was joined on the continent by Archibald, fourth Earl of Douglas, the veteran of Homildon Hill, whom the dauphin created Earl of Touraine. New encouragement was given the following August when Henry V died after contracting what is believed to be dysentery while conducting the siege of Meaux. He had returned to France to restore English fortunes after Clarence's death, and had begun the work speedily and brilliantly. Now his brother, John, Duke of Bedford, had to keep the operations going.

The following October the King of England was joined in death by the poor, mad King of France. Naturally enough the dauphin proclaimed himself to be King Charles VII, but under the terms of the Treaty of Troyes the new King of France was the English infant Henry VI. The motivation for war was now crystal clear.

In mid-1423 the dauphin made his first moves against Burgundy, and an army under Sir John Stewart of Darnley besieged Cravant. The army was chiefly composed of Scots, with the addition of mercenaries recruited in Lombardy and Spain. It was a shrewd move on the dauphin's part. The Burgundians were less formidable than the English, and Cravant was isolated from any English garrison. Bedford immediately sent 4,000 English to Cravant's relief under the general command of the Earl of Salisbury. Should the matter come to a pitched battle, it would be the first to be carried out by English and Burgundians working together, so a council of war was held in the cathedral of Auxerre to work out harmonious arrangements for cooperation. This shows good judgement on Salisbury's part, and it was certainly beneficial to the armies to know that such planning had taken place at all. The plans involved the welding together of the armies of two separate nationalities, which was not an easy task. Among the details recorded are that each man was to carry two days' food and that no prisoners were to be taken until the issue of the battle was decided – a wise precaution as the arranging of ransom took time.

The Anglo-Burgundian army found the Franco-Scottish army lining the far side of the River Yonne at Cravant. While the archers provided covering fire the English men-at-arms dismounted and began to ford the river led by the Earl of

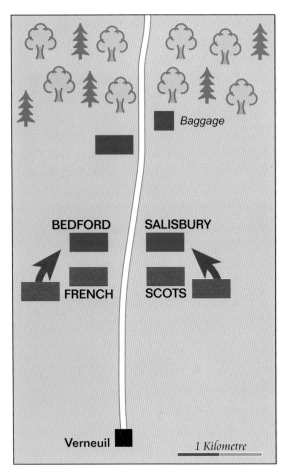

Baggage

BEDFORD

SALISBURY

FRENCH

SCOTS

Verneuil

1 Kilometre

Map of the Battle of
Verneuil.

Salisbury, while the right wing, under Lord Willoughby, contested the bridge. In spite of being forced back initially by the Scots, the Anglo-Burgundians carried the day, the decisive push being provided by the castle garrison who took the Scots in the rear. The mercenaries were the first to flee, after which John Stewart of Darnley lost an eye and was captured. It was a victory for careful planning, good communication and dashing leadership, all of which had been demonstrated by the Earl of Salisbury that day.

The defeat at Cravant did not, however, destroy Charles's faith in the fighting qualities of the Scots, and in 1424 another army, this time consisting of 6,500 troops, landed at La Rochelle and joined forces with the dauphin in the south, where their commander was said to have been welcomed 'as another Messiah'. Unfortunately his countrymen did not take so kindly to this sudden incursion by thousands of foreign troops, whom they denounced as *sacs de vin* and *mangeurs de mouton*. One chronicler went as far as to say that their eventual defeat at Verneuil saved the French from being slaughtered by them!

Verneuil, where the classic battle that is often referred to as the second Agincourt was fought, was a castle in Normandy, and it was the memory of that great defeat that brought Verneuil into the history books at all. A deal had been done with the defenders of Ivry, 30 miles west of Paris, that it would surrender if not relieved by a certain date. The relieving army was that of the dauphin with a large Scottish component, whom the Duke of Bedford eagerly desired to catch in a pitched battle. There lay the French dilemma. Their leaders, naturally enough, wished to avoid another Agincourt, and were content just to capture as many English-held towns as possible, beginning with Verneuil, hoping thus to draw the English from Ivry. But the Scottish leaders were eager for a fight, and their wishes prevailed, so that on 17 August 1424, the allied army stood arrayed on the open plain 1 mile north of the castle of Verneuil. Leading the Scottish army was Archibald, fourth Earl of Douglas.

The second Agincourt was so like the first as to require only brief details of its execution. The Duke of Bedford was a conventional soldier and not one for

A reconstruction of the probable appearance of the mechanism of the gateway and portcullis of the White Castle in Monmouthshire. The drawbridge could be raised so that the gateway was protected by a deep pit. (Illustration by Chris Jones-Jenkins 1991, Cadw: *Welsh Historic Monuments* Crown Copyright)

surprise attacks or complicated flank movements. His battle formation was therefore very similar to that of his brother's at Agincourt, but with the addition of a stronger guard on the baggage train, which he had arranged in a circle at the rear. The chronicler, Jean de Waurin, who was present at both battles, declared that Verneuil was the more strongly fought of the two. There was a worrying moment early in the fight when the French cavalry advanced on the English archers while they were still planting their trusty stakes (the French had obviously learned a lesson from Agincourt) but, in spite of a day of fierce fighting, that initial charge did not decide the victory. Almost the entire Scottish army were killed, including Douglas, his son James, and his son-in-law, the Earl of Buchan.

The Battle of Verneuil was the last time in the Hundred Years' War that a large Scottish army was to take the field, and their defeat meant that the dauphin Charles was now totally isolated south of the Loire. Even his great fortress town of Orléans was now likely to be captured by the English unless some sort of miracle happened.

The Long, Losing War

9

The campaigns of the 1380s, which brought to a halt the first phase of the Hundred Years' War, came to an end from an exhaustion of will, of resources, and of great leaders on both sides. During the second phase in the 1420s, the decade from which the decline of English power in France is usually traced, any portents of a future collapse were either absent or unheeded. Henry V may have been dead, but of great leaders there was no shortage, and once again we see the emergence of talent on the French side from an unconventional direction. Poton de Xaintrailles began his career as a mercenary. So did his comrade in arms, Etienne Vignolles, called La Hire. Jean Dunois, Count of Longueville, bastard son of the Duke of Orléans, overcame the handicap of his illegitimacy to lead French armies to glory. Others had more exalted backgrounds. Arthur de Richemont, brother of the then Duke of Brittany, and son of the duke victorious at Auray, was created Constable of France in 1436.

On the English side the war flung into prominence one name above all others: John Talbot, who from 1442 onwards held the title of Earl of Shrewsbury. Talbot was born in about 1387, and may well have received his first taste of action at the Battle of Shrewsbury in 1403. We know that he was present at the sieges of Aberystwyth in 1407/08 and Harlech in 1409. His time in Wales was marked by no great victories, but showed grim determination and ruthlessness that marked the beginning of a legendary aura. He served at Melun and Meaux under Henry V, and on his return to France in 1427 began the phase of his career for which he is best remembered and feared. His first engagement was at the capture of Pontorson by the Earl of Warwick. At the subsequent siege of Montargis he was forced to withdraw, and hearing that La Hire had captured Le Mans marched to its rescue with only 300 men. His small band arrived outside the walls just as dawn was breaking, and swiftly assaulted the sleepy guards. Le Mans was retaken, and Talbot acquired a reputation for rapid action that was to endear him to the soldiers who fought under his banner. He was shortly to be tested in a series of attacks which were the preliminary to what was planned as the first major English advance since Henry V's Normandy campaign.

Opposite: This fine equestrian statue outside the Town Hall in Vannes represents Arthur de Richemont, Duke of Brittany and Constable of France. De Richemont fought at Agincourt, was a companion of Jeanne d'Arc, and played a decisive part in the great French victory of Formigny (1450), which drove the English from Normandy. The surname of this French hero is particularly ironic, as it is the French version of Richmond, the title bestowed upon the Dukes of Brittany by the English sovereign.

THE SIEGE OF ORLÉANS

By the year 1428 the dauphin Charles had reached his lowest ebb. As the English now occupied all the area between the Seine and the Loire, the latter river marked a very genuine frontier between their Anglo-Burgundian occupied territory and his French kingdom of Berry. For the English conquest to continue, and in particular for the late Henry's long-term aim of removing the rival king from the throne of France, the Loire had to be crossed and the fight taken to him in his own territory. From all the available crossing-points the Duke of Bedford boldly selected one that would have tremendous psychological effect in addition to its military advantage – the city of Orléans.

Orléans is the nearest point to Paris on the River Loire. Strategically it had much to recommend it. English armies advancing south from Orléans could be easily supplied from Paris, and its capture would be as great a boost to English morale as it would be depressing to the French. The decision to attack was therefore taken, after a brief pause for consideration of a moral point. Orléans, apparently, did not belong to Charles VII, but to his brother the Duke of Orléans, who had been held captive in England since Agincourt. It was an act without precedent in what remained of the rules of war to attack the territory of a knight held captive, but it illustrates the importance in which Orléans was held that this particular objection was brushed aside.

The summer of 1428 was spent in raising the army, which eventually numbered about 5,000 men under the command of Thomas Montagu, Earl of Salisbury. Salisbury was the experienced soldier who had commanded at Cravant, and his excellent eye for strategy is well illustrated in the preliminaries to his campaign. His first major objective was the town of Janville, which lies 15 miles north of Orléans, to use it as a forward base for what he foresaw as a long siege. Janville fell after a brisk attack, enabling Salisbury to begin the isolation of Orléans by capturing Jargeau upstream and Beaugency and Meung downstream. The road to the latter two towns passes quite close to Orléans, so on 8 September the city had its first glimpse of the English army in the form of a small detachment guarding the road along which the artillery train would have to pass. As it happened Meung surrendered at the threat of artillery fire, but Beaugency proved a much more difficult operation. Its castle and its abbey, which had been fortified, were just within range of the long bridge. A siege of the castle began on 20 September, and on the 25th a simultaneous attack was launched on the castle from the north, and on the opposite end of the bridge from the south, the possession of Meung having enabled the English army to cross the river. There was a fierce hand-to-hand fight on the bridge (pieces of armour have been dredged from the river) and with the bridge in English hands the garrison

Jean Dunois, Count of Longueville, bastard son of the Duke of Orléans, was a companion of Jeanne d'Arc and played a prominent part in the long campaign against the English.

surrendered the following day. A week later Jargeau surrendered to Sir William de la Pole and the isolation of Orléans was complete. The English army joined forces and made camp on the southern bank of the Loire opposite the city.

The defences of Orléans matched its strategic importance. The city was naturally strong, the river being 400 yards wide where it was crossed by the

Map of the later Hundred Years' War.

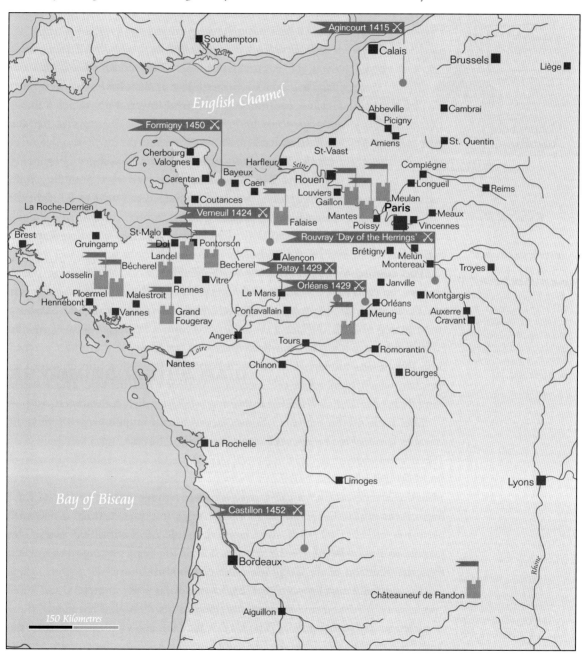

kingdom of France and drive the English out of her country. She was told to accomplish this by going to see the dauphin at Chinon, raising the siege of Orléans, and crowning him King of France at Reims. As to the great siege, the winter operations had been going on for some time when Jeanne acted. Her interview with the dauphin at Chinon, during which she convinced him of the genuine nature of her mission, took place about a fortnight after the Day of the Herrings, a time when French morale was at its lowest. As his original relieving army had been cut to pieces by what was virtually the guard of a baggage train, the dauphin's decision to raise another army, with or without Jeanne at its head, represented a considerable act of faith.

The assembling of the new army took time, a fact which irritated Jeanne, for she was eager to be in action, and they eventually left for Orléans on 27 April 1429. As a collection of fighting men some 4,000 strong, the army was nothing remarkable, but as a cohesive group of inspired individuals it was unique in

The statue of Jeanne d'Arc at Orléans marks the site of the unexpected reversal in English fortunes which will for ever be associated with the name of the Maid. It was her inspiration which turned the inhabitants of a defeated city into a fighting force, and set in motion the long process by which the Hundred Years' War was brought to an end.

A tapestry in the Museum of Orléans, depicting Jeanne d'Arc with her famous banner, entering Orléans in 1429.

history. The army marched with the devotion of pilgrims, happy and elated. Whatever the ordinary soldiers thought she was, saint, mascot or magician, she gave them an inspiration they had never had before, and strict discipline. Swearing was forbidden, prostitutes were banned, and everyone attended Mass and made confession. In a spirit of confidence and ecstasy the army advanced. Her army, with its train of supplies, marched proudly on to Orléans through the incomplete English lines, and she began to inspire the defenders of the city by her self-confidence. Perhaps inevitably, however, the deep trust in her did not extend as far as the French commanders, whose charisma she had totally supplanted. They may have been demoralized by recent events, but their years of experience as hard-bitten soldiers made them very reluctant to accept Jeanne's military advice or direction. Certainly they recognized her contribution to morale, her role as a figurehead and an example, but she was not admitted to their councils of war. For example, one problem facing the French forces was the need to get a further large train of supplies safely into Orléans. The plan worked out by the Duke of Alençon, supposedly in command of Jeanne's army, and Dunois of Orléans, the commander of the garrison, was for a number of barges to be brought a few miles upstream, loaded away from the English lines, then floated on the current downstream to the city, while Alençon's army proceeded along the southern bank. The scheme worked perfectly, but the presence of Jeanne d'Arc has tended to obscure a straightforward and successful military operation for which Dunois and Alençon deserve more credit than they have ever received.

Sir Richard Redman's tomb at Harewood in Yorkshire bears this monumental effigy of a knight dressed in a suit of armour typical of that worn in the years of the 'Long, Losing War'. His helmet is a great bascinet, and he wears a collar of the supporter of the House of Lancaster, which consisted of a series of 'S's. He died in 1425.

If Jeanne wrought any miracle at Orléans it was in the hearts and minds of the ordinary French soldiers and civilians – and that was wonder enough. As she had transformed the relieving army so she transformed the inhabitants of Orléans from a broken-down, weary and starving mass into a fighting community. The very day that she entered the city an attack was being mounted on the English Fort Saint-Loup, probably as a diversion to cover the arrival of the rest of the supplies. Jeanne galloped out of the town and so heartened the attackers that they actually captured and burned the fort, probably greatly surprising themselves into the bargain. Admittedly Saint-Loup was isolated outside the English lines, evidence indeed of the disdain the English had for the French military capacity prior to Jeanne's arrival, but once smoke was seen rising from the fort, Talbot, who had advanced with a small relieving force, prudently withdrew.

The capacity of the French to fight was dramatically confirmed a few days later. South of the bridge was an English fortress converted from the Convent of the Augustins. In a well planned operation the Orléans army moved against this fortress and the mid-river fort of Les Tourelles. Under the direction of Dunois a bridge of boats was constructed from the little island of Saint-Aignan to the southern bank, while the Tourelles garrison was engaged. After a day of fierce fighting led by the Maid the Augustins fort was captured, and the following day the full strength of 4,000 French troops was launched against Les Tourelles, which with the remnants of the Augustins garrison held about 500 men. The barbican earthwork was first to fall, and as the English retreated across the drawbridge to Les Tourelles it collapsed under their weight. A poignant touch was provided by a gallant English knight called Glasdale, who was cast into the river and drowned, bearing in his hand the banner of the late great English captain, John Chandos. The French were able to redouble their attack by constructing a temporary bridge across the arches they had previously destroyed, and Les Tourelles was taken. The English were now isolated on the southern bank, and within a few days they decided to raise the siege. Enough was enough.

Orléans was the turning-point in the long, losing war. The miracle that was Jeanne d'Arc had shown that victory was not only possible, but almost inevitable. Years later her companion-in-arms, Dunois, was willing to testify that prior to the coming of Jeanne d'Arc 200 Englishmen would put to flight 800 or 1,000 Frenchmen. Now all was changed.

One other transformation now occurred – in the attitude of the French commanders towards her. She had won her spurs at Orléans, and could be trusted and consulted. They began a furious week of campaigning and fighting, as Jeanne speedily retook the fortresses along the Loire which Salisbury and Talbot had so methodically reduced before Orléans. Jargeau was the first to be liberated. Three shots from a bombard practically demolished one of the main towers, and at Jeanne's insistence an immediate assault was mounted, during which the Maid herself ascended one of the scaling ladders. The Earl of Suffolk was captured on the bridge as the English army escaped, and like a true knight, enquired anxiously of his captor if he too were a knight. When the Frenchman confessed that he was only a squire, Suffolk knighted him on the spot and surrendered.

Beaugency fell after a short artillery bombardment of its huge twelfth-century keep. To shorten the range some guns were floated by barge into the middle of the river. But the vital factor was the presence of Jeanne d'Arc which seems to have brought the domino theory into effect. On hearing the news that Beaugency had fallen, the garrison at Meung lost heart and withdrew towards Patay, 18 miles due north. At this point Jeanne received reinforcements in the shape of 1,000 Bretons under Arthur de Richemont, Constable of France. It was his first meeting with the redoubtable Maid, and his words as she embraced him give a vivid illustration of the ambivalent attitude of the French commanders towards her. 'Whether you are sent from God I know not: if you are I do not fear you, for God knows that my heart is pure. If you come from the Devil I fear you still less.' In common with all his contemporaries he would use Jeanne, but he could not understand her.

The gilt-bronze effigy of Sir Richard Beauchamp, Earl of Warwick, in the Beauchamp, Chapel, St Mary's Church, Warwick. Sir Richard Beauchamp was a loyal servant of the English cause in France during the minority of Henry VI.

Once again Jeanne's boldness prevailed, and the French army, now about 6,000 strong, set off in vigorous pursuit of the retreating English. As the latter were encumbered by a slow baggage-train the French rapidly gained ground, and Sir John Fastolf decided to make a stand near Patay. While Fastolf deployed his troops on a ridge, Talbot stationed himself with a company of archers to the south. Both knew the precarious nature of their position. Theirs was the only English field army in France at the time, and they were being approached by a large French force elated after a week of victories.

A statue of Jeanne d'Arc at Mont Saint-Michel.

For some reason Jeanne did not lead the attack at Patay. This may well have been a wise precaution in view of the number of English archers who would be operating unencumbered by siege works, and any of them would have been eager to bring down the witch who had plagued them. Instead La Hire and Poton de Xaintrailles led the vanguard, followed by the main body under Alençon and Dunois, with de Richemont and Jeanne d'Arc at the rear. La Hire and Xaintrailles led the French knights in a well-conducted cavalry charge, which swept round the archers' stakes to attack them from the flanks. It was a bold move which paid off. The unprepared archers were caught, and the main body lay open to attack. The engagement was over very quickly. Sir John Talbot was captured, as was Lord Scales, and Sir John Fastolf led an ignominious withdrawal with the survivors. Defeated and disgraced, he was deprived of his Garter, but this was later revoked.

On 17 July, after a march in strength that was more like a military parade, Charles the Dauphin was anointed and crowned King Charles VII at Reims Cathedral. It was a political masterstroke. According to the English, the rightful King of France was a boy of seven who held court in London and whom his so-called subjects had never seen. The legitimacy of the new Charles VII was a statement of intent to the French people and to the Burgundians who had English sympathies. Could anything now stop his progress?

Had the king been willing to risk the hazards of war against the English a little longer, the campaigns might well have gone from strength to strength, but he preferred to receive the surrender of Burgundian towns, hoping thereby to prise Burgundy from his English allies. In September Jeanne led an attack on Paris. While Alençon maintained observation over the Porte Saint-Denis, Jeanne launched her army against the Porte Saint-Honoré. This time things did not go her way. Wounded in the leg by a crossbow bolt, she lay in the open until dark, as none of her erstwhile companions would come to her rescue.

When winter came Charles VII disbanded his army, leaving the conduct of

Model by Peter Wroe of Richard Beauchamp's armour, which is in the Milanese style of about 1450. (Board of the Trustees of the Royal Armouries II 194)

the war to a few garrisons and mercenary bands whom Jeanne was permitted to lead. But the spirit which she had earlier supplied in the cause of France did not work with these forces. In May she took part in a sortie from the beleaguered town of Compiègne. The French lingered to pillage, giving the Burgundian troops time to rally. They put the French to flight, and the commander of Compiègne, fearing that the Anglo-Burgundians would enter the town, was forced to close its gates before all his army had returned. Jeanne d'Arc was one of those left outside, and soon she was in the hands of her enemies.

The subsequent story of Jeanne, of her imprisonment and trial, and execution at the stake, is one from which no one emerges with any credit. The most amazing and disgraceful feature is that King Charles VII made no attempt to negotiate for her, or in any way to liberate her. There exists the possibility that Charles may have considered exchanging Jeanne for Talbot, who had been captured at Patay, because it is recorded that Charles bought Talbot in May, shortly after Jeanne's trial began. But nothing was set in motion, and Talbot was not in fact liberated until 1433, when he was exchanged for Poton de Xaintrailles.

For their part, the English regarded the capture of the Maid as an event of immense importance. They sensed that the spell could be broken, perhaps even interpreting that in the literal sense, considering the reputation she had acquired. A brief attempt was made to assert English kingly authority by arranging for Henry VI's coronation in Paris, but the event, though carefully stage-managed, lacked the authenticity which the pious masses demanded, and achieved nothing. The trial of Jeanne had greater potential. If she could be denounced by an ecclesiastical court as a witch and a heretic, her achievements would be degraded along with her own reputation.

THE COMPANIONS FIGHT ON

King Charles VII of France, whose throne was secured by the activities of Jeanne d'Arc. Although history reviles Dauphin Charles for abandoning the Maid, it was he who began a long, slow series of reforms in French military life which prepared the country for its time of greatness in the succeeding century.

Though deprived of her presence, the Maid's companions continued her work. In February 1436 Arthur de Richemont attacked Paris and began a carefully planned siege. A well-timed riot in the city enabled the French troops to enter unmolested, and the English garrison, who had taken refuge in the Bastille, were allowed to withdraw. At the same time as the submission of Paris came the long-awaited and planned reconciliation with Burgundy. The English in France were now totally isolated, yet the war still had nearly twenty years left to run.

During these twenty years France gradually recovered from two crises. The immediate one of the expulsion of the English was a long, slow process, the government's exhaustion allowing it to take little initiative, but rather to wait for the English generals to make the first move. The other crisis was more insidious. The long-lasting plague of unemployed mercenaries continuing their own private wars for their own ends once again threw the people of France into terror. In 1444 the Treaty of Tours was concluded. It achieved a truce (a lasting peace was still out of the question) and a marriage between England's King Henry VI, now twenty-three, and Charles VII's niece, Margaret of Anjou. It was a match well regarded on both sides of the Channel, none suspecting the effect it would have in England in the years to come.

THE END IN NORMANDY

When the war resumed in what was to prove its final phase, it was the French king who took the initiative by besieging Le Mans. His army was impatient for action, and his councillors were impatient for results. England was presently undergoing the internal political turmoil which was shortly to emerge in armed conflict as the Wars of the Roses. In 1450 a new Lieutenant of Henry VI arrived in France – Edmund Beaufort, Duke of Somerset, who embarked upon a rash policy of provocation, which suited ideally the French king's aims. Instead of

This photograph shows the interior of the main gate to the castle of Fougères, one of the three fortresses on the border between Brittany and the rest of France.

Falaise Castle, in Normandy, was the birthplace of William the Conqueror. In 1450 it became associated with another French hero when it was surrendered to Poton de Xaintrailles in exchange for the captured John Talbot, the leading English commander of his day. (Photograph by Ian Clark)

withdrawing the ousted English garrisons of Maine to Caen or Rouen, he moved them to erstwhile neutral territory on the borders with Brittany. He also entrusted an Aragonese leader of mercenaries, François de Surenne, with a revenge attack for Maine. In March 1449 de Surenne captured the border fortress of Fougères, which was owned by the Duke of Brittany whose uncle, Arthur de Richemont, had already done so much for the French cause. The capture of Fougères was the final break between England and Brittany.

Charles VII entrusted the final campaign to drive the English out of Normandy to the veteran Dunois of Orléans. For twelve months the French

progressed steadily in a campaign of brief sieges that was everywhere successful. Three columns operated separately but in concert: the Counts of Eu and Saint-Pol in the North; Dunois in the centre, supported by the Duke of Alençon; and in the west, where Normandy borders Brittany, Arthur de Richemont and his nephew, the duke. This latter also had the satisfaction of retaking Fougères in November. Rouen had fallen in October, and as winter wore on it was joined by the symbolic prize of Harfleur, Henry V's first victory on French soil.

English resistance was feeble. Talbot tried to harry the French armies, but his resources were insufficient, and in March 1450 reinforcements under Sir Thomas Kyriell had to be sent to Normandy. Kyriell's army consisted of a mere 2,500 men. Note how it was commanded by a commoner – just as in the *chevauchée* of 1370 led by Sir Robert Knowles. Perhaps no one of noble birth was willing to risk his reputation by leading what was likely to be a forlorn hope. Kyriell made a bad start. Instead of advancing on Bayeux he responded to local requests to reduce the town of Valognes, which he accomplished, though not without the help of reinforcements sent from other parts of Normandy, which the beleaguered forces could scarce afford. But the loss of time far outweighed any gain. Four weeks had elapsed since his landing, giving time for two separate French armies to advance on the Cotentin peninsula in search of him.

The first French army of about 3,000 men was under the command of the Count of Clermont. Being outnumbered by Kyriell's augmented force, he made no attempt to stop his advance across the estuary of the River Vire, where the English army was for a time delayed by the high tide. Instead he waited to be joined by the army commanded by Arthur de Richemont, whose 2,000-strong contingent was about 20 miles south-west of Clermont's at Coutances.

By 15 April 1450, Kyriell's army was encamped by the little village of Formigny. Yet during that morning the English army did not continue on its way. Perhaps Kyriell wished to emulate his predecessors at Agincourt and Verneuil, and destroy Clermont's army in a field battle. What, of course, he did not know was that he was opposed not by one army but two, the second of which was moving towards him with great rapidity. The communications between Clermont and Richemont must have been of the highest order by any standards, and remarkable by medieval ones, for as Clermont advanced from the west de Richemont seems to have pinpointed the exact spot where Kyriell would be, and moved upon it, shadowing his comrade's moves perfectly. Sir Thomas, for his part, formed a line of battle strikingly similar to that employed at Agincourt, and prepared to meet the threat from the east.

The analogy with Agincourt might well have extended as far as another crushing English victory, had the day continued the way it began, because the headstrong young Clermont disregarded the advice of his older colleagues and led an impetuous attack on foot against the lines of English archers. The archers managed to hold them off, and after two hours of fighting, during which a counter-attack by the archers captured two French field guns – an ironic comment on Charles VII's modernization programme – the French army began to give way. At this point de Richemont appeared from the south approaching Kyriell's left flank. With great difficulty Kyriell redressed his line to face the new threat, but the fresh troops carried the day.

The battle of Formigny sounded the death knell for the English occupation of Normandy, and the remaining fortresses fell like houses of cards. Caen, held by the Duke of Somerset, capitulated to four columns of troops and artillery fire. Falaise surrendered to Xaintrailles as an exchange for the captured John Talbot. Finally Cherbourg collapsed under a remarkable bombardment from the artilleryman Jean Bureau, who waterproofed his shore-based guns before every high tide by covering them with tallow and hides. On 11 August 1450 English rule in Normandy came to an end.

FAREWELL TO AQUITAINE

The loss of Gascony was even more poignant. Charles VII's army entered Bordeaux as liberators, but were received as invaders. Aquitaine, after all, had been English for three centuries, and the burgesses had sent a request for help to Henry VI when Charles was on his way. Henry's response was to send them his greatest soldier: John Talbot, since 1442 Earl of Shrewbury, and now in his mid-sixties. Henry VI could scarcely afford to let him go, because the turbulent events which later became known as the Wars of the Roses were beginning to cast a shadow across his realm. The army which Talbot took to Gascony was only about 3,000 strong in all, but it was considered sufficient for the job. Gascony welcomed him, and most of the western parts of the province were back in English hands by the autumn of 1452. During the winter Charles VII gathered his forces for a final reckoning with the man whose name had already become a legend, and three separate French armies converged on Bordeaux. The centre column was under the command of Jean Bureau, who had already made his name for good artillery work, and it was with a considerable artillery train that Bureau's army approached the small walled town of Castillon.

Even though Bureau's army was formidable (some chroniclers claim he had 300 guns with him), the reputation of Talbot was sufficient to make him adopt a fundamentally defensive posture before Castillon. Instead of attempting to surround the town his men constructed a palisaded earthwork to the south, out of range of the defenders' guns. It was a considerable work, using the little

John Talbot, Earl of Shrewsbury, killed at the Battle of Castillon in 1453. So disfigured was his corpse that the herald could identify him only by his teeth. This cast of his effigy is in the Victoria and Albert Museum.

River Lidoire as one side and with deep ditches and ramparts on the others. The numerous guns were placed around the perimeter and the base was ready for an assault on the town, or to resist an attack by the famous Talbot. Talbot's advance on Castillon was rapid and tiring. His army left Bordeaux in the early hours of 16 July, and marched throughout the day and most of the night. At daybreak on the 17th, the French advance guard (mostly archers) in the Priory of Saint-Laurent were taken completely by surprise and overwhelmed. It was a fitting climax to the long and difficult march.

Could the impetus be continued? Sensibly, Talbot decided to let his men rest, while his scouts investigated the dispositions of the French main body in their earthwork. Their respite was short-lived because just as Talbot was preparing to attend Mass prior to setting out again, a report arrived that the French were abandoning the position and moving away. But what the scouts had actually seen were servants riding the horses away from the French camp to make room within for the archers fleeing from the earlier action at the priory.

The French army and its guns, secure behind the ditch and palisades, and outnumbering the English by six to one, must have provided a

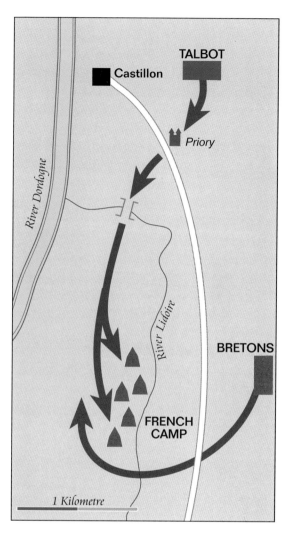

Map of the Battle of Castillon.

chilling sight, but Talbot could not bring himself to call a retreat. Instead he led an attack in the teeth of cannon fire. Such a move could ultimately have only one result, but the struggle continued for some time, until a detachment of Bretons, whom the French had stationed some distance away, took Talbot in the right flank. As he fought to organize a withdrawal Talbot's horse was struck by a cannonball; the animal fell, trapping the aged knight beneath it. A French soldier seized the opportunity to drive his battleaxe into Talbot's skull. That was the end of the battle. The Anglo-Gascon army dispersed, and the long history of 'England's first colony' came to an end. The body of the earl was found the next day, recognizable only because a certain tooth was missing. His remains were taken home to England, and interred at Whitchurch. The death of Talbot at the Battle of Castillon had ended the Hundred Years' War.

The Wars of   10
the Roses

When Henry Tudor eventually succeeded to the English throne in 1485 he took as his badge the Tudor Rose, which, in heraldic terms, is parti-coloured red and white. It symbolized his marriage to Elizabeth of York, a union popularly regarded as uniting York and Lancaster, the warring factions indicated by the two roses. There is still some controversy as to who first coined the phrase 'The Wars of the Roses' for the conflict that had preceded this union. Sir Walter Scott has been suggested, but his actual words, in the novel *Anne of Gierstein* are: '. . . the civil discords so dreadfully prosecuted in the wars of the White and Red Roses', which is not quite the phrase we are used to. Nevertheless, it has passed into common usage, leaving generations of schoolchildren convinced that it was all something to do with Yorkshire and Lancashire and commemorated every year by a cricket match.

The red rose was a very ancient badge of the House of Lancaster. A golden rose had been brought into English heraldry by Eleanor, the queen of Edward I, and was used as a badge by Edward II and Edward III. Edward I's brother, the first Duke of Lancaster, changed the colour to red for his own badge, and a red rose was flown on the standard of Henry Bolingbroke, who became Henry IV. Strangely enough, little, if any use seems to have been made of the red rose during the Wars of the Roses until the astute Henry Tudor advanced his claim. This was largely because no one during this period was actually Duke of Lancaster, so the Lancastrians fought and died under the banners of the King of England.

There were, however, Dukes of York who used the white rose, obtained originally from the Mortimers, so of great potency in advancing kingly claims. But the white rose was one badge among many others, including the sun in splendour and a rather fine-looking falcon. It was the happy coincidence of two similar badges that led to the famous association being made when Henry Tudor to realize the power of explanation it could have.

So much for the Roses, what of the Wars? Was England really split in two for a generation with the country laid waste and trade suspended? Apparently not, because

The seal of Henry VI of England. Son of the warrior King Henry V, the pious and studious Henry VI presided over the English withdrawal from France, and suffered the upheaval of the Wars of the Roses.

Opposite: The Great Gate of the castle of Raglan, which served as the principal entrance from the 1460s onwards. It was built by Sir William Herbert, a veteran of the French Wars, and showing as a result some considerable French influence in its design.

an analysis of the fighting shows brief and sporadic outbreaks of activity which were largely confined within short periods of years. The longest continuous time which could be called a war lasted for just one year from the landing of the Yorkists in Kent in June 1460 and the advance on Northampton, to the final mopping-up after Towton the following April and May. The floods which occurred in November 1460 probably caused more disruption to normal life. The suggestion that most of England was very peaceful during the latter half of the fifteenth century is in fact supported by the Burgundian Commynes (1447–1511) who commented that '. . . out of all the countries which I have personally known England is the one where public affairs are best conducted and regulated with least damage to the people'.

The first war is usually regarded as beginning with the First Battle of St Albans in 1455. This engagement was one more example of a process which had occurred several times before – the attempt by an aggrieved baron to put his case before the king. York had, in fact, tried a similar exercise in 1451, and in spite of raising a large army was forced to abandon his plans before any fighting took place. Where the 1455 incident differed from the much larger strategic conflict of 1451 was in the way it ended in violence. The 1451 affair had ended with the humiliation of the leader of the protesting party: the Duke of York. This was two years before the Battle of Castillon. English armies were still engaged in France while this domestic quarrel was going on. In fact, John Talbot, Earl of Shrewsbury, was instrumental in bringing it to a peaceful and successful conclusion in favour of the king. But by 1455 he was dead, and York had much less to fear.

YORK AND LANCASTER

Richard Plantagenet, Duke of York, was born in 1411, and before he reached his sixth birthday both his father and his uncle had met violent deaths. His father, the Earl of Cambridge, was executed by Henry V in 1415 following the failure of a conspiracy to put Edmund Mortimer on the throne, while Richard's uncle, the Duke of York, paid for his staunch loyalty to Henry V by being suffocated to death on the field of Agincourt. He died childless, so the title of Duke of York passed to the boy Richard.

In 1424 Richard's other uncle, Edmund Mortimer, in whose name so many rebellions had been plotted and so many lives had already been lost, also died childless, so the two separate lines of descent from Edward III now came together in Richard's inheritance. Richard of York was now the sole personification of the union between York and Mortimer, the sole legitimate Mortimer heir and the sole York heir. He received the Earldom of March to add to his titles, the castle of Wigmore, and the Mortimer's Earldom of Ulster – giving him a useful sanctuary in Ireland should he ever contemplate rebellion.

The statue of Richard, Duke of York, on the site of the Battle of Wakefield, 1460, where he met his death. An accomplished soldier who served with distinction in France, Richard of York was the inheritor of both the Mortimer and the Yorkist claims to the throne of England. His death on the fields below Sandal Castle marked the end of the first phase of the Wars of the Roses. The statue is a faithful copy of a contemporary one which was formerly on the old Welsh bridge in Shrewsbury.

In 1438 Richard married Cecily Neville, of the powerful Marcher family. She gave Richard children and a collection of relatives who would alternately help and hinder the House of York for the next thirty years. Among these Richard acquired a brother-in-law, the Earl of Salisbury, who was to fight beside him at Wakefield, and a young nephew of ten, another Richard, who in time would inherit the titles of Salisbury and Warwick, and, with the epithet of 'Kingmaker', play a decisive part in the fate of his uncle's house.

During the English withdrawal from France Richard of York served with great distinction, and by 1452 he had become the richest magnate in England. The statue of him at Wakefield, a faithful copy of a contemporary effigy formerly in Shrewsbury, shows a proud man, successful in war and peace, and the only man in England with a lineage that could seriously threaten the overpowering position which the Lancastrian line had secured for itself.

The only other serious rivals to York were the Lancastrian branch who had become the Dukes of Somerset. They were the Beaufort family, descended, like York, from Edward III, but through John of Gaunt. The Beauforts were originally Gaunt's illegitimate offspring legitimized by his marriage to their mother following the death of his first wife, Blanche, the mother of Henry IV. Just as the Mortimer and York families had come together in the person of Richard, so would the Beaufort and the main Lancastrian line do the same many years later, when Margaret Beaufort married Edmund Tudor, son of Owen Tudor and Queen Catherine, widow of Henry V, and produced the future Henry VII.

York's present concern was not with Margaret, but with her uncle, Edmund Beaufort, the second Duke of Somerset, because he and Richard of York were the main candidates for the position of Protector of the Realm during Henry VI's periodic bouts of insanity. Their fortunes varied, and each fell into and out of favour. In 1448 Edmund Beaufort replaced York as Lieutenant in France and York was posted to Ireland – an unfortunate choice for a virtual exile, as there were large Mortimer estates of Ulster. So the rivalry continued, the Yorkist faction taking the offensive by suggesting that the new Prince of Wales, Prince Edward, born to Queen Margaret and her chaste, saintly king, was in fact the son of Edmund Beaufort. The truth or otherwise of the suggestion was never established, but such a liaison could well explain the almost fanatical attachment the Beauforts had to the main Lancastrian line.

In May 1455 the political struggles between Beaufort and York broke into physical violence at St Albans, the protagonists in the brief conflict little suspecting that to future historians they were launching the Wars of the Roses. St Albans represented an attempt by York to secure the person of the king, then under the protection of Edmund Beaufort, and St Albans is where the Yorkist army caught up with King Henry and his Lancastrian supporters.

The clock tower at St Albans. The brief Battle of St Albans in 1455 was fought in the streets around this tower.

The First Battle of St Albans was unlike any other battle in the wars to come. It was, first of all, extremely brief, and fought entirely within the confines of the historic town. We have been left a description of it written by the abbot of St Albans Abbey, John Whethamstede. It may well be a literal eyewitness account, for one can imagine the worthy abbot stationed on top of the great abbey gateway, noting every detail of the conflict raging below.

When the approach of the Yorkists was noted the Lancastrians began to fortify the town as best they could, dropping tree trunks across the streets, and reinforcing the old town ditch. The attacks began at ten o'clock, and were held off until the Duke of York's nephew, Richard of Warwick, found a weak spot in the defences, apparently by breaking through some houses beside the Chequers Inn. Their sudden arrival in the marketplace caused great alarm, so a warning bell (probably the bell in the four-teenth-century clock tower) was rung to call every man to arms. Once the Yorkists were in the main streets a fierce fight developed. The royal banner was flung to one side and the king himself was wounded in the neck by an arrow. In the thick of the action fell the very man on whose behalf the fighting had taken place. Edmund Beaufort, second Duke of Somerset, had received a prophecy that he would die at Easter. Easter had passed, but he had since had a recurrent dream of Windsor Castle, a place which he had subsequently avoided. When the battle was over he was found slumped in the doorway of the Castle Inn, beneath a swinging sign bearing a picture of Windsor Castle.

RAISING ARMIES

The St Albans affair begs one particular question. How was it that a wealthy landowner could so easily raise an army to oppose the king, when for a generation it had been the monarch alone who had raised armies for the wars in France? Were lords such as York so powerful that they had a standing army who would fight for them alone? The surprising answer is yes, they did effectively possess a standing army, or at least one that could be quickly assembled. Even more strange is the fact that they were able to muster troops more easily than the king himself.

This strange paradox arose out of the organizational arrangements set up during the latter part of the Hundred Years' War and now transferred from the need for foreign invasion and occupation to purely domestic quarrels. I have noted earlier the system of raising armies by contract, the brainchild of Edward

III for launching his campaigns in France which proved its real worth in the ease with which armies could be quickly raised and garrisons maintained. To sum up the original working of the system: a number of contract captains, usually nobles, settled individual terms of service by negotiation with the king, drawing up a fairly standard form of contract specifying rates of pay, profit to be expected from plunder and so on. The reader will recall that quite early after such systems were adopted Sir John Chandos had acquired a reputation for being a good 'employer'. Such men had no difficulty in finding troops for the king's service.

But one side in the Wars of the Roses was not for the king, and it is a measure of how successful the system had been in producing soldiers quickly that the loyalty properly due to the king could be channelled elsewhere, or rather, halted at an intermediate stage. To be seen to respond quickly and loyally to a king's demands had always been a good recommendation for advancement, so there was an incentive to take measures that would ensure a permanent supply of troops for the contract captain. The practical result was that the captain would quite simply contract the service of soldiers for life, so that when trouble arose there was no need of lengthy negotiations. The men whose loyalty was thus retained received a retainer fee, sometimes a quite substantial sum. In this way Sir Edward Grey was contracted for life to Humphrey Stafford, the first Duke of Buckingham, who was to meet his death at Northampton. Grey's contract had lasted from 1440 when he had agreed terms of £40 per annum. His was the best paid. Two other knights received £20 per annum, and the remaining seven knights in Buckingham's personal retinue received £10. The esquires were more numerous and were paid at a lower rate. Each of these knights and esquires could themselves subcontract for archers and men-at-arms, many of whom would be personally known to the hirer, so there was a potential for creating a large cohesive army. In the case of the Duke of Buckingham we know that prior to the Battle of St Albans 2,000 badges of the Stafford knot were produced for distribution to his men.

There was, however, one great disadvantage in the Wars of the Roses compared to the Hundred Years' War, and this was the time factor. A contract captain who undertook to raise armies for France

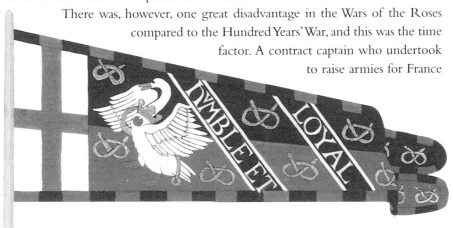

The standard of Henry, Second Duke of Buckingham, who was beheaded by order of Richard III in 1483. The standard shows the Stafford knot, the badge worn by the Stafford retainers at St Albans and Northampton, where Henry's father, and later his grandfather, met their deaths.

could expect weeks, perhaps even months, to select and train his troops, and for the soldiers to get to know their commanders. Once the First War of the Roses began, events moved at such a rapid pace that armies were hastily recruited and equally hastily used. The presence in such a force of experienced, well-trained veterans of the French wars was a godsend to a desperate commander, provided that their speedily sought allegiance remained steadfast, and we will see several occasions in the following pages when it did not. But there were literally thousands of such men to be called upon, and their usefulness was fully recognized.

For experienced soldiers and recruits alike, loyalty to the point of death had a strong mercenary aspect. There is a recorded case from 1464 of the wages for Henry VI's army being intercepted near Newcastle. The army which the king had assembled were fully equipped and ready to move off, but '. . .would not go one foot with him till they had money'. If financial considerations could hinder a king's army, what had become of the loyalty due to the sovereign's person? Did the king have any troops on whom he could utterly depend?

The position was that the only permanent military forces were those concerned with guarding England's borders. One thousand of these were permanently stationed in Calais, defending the last possession of Henry VI in France, while others, based respectively at Berwick and Carlisle, kept a constant watch on the Scots. To a large extent, therefore, the king had to go to the marketplace for his armies as did his rebellious subjects, with perhaps the slight advantage that early on in the Wars of the Roses the name of the king still had a considerable influence on professional troops, as the Earl of Warwick was to find when he took the Calais garrison to oppose the king at Ludlow. From 1461, of course, there were two kings demanding absolute loyalty.

In addition to the contract captains there were two other ways of raising armies. The first was the employment of foreign mercenaries. The Earl of Warwick employed Burgundian handgunners at St Albans in 1461, and both sides employed specialist and expensive German gunners when artillery came into the wars in the mid-1460s. Large numbers of Swiss and Flemings, armed with their characteristic pikes, were also recruited. On one occasion at least during the Wars of the Roses the paid foreign troops included Scots. In 1462 Henry VI, whose military operations were by then confined to the north, came to an agreement with George Douglas, the Earl of Angus, for the supply of troops. Within a month of winning, Henry promised, Douglas would receive a dukedom in England, with a value of 2,000 marks, which he would be free to hold in time of peace or war (war no doubt referring to the ever-present likelihood of hostilities between England and Scotland). In the latter case, Douglas would be entitled to send twenty Scotsmen to govern his lands, who would be treated as honorary Englishmen!

Opposite: This restored drawbridge, at the Fort la Latte in Brittany, is an excellent example of what a working drawbridge would have looked like.

The final means of raising armies, that of a commission of array, was, strictly speaking, only available to the king, a consideration that was subject to some interpretation after 1461 when there were two rival kings. Commissions of array were the ancient means of raising troops for the defence of the realm, and were revived by Henry VI in 1459 on the grounds that his realm was in peril from rebellion. It was something of a haphazard affair compared to the methods of contract captaincy. The quality of troops arrayed depended almost totally on the enthusiasm and loyalty to the sovereign of the person appointed as commissioner. Nor was there any guarantee that the army subsequently arrayed would be used in the manner for which it was intended. An odd case occurred in 1460 when the Duke of York, declaring himself the loyal servant of King Henry and desirous of rescuing the king from his enemies, claimed defence of the realm, and gave one of his more distant Neville kinsmen the job of commissioning an array. This Neville did, and then used the troops so arrayed to attack York on the king's behalf!

Arrayed men depended upon the commissioner for their military equipment. Some were very poorly kitted out, with the chroniclers referring to them as 'naked men'. Other contingents were well provided for, their equipment exceeding the minimum standards laid down by regulation. The surviving account of a muster of this sort at Bridport in Dorset indicates a reasonably equipped army for one so hastily assembled. Of 180 men arrayed, 100 had some form of weapon, including about 70 with bows and arrows. Seventy had some or all of the following: a sallet (helmet), jack (reinforced coat), sword, buckler (small shield) and dagger. Ten of the muster had all of the items mentioned. There were also a sprinkling of poleaxes, spears, axes and one handgun, together with odd bits of armour. Such were the ways in which the armies of the Wars of the Roses were formed, but whatever means the commanders used to persuade, shame or pay men to join them, there was certainly no shortage of the basic raw material. The end of the French wars had seen the return of large numbers of men whose only trade was that of soldier. Bored, unemployed and disillusioned by the transience of their achievements and the decline in their own skills, they were readily available to the recruiting officer.

VETERAN WARRIORS

Warfare has many aspects, and there was much more to the Wars of the Roses than two lines of levied men facing one another for a series of battles. Civil war was a matter of political chicanery, desperate strategy and subtle manoeuvring on and off the battlefield in which the personalities and experience of the commanders played a vital part. When the wars began the commanders on both sides shared a common experience – that of fighting in the Hundred Years' War.

They respected the power of the English longbow, understood the strength of a fortified position, and had the patience needed for the formalities and discomfort of siegework. They also knew the limitations of heavy cavalry, could select and train loyal troops, and had never experienced the insult of desertion. How, therefore, would these old soldiers react to a totally new situation, where archer was to be pitted against archer, where troops had to be raised in days, where few massive fortifications existed, and where the enemy were the troops of a neighbour beside whom they had lived and fought in France?

After St Albans four years went by before fighting restarted and it was the king's side which took the initiative. York was seen to be gathering his forces once more, but his armies were divided geographically. Richard of York was in Ludlow, with an additional garrison at nearby Wigmore. His brother-in-law Richard Neville, Earl of Salisbury, was at Middleham Castle in Yorkshire, while the third Richard of the trio, Richard of Warwick, Salisbury's son, was serving a term as Captain of Calais. For the two earls to join forces with the duke they would have to pass through the Midlands. Henry VI accordingly raised his standard at Coventry. When the Yorkists responded the king could hit them while they were still divided.

For such a plan to succeed required considerable political manoeuvring to ensure that York could not obtain help nearer than his distant kinsmen, and in this context Queen Margaret had already been active. She had entrusted the awakening of Lancastrian sympathies in Wales to a Welsh family with royal connections: the Tudors. The Tudor rise to power had begun with Owen Tudor's marriage to Henry V's widow, Queen Catherine, which bound them as close to the Lancastrian line as the Beauforts. Owen's son Edmund was therefore Henry VI's half-brother, whom the king honoured by investing him as Earl of Richmond. He died soon afterwards, just two months before the birth of his son Henry, who was destined to raise the Tudors to undreamed of heights. Edmund's work was continued by his brother Jasper, a skilled politician and one of the few major leaders in the Wars of the Roses to see their completion. By 1459 he had managed to secure most of west and south-west Wales for the Lancastrian cause including the fortresses of Carmarthen and Aberystwyth, and heard his praises loudly sung by the Welsh bards, who emphasized his royal blood, his Welsh ancestry and his efforts to unite Wales for the king.

Meanwhile, Queen Margaret directed her own energies towards improving her position in Cheshire and North Wales, thus progressively isolating York in the Marches. In the spring of 1459, we read, the queen 'allied unto her all the knights and squires of Cheshire for to have their benevolence, and held open household among them; and made her son the Prince give a livery of swans to all the gentlemen of the countryside'. In an age that appreciated omens, in a 'little town in Bedfordshire' there fell a 'blody rayne', the red drops appearing on sheets which a woman had hung out to dry.

At the same time Richard, Earl of Warwick, was preparing to come to the aid of his father and uncle with 600 men of the Calais garrison. This was a bold gesture considering that the Yorkist faction were regarded as rebels and the Calais garrison were the only official royal standing army. This was also the interpretation put upon it by Warwick's followers, who were most reluctant to accept his bland statement that the Yorkists were acting solely in self-defence. Eventually they sailed for England leaving Warwick's uncle, William, Lord Fauconberg, in charge in Calais, but only after Warwick had sworn an oath that he would not lead them against their king. Warwick's father, Richard of Salisbury, was likewise on the move, hurrying from Middleham Castle across England to Ludlow. His route took him through Staffordshire on the road to Shrewsbury, where the Lancastrians caught him just as they had planned, isolated from any other Yorkist support, at a field called Blore Heath.

The battle which followed, however, did not go as the Lancastrians would have wished. After heavy fighting, from 'one of the clock till five afternoon', the Earl of Salisbury was able to continue his journey under cover of darkness. It is evident that at Blore Heath Salisbury did not encounter the full Lancastrian host, for we read that Queen Margaret was with the main body only 5 miles distant, and presumably entrusted the stopping of Salisbury to a

The cross commemorating the death of Lord Audley at the Battle of Blore Heath in 1459. Blore Heath arose from Queen Margaret's attempt to intercept the Yorkist forces under the Earl of Salisbury who were marching to join his brother the Duke of York in Ludlow. Because of the unusual position of the cross, halfway down a hill and invisible from the road which passes the site, it is more than likely that it represents the actual spot where Lord Audley was killed.

detachment thought sufficient for the purpose. The commander of the force, Lord Audley, was slain during the battle, the presumed spot where he fell being marked by a stone cross. The longest account of Blore Heath, in Gregory's *Chronicle*, gives part of the credit for Salisbury's escape to a certain Friar Austin, who remained on the battlefield and 'shot guns all that night', to cover the retreat. By the time the Lancastrian main body dared to sent scouts to investigate the mysterious artillery fire, the victorious Salisbury was well on his way, leaving the ambushers with the problem of what to do with the brave friar.

A major Yorkist army had therefore slipped through the net which the Lancastrians had been so patiently weaving, and two days later Richard of Warwick did the same when he avoided a royal ambush near Coleshill. By the end of September 1459, the Yorkists were safely within the 12-foot thick walls of Ludlow Castle, and had dispatched a letter to their king, claiming that they bore him no personal malice, but stressing their determination to fight for what they saw as their cause, '. . . having regard to the effusion of Christian blood, . . . which that God defend which knoweth our intent, and that we have avoided . . .'

The castle of Ludlow viewed from Whitcliffe Hill. Ludlow was one of the two great Yorkist fortresses of the Welsh Marches.

THE LUDLOW INCIDENT

From Worcester the king's army advanced on Ludlow for the reckoning. According to Gregory's *Chronicle* there were 30,000 'harnessed men', together with 'naked men that were compelled to come with the King' – an obvious reference to poorly equipped levies. The road to Ludlow from the south crosses the River Teme by a fine fourteenth-century bridge at Ludford. It was at Ludford Bridge, rather than from within Ludlow itself, that Richard of York prepared his position, digging a deep ditch and fortifying it with guns, carts and stakes. No doubt the Lancastrian commanders would have ascended Whitcliffe Hill on their left flank to gaze down upon the mighty fortress and consider how, having disposed of York's field fortifications, they might besiege it. But military skill was not to be the decisive factor at Ludlow. There was some fighting on the bridge, raids and skirmishes against the Yorkist line, but Yorkist morale was running low, and their rivals brilliantly exploited the situation. With a particular eye to the Calais troops, Henry proclaimed a pardon to any Yorkist who would join him. In desperation the Ludlow commanders turned to bluff, telling their troops that Henry was dead. But their men were not fooled, and as darkness fell on 12 October 1459 the first Yorkist deserters began to slip across Ludford bridge to the king's peace.

Ludford Bridges, which crosses the River Teme below Ludlow. This is the actual medieval bridge over which was fought the brief Battle of Ludford Bridge in 1459, when the Lancastrians forced their way into Ludlow.

The last remaining of the former seven gates of the town of Ludlow. The grooves for the porticullis are still visible. The Lancastrian army entered by this gate after the Battle of Ludford Bridge in 1459.

The arms of the town of Ludlow commemorate its association with the Yorkist kings. The white rose and the lion of March were both badges used by the House of York.

Once the Calais men followed them the débâcle was complete. Led by Andrew Trollope, another veteran of the French wars, they abandoned Warwick and his muddled, apparently motiveless rebellion for the security of their monarch. It is not difficult to see why. As Captain of Calais, Warwick was a king's man; but, seeing the danger to his father and uncle, the needs of his family had overridden his normal duty. Once the point had been made, he would have been able to assure the king that the Yorkist quarrel was not with him but with the evildoers who advised him, just as they had at St Albans. However, the Ludlow campaign had not been so speedily settled, and to an ordinary soldier from the Calais garrison the feeling that they were engaging in rebellion must have grown from day to day, until the choice had to be made between the immediate leader and the ultimate object of their loyalty. Seeing his army disintegrate about him, Richard of York had little choice. To stay within Ludlow was to offer himself as a prisoner by siege, so that night he too slipped away and 'fled from place to place in Wales, and broke down the bridges so that the King's men should not come after them'.

By morning the Yorkist army had disappeared, and the Lancastrians took their revenge for Blore Heath on the town of Ludlow, which was 'robbed to the bare walls'. Another account tells how the royalist troops went on a drunken spree, 'and when they had drunken enough of the wine that was in the taverns and other places, they full ungodly smote out the heads of the pipes and hogsheads of wine, that men went wet-shod in wine, and then they robbed the town, and bare away bedding, cloth and other stuff, and defouled many women'. To the veterans from France it must have seemed like the good old days again.

Ludlow was essentially a triumph for Queen Margaret's Tudor-led propaganda, which proved to have neutralized York's local support. It is also likely that Jasper Tudor was advancing on Ludlow with an army when the defections occurred, for we know he was late arriving at Coventry on 20 November, where a parliament was held and passed an Act of Attainder against the Yorkist leaders. The Act proclaimed:

> ... that the said Richard, Duke of York, Edward, Earl of March, Richard, Earl of Salisbury, Edmund, Earl of Rutland, etc., for their traitorous levying of war against your said most noble person, at Ludford specified above, be declared attainted of high treason against your most noble person ...

Defeated, out-generalled, and now officially attainted with treason, the Yorkist leaders dispersed far and wide. Richard of York went to Ireland and Warwick went back to Calais.

A reproduction cannon of the fifteenth century, operated by the re-enactment group '1471 Tower Ordnance'.

THE BATTLE OF NORTHAMPTON

Richard, Duke of York remained in Ireland when his kinsmen returned to take up the challenge once again. In the summer of 1460 the Earl of Salisbury landed at Sandwich with his son Warwick and his nephew, Edward, Earl of March, Richard of York's heir, who was a promising soldier. They had returned to an England sodden by the wettest summer the country had experienced in many years. Communications everywhere were difficult, with horses and men becoming mired in the mud of the ill-made roads. Warwick's father, Salisbury, remained behind in London, besieging the Tower, while the younger warriors of York set off to capture the king. Henry, perhaps in direct response to the invasion, had moved his headquarters south from Kenilworth to Northampton. His army, under Humphrey, Duke of Buckingham, whose son had been killed at St Albans, had constructed a formidable field fortification on a bend in the River Nene, cutting into the river banks to flood a moat in front of the palisades. We

Kenilworth Castle, from where the Lancastrian army marched to Northampton.

know that these fortifications bristled with guns, as at Castillon, because it is recorded that they were brought from Kenilworth, and the difficulty of transporting them any further is probably why Northampton was chosen for a stand. When Richard of Warwick ascended the rising ground which overlooks the position he must have recalled Ludford Bridge, but this time the defensive army was holding an artificial position, not merely strengthening a natural one with a fortress behind. The river, traversed by a small bridge, was at their backs. Even though the earthen walls looked formidable, the pouring rain indicated that the guns, brought at such enormous cost in time and manpower, were probably sinking into the mud and would be unworkable.

On 10 July 1460, the Yorkists attacked. Edward, Earl of March, carrying the banner of his absent father, took the left flank, William Neville, Lord Fauconberg (Warwick's uncle and a veteran of France) the right, and Warwick himself the centre. They advanced on a narrow front, waded the ditch under heavy archery fire and the occasional ball from the few guns left in action, then slipped and squelched

their way up the slimy embankment to the Lancastrian defenders. At first there was fierce hand-to-hand fighting, but suddenly the Lancastrian right wing, under Lord Grey of Ruthin, signalled to the Earl of March to advance unhindered. Hands reached down to help his exhilarated troops scale the palisades. Field fortifications were pushed over, and the united Yorkist left and Lancastrian right turned on to Buckingham in the centre. The panic-stricken Lancastrian troops fought one another for the narrow passage of the bridge. In the confusion the Duke of Buckingham was killed, and the king was taken prisoner by the Yorkist faction.

Northampton was a victory for the younger generation of the House of York, because Richard of York was still in Ireland and Richard of Salisbury was besieging the Tower when the fight took place. The hero of the hour was Warwick the Kingmaker, and it was largely a Neville government that was formed out of the survivors and victors of Northampton. Ludlow and Northampton had two points in common. First, they involved the use of a fortified camp which controlled local communications with the object of challenging an enemy to launch a costly assault or talk terms. This defensive approach had worked well in France, but now we come to the second point. This was civil war, and in both cases defeat had come about because certain bodies of troops changed sides. This remorseless self-interest, ensuring one's survival by ending up on the winning side – which, because it then held the king's person, became the royal party – was to become a feature of the wars.

Opposite: This is the Gobelin Tower of Fougères. In the foreground is the site of the former keep, destroyed by Henry II of England in 1166.

While Edward and Warwick had been crushing the fortified camp of the Lancastrians at Northampton, Warwick's father, Salisbury, had been attempting to capture the Tower of London. It was bitterly defended by Lord Scales, whose men 'cast wild fire into the city, and shot in small guns, and burnt and hurt women and children . . .' Salisbury eventually forced a negotiated surrender, having met fire with fire by using great bombards, but if the Battle of Northampton had had a different result Scales might well have held out longer, preventing any Yorkist supremacy. As it turned out, the siege of the Tower provided a timely reminder of the importance of a strategic, well-defended base, so Yorkist attention turned rapidly towards the Welsh castles. In August 1460, the Constables of Beaumaris, Conwy, Flint, Holt, Ruthin and Hawarden received official orders to keep the castles secure, lest any should be appropriated by the Lancastrians and used as a base for future operations. In the following year, Queen Margaret realized the importance of castles when she failed to take London after the Battle of St Albans, a reverse which rendered her victory a Pyrrhic one.

If Henry VI had been childless the Wars of the Roses would have ended at Northampton, because an Act of Parliament, carried by the Yorkist majority, reversed the Act of Attainder, and proclaimed the loyal Richard of York as Henry's successor, for which Richard returned to England in September 1460. But Henry, of course, did have an heir, Edward, Prince of Wales. More importantly he had a wife, the indomitable and talented Queen Margaret of Anjou. From the moment that the Act was passed her devotion to the cause became passionate. The older Lancastrian leaders, such as Buckingham and her supposed lover, Beaufort, were dead. The new ones now had a cause, and a fierce spokesperson in the queen, who would suffer any hardship for her son's throne. She was determined to prove that in disinheriting him, the Yorkists had made a rod for their own backs.

Queen Margaret, already skilled in propaganda in Wales, set about recruiting a new army. This time she concentrated on the north of England and Scotland, helped by the Percy family, whose long rivalry with the Nevilles was rapidly coming to a head. As the army grew in size she tried it out by raiding and skirmishing in Yorkshire, York's second power base, where the destructive presence would have the maximum psychological effect. It was a challenge that Richard of York could not long ignore, and in December he headed north accompanied by his brother-in-law, the Earl of Salisbury. York's march was a double challenge – to Margaret, busily arranging a Lancastrian rendezvous at Hull, and whose rough troops were pillaging York's estates, and to Warwick, to assert his seniority and military skill which had been somewhat eclipsed by his son's and nephew's dash at Northampton.

The ruins of Sandal Castle, near Wakefield, looking north towards the city. The slope leading from Sandal down to the River Calder was the site of the Battle of Wakefield in 1460.

THE END AT WAKEFIELD

The events which followed marked the end of an era in the Wars of the Roses. Perhaps York overreached himself in his determination to get to his capital, instead of settling for safer havens at Doncaster or Nottingham. But pride dictated that he alone should rescue his tenants from the intimidating assaults of the Lancastrians, and he needed to show the next generation of Yorkist leaders that he was still the old master. He spent

The chantry on the bridge over the River Calder at Wakefield. Following the Battle of Wakefield, Edmund Earl of Rutland, son of the Duke of York, was murdered by Thomas 'The Butcher', Earl Clifford, on the bridge outside the chapel.

a merry and peaceful Christmas at Sandal Castle, even though the countryside was swarming with Lancastrian warbands, supplied from the massive royal fortress of Pontefract scarcely 10 miles away. Sandal was much smaller, and it is quite likely that the Lancastrian army were prepared for a full assault. Somehow that assault never took place, because on the fields between Sandal Castle and the city of Wakefield was fought a battle which decimated the Yorkist army and totally wiped out the older generation of Yorkist leaders.

There are various accounts of the Lancastrian attempts to lure York out of Sandal to fight. One holds that Sir Andrew Trollope, who had changed sides at Ludlow, led a large contingent of Lancastrians flaunting spurious badges and claiming to be a reinforcement from Warwick, and that the Battle of Wakefield took place when the defenders moved outside the walls to greet them. Others suggest that the Yorkists were caught while out foraging, or that the Lancastrians taunted York into attacking an isolated group of Lancastrian soldiers. What these accounts have in common is the implication that here was a new, aggressive young Lancastrian leadership, able to employ psychological warfare and play upon the fear and pride of an old soldier. They also make it clear that when the Yorkists were lured out of Sandal the main body of the Lancastrians was well out of sight of the castle. Their leader was Henry Beaufort, third Duke of Somerset, whose father had been killed at St Albans, and as the year 1459 drew to its close, the troops of Richard of York burst through the Lancastrian

Sir William Gascoigne, who died in 1465, was one knight of the Wars of the Roses who received his knighthood on the field of battle. In William's case it was bestowed upon him at the Battle of Wakefield in 1460. He continued to support the House of York until his death, and his collar bears the alternate suns and roses of the Yorkists.

vanguard. It was then that the main body, under Thomas, Earl of Clifford, whose father had been killed by York at St Albans, emerged in the poor light, catching York 'like a fish in a net'.

Richard of York died on the battlefield and a savage pursuit began as the Yorkists fled in all directions. York's second son, Edmund, Earl of Rutland, (the only one of his children to be present), headed for Wakefield, crossing the Calder by the city's main bridge to the south. Projecting from it, its foundations in the river bed, was a small chantry, its fine west front part of the bridge itself. It promised sanctuary and a hiding-place, but before the young man could scramble inside he was seized by Clifford, who plunged a dagger into Edmund's back.

So perished a young member of the House of York at Wakefield, and for his uncle, Richard Neville, Earl of Salisbury, an equally savage fate was in store. Taken to the dungeons of Pontefract to await a possible ransom, he was dragged from his brief incarceration by a mob and beheaded. His grizzled old skull joined the severed heads of Richard and Edmund on the Micklegate in York. 'York', said the vengeful Lancastrians who had spoiled the county, 'may now look upon York.' Richard of York, the man who had been declared heir to Henry, was crowned in death – stuck high on a gate, and the crown was of paper.

Opposite: The massive square keep of the castle of Brougham in Cumbria, owned by the Clifford family. Their involvement in the Wars of the Roses was to prove disastrous for this staunch Lancastrian family. Thomas, the Eighth Lord, was killed at the Battle of St Albans. The Ninth Lord, Thomas 'The Butcher', killed the son of the Duke of York on the bridge at Wakefield, then perished himself while attempting to hold the northern bank of the River Aire against the Yorkist advance northwards, a move which led to the Battle of Towton. Following his death all the Clifford lands were confiscated.

The Sun in Splendour 11

Wakefield did for the House of York what Northampton and St Albans had done for Lancaster: it deprived them of the older generation of commanders. From the beginning of 1461 onwards the Wars of the Roses entered a new and savage phase, when the leaders were young, unhampered by ideas appropriate only to foreign wars, and were playing for much higher stakes than merely to be in the king's favour. The new spirit showed itself first on the Lancastrian side, as Queen Margaret launched what can only be described as a *chevauchée* in her own country. The soldiers she had recruited in the north were rough, hard men used to border raiding and feuds. They began to sweep southwards in the depths of winter like a horde of ravaging locusts, towards London, still held by the Yorkists. As Whethamstede's Chronicle relates:

> . . . they robbed, despoiled and devastated, and carried off with them whatever they could come upon or discover, whether garments or money, herds of cattle or single animals, sparing neither churches nor clergy . . .

When they were only a week's march from the capital Warwick set out to meet them. It must have been difficult for him to decide how to combat such a heterogeneous band moving on a 30-mile wide front. He had no shortage of troops, because the fear of the approaching northerners had made recruitment very easy. But such a large and hastily assembled army was difficult to garrison in London, where Warwick might have been safer. His cousin Edward would be on his way from the Marches, eager to avenge his father's death, and the Lancastrians had shown how they were now able to pounce on an isolated Yorkist position and destroy it quickly before reinforcements could arrive. His uncle had paid with his head for abandoning a fortified position at Sandal, but Warwick himself had overcome one at Northampton! What was he to do? Warwick's final decision, to move to St Albans and erect field fortifications on a wide front, smacks of compromise.

Opposite: The effigy of Sir Richard Croft in Croft Church, Herefordshire. Sir Richard Croft was Edward IV's tutor in childhood, and later fought alongside him in the Wars of the Roses. It is probably to Sir Richard's experience and local knowledge that Edward owed his victory of Mortimer's Cross.

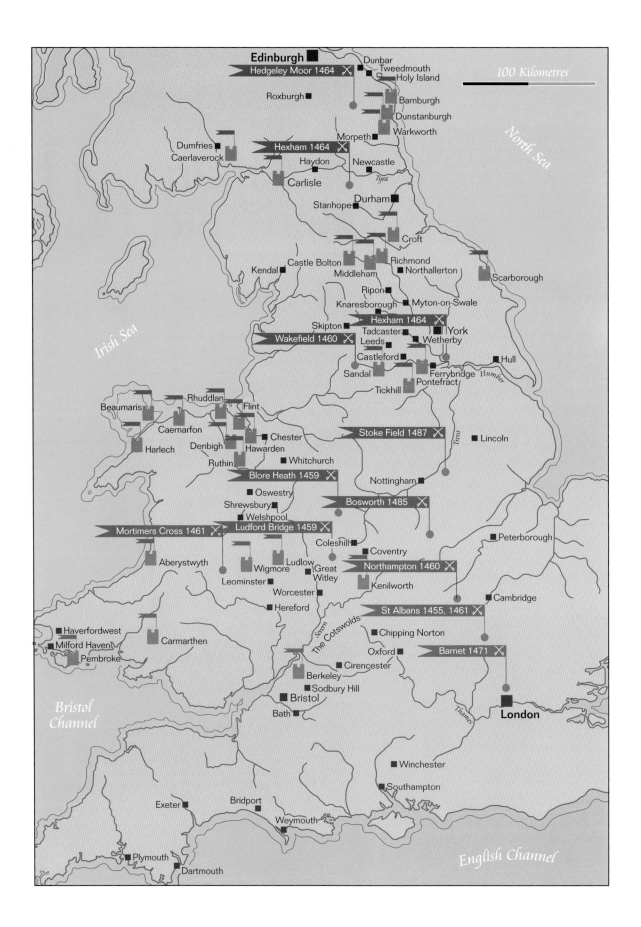

Edinburgh

Hedgeley Moor 1464 ✗

Dunbar
Tweedmouth
Holy Island

Roxburgh

Bamburgh
Dunstanburgh
Warkwarth

Morpeth

Dumfries
Caerlaverock

Hexham 1464 ✗

Haydon

Newcastle

Tyne

Carlisle

Durham

Stanhope

Croft

Kendal

Castle Bolton

Richmond
Northallerton

Middleham

Scarborough

Ripon

Knaresborough
Myton-on-Swale

Skipton

Hexham 1464 ✗

Tadcaster
York
Leeds
Wetherby

Wakefield 1460 ✗

Castleford

Sandal

Ferrybridge
Pontefract

Hull

Tickhill

Humber

Beaumaris

Rhuddlan

Flint

Caernarfon

Chester

Stoke Field 1487 ✗

Lincoln

Harlech

Denbigh

Hawarden

Ruthin

Whitchurch

Blore Heath 1459 ✗

Nottingham

Trent

Oswestry

Shrewsbury

Bosworth 1485 ✗

Welshpool

Mortimers Cross 1461 ✗

Ludford Bridge 1459 ✗

Coleshill

Peterborough

Aberystwyth

Wigmore

Ludlow
Great
Witley

Coventry

Northampton 1460 ✗

Leominster

Worcester

Kenilworth

Cambridge

Hereford

St Albans 1455, 1461 ✗

Haverfordwest

Carmarthen

Severn
The Cotswolds

Chipping Norton

Milford Haven
Pembroke

Oxford

Barnet 1471 ✗

Cirencester

Berkeley

Sodbury Hill

*Bristol
Channel*

Bristol

Bath

Thames

London

Winchester

Southampton

Exeter

Bridport

Weymouth

Plymouth

Dartmouth

English Channel

North Sea

Irish Sea

100 Kilometres

Perhaps he relied on bringing the northern army to a pitched battle on ground of his choosing. If they encountered the Yorkist army, the Lancastrians would surely engage them, because to pass them by and continue towards London would invite an attack from the flank. Fighting would at least slow down the Lancastrian advance, perhaps until his cousin Edward, Earl of March, and now Duke of York, could come from the Welsh Marches to join him. Warwick had no means of knowing that Edward was indeed on his way, still less that he was in fact advancing to meet Warwick having just fought and won a decisive battle!

THE BATTLE OF MORTIMER'S CROSS

The background to this surprising improvement in Yorkist fortunes is as follows. Edward, Earl of March, was in Gloucester when the news reached him of his family's tragedy. He immediately began to levy troops from various shires, and succeeded in assembling a large host, which is perhaps surprising in view of the queen's previous efforts. However, the Marches proved loyal, and the Lancastrian behaviour at Ludlow can only have inclined any local waverers to follow the dashing young Duke. Edward also had the advantage of being well known in the vicinity. He had spent his boyhood in the Marches under the tutelage of Sir Richard Croft, whose simple castle of Croft had become a second home for the Yorkist heir. So many local knights flocked to his standard, in particular Sir William Herbert, Sir Walter Devereux and Sir Roger Vaughan. All were veterans from France and familiar with the Marches. Herbert and Vaughan in particular could appeal to Welsh sentiment in a much-needed counter to the Tudor propaganda from the other side.

Opposite: Map of the Wars of the Roses.

It soon proved that the Tudors were Edward's nearest and deadliest threat. Having set out eastwards to seek Margaret's army, Edward was forced to turn and engage the force that had appeared in his rear. It was a motley band, consisting of Welsh troops under Jasper Tudor, Earl of Pembroke, accompanied by his father Owen, and Irish, French and Bretons who had probably been brought in via Milford Haven by James Butler, the Earl of Wiltshire.

The two armies came face to face at a crossroads known as Mortimer's Cross, about 6 miles from Leominster, and not far from the castles of Wigmore and Croft. Here Edward fought his first battle as Duke of York under the azure and murrey standard of his house, ornamented with the white rose. Early in the morning of 2 February 1461 his troops were startled by a strange dawn phenomenon, probably caused by mist in a frosty sky. They saw 'three suns in the firmament shining full clear, whereof the people had great marvel, and thereof were aghast'. For a brief moment the three suns shone, then came together as one. Seeing his men alarmed, but knowing the psychological value of a good omen, 'the noble Earl Edward them comforted and said, "Be thee of good comfort and dread not; this is a good sign, for these three suns betoken the Father, the Son and the Holy Ghost, and therefore let us have a good heart and in the name of Almighty God go we against our enemies"'.

The reaction of the Tudor army to the three suns is not recorded, but it seems to have been an equally positive one, for they were the first to move into the attack. Little is known of the details of the battle, but we may assume that Edward drew up his army on the east bank of the River Lugg, using it, and the Wig marsh on its west bank, as natural defences between them and the Lancastrians, who descended from the hills which sweep down to the Wigmore road. The attack was fiercest from the Tudor left flank where Sir Richard Croft, acting as Edward's military adviser, allowed them to advance. The Yorkist right wing was in fact driven from the field in the direction of Croft, but the net result was to deprive the Tudor forces of a third of their army, and by the time they returned the battle was lost and 3,000 of Tudor's men lay dead. Jasper Tudor and the Earl of Wiltshire stole away in disguise, and old Owen Tudor was captured.

Owen Tudor, the chronicler tells us, did not believe that he would then be executed by his captors. Perhaps he counted on being ransomed. The stepfather of King Henry, after all, would command a pretty price. But this was a civil war,

The bridge over the River Lugg, site of the Battle of Mortimer's Cross, 1461.

A knight arming c. 1450. The manuscript depicts Sir John Astley, assisted by his squire, a boy training to be a knight and acting as a servant. (The term esquire denoted a fighting man of a rank lower than a knight.)

and much had changed even since the gentlemanly days of St Albans, and the heads of Edward's father and brother were rotting on the spikes of the gates of York. It was not until he saw the axe and the block, and felt the headsman rip away the collar of his fine red doublet that the grandfather of the future king accepted the inevitable. His last words were, 'that head shall lie on the block that was wont to lie on Queen Catherine's lap'. His severed head was displayed in the marketplace at Hereford, where, a chronicler relates, a mad woman combed his hair and washed away the blood from his face, then surrounded the ghastly trophy with a hundred burning candles.

The Welsh bards lamented the loss of the sire of the Tudors. Robin Ddu refers to his death, and speaks of Jasper Tudor, Earl of Pembroke, as their great hope for the future. In a curious passage he compares the white of the Yorkists and the red of the Welsh dragon: '*Draig wen ddibarch yn gwarchae, A draig goch a dyr y cae*'. (The dishonourable white dragon has triumphed, but the red dragon will yet win the field). It is interesting to note the contrast of the red and white, particularly in view of the traditional allusion of York and Lancaster. One addition was in fact made to the Yorkist heraldry not long after the battle, when Edward combined the white rose of York with the badge of the sun in splendour, producing the beautiful effect of the white rose *en soleil* on the standard of Richard III. Was it perhaps a direct reminder of the 'Glorious Sun of York' which had smiled on them threefold that morning?

ARMS AND ARMOUR

As the Wars of the Roses progressed, developments in armour continued the trend towards total plate armour that has been discussed throughout this book, but in an army consisting of veterans of the French campaigns hungry for work, and hastily recruited levies who kept the odd helmet in the barn in case of action, the notion of a 'suit of armour' was probably meaningless to 95 per cent of the soldiers engaged. Armour was always expensive, so parts of armour that were serviceable and comfortable would be retained, and broken pieces replaced. If the knight could afford it he would choose the latest refinements, and if he were fashion-conscious seek out the latest style from Germany or Italy. Throughout the fifteenth century, however, it was practical considerations which produced new fashions. The attractive fluting on the surfaces of the so-called Gothic style of armour helped to give additional strength and deflected blows aimed at it.

The most noticeable innovation in armour at this time was concerned with the helmet. The great bascinet, which prevented the knight from turning his head independently of his body, was finally replaced by something more suitable for fighting on foot. This was the armet, a round helmet which fitted closely to the head and allowed much more sideways movement than the great bascinet and was without its ponderous weight. The alternative style, called a sallet, resembled a modern infantryman's helmet. It was fastened with a strong chinstrap, and additional protection for the lower face was provided by a bevor, a reinforced chin and neck-piece which came up to the mouth. In combat several knights abandoned the bevor and suffered the consequences of a throat or neck injury.

These later suits of armour were superbly articulated with the weight being more evenly distributed than ever. A reasonably fit man would have experienced little restriction of movement from weight alone, but prolonged bouts of combat on foot would have caused him to sweat profusely, which would have weakened him very quickly. This happened at Towton, even though snow was falling.

The completeness of plate armour and its strengthening by fluting led to the decline of the sword as a cutting weapon and its relegation to use as a piercing weapon for delivering the *coup de grâce*. Grappling between knights would be carried on with a variety of weapons designed to crush armour surfaces rather than cut mail or thin plate. Various combinations of axe head, hammerhead and spike were used.

A late fifteenth-century helmet for a foot-soldier. It is German, and is in the Wallace Collection, London.

THE SECOND BATTLE OF ST ALBANS

Knights armoured in such a fashion would have been standing with Edward's cousin as he waited at St Albans behind the field defences he had erected. There were guns to fire balls and arrows, and various sorts of nets with nails thrust through the interstices so that when laid down they would present a carpet of spikes. 'Also they had pavises . . . with shutting windows to shoot out of, they standing behind the pavis, and the pavis as full of threepenny nails as they might stand. And when their shot was spent and done they cast the pavis before them: then there might no man come over the pavis at them for the nails that stood upright, but if he would mischief himself'. Warwick also had a plentiful supply of caltrops, devices consisting of four spikes arranged in a solid tetrahedron, so that however it fell one spike was sticking straight upwards. To supplement his firepower he also had under arms a small contingent of Burgundian handgunners firing primitive arquebuses.

Thus prepared, Warwick waited for whichever army arrived first, his cousin's, or the queen's, but a traitor in Warwick's ranks defected to Margaret and disclosed the precise layout of Warwick's defences. Such treachery is perhaps not surprising. What is remarkable is the sophisticated way in which the Lancastrian leaders made use of the information. Her army had already veered to the west from the direct route to London. Now it was to turn back towards the east, to attempt a surprise attack on Warwick's right flank, avoiding the spiked defence line. The northern army therefore headed for Dunstable, taking a Yorkist detachment completely by surprise and either killing or taking prisoner their entire number. Consequently none got back with any news for Warwick, and that night, 16/17 February, the Lancastrian leaders organized their loosely disciplined army in a night march which fell upon the unsuspecting Warwick shortly before dawn.

Opposite: Suit of armour. (Wallace Collection, London)

The untidy and bloody battle which followed was a Lancastrian victory, but an incomplete one. It was a victory in terms of the numbers slain across Warwick's wide front, though a Yorkist-biased chronicler noted with some satisfaction that Sir Andrew Trollope suffered a caltrop in his foot. The Burgundian handgunners do not seem to have come into the story at all. Whoever it was among the Lancastrian leaders deserved the credit for the flank attack, for it is clear that Warwick was totally outmanoeuvred.

TOWTON – THE DAY OF RECKONING

Warwick escaped from St Albans with a small band to link up with Edward at Chipping Norton, and from the moment of their reunion fortune seemed to favour them once again. They returned boldly to London, finding to their delight that it had not fallen to the Lancastrians, where Edward of York was proclaimed King Edward IV. Realising the precarious nature of the reign he had just initiated, Edward stayed in the capital only long enough to complete the formalities of kingship, then was off campaigning again.

Frustrated at her failure to take London, and with her army idle in the south, Queen Margaret began an orderly withdrawal. By 22 March Edward had followed them as far as Nottingham, where reports reached him that the Lancastrian army

The battlefield of Towton in summer, looking down the slope on the right of the Lancastrian lines to Bloody Meadow, and bordering it the sinuous River Cock, a death-trap for many a Lancastrian soldier.

had halted north of the River Aire, where they were holding the bridge at Ferrybridge near Pontefract. A few days later, on 28 March, the Yorkist vanguard under the Duke of Suffolk encountered the Lancastrian guards, and under orders from Edward, who arrived with the main body, began a fierce fight for the bridge. As soon as the Yorkists looked like winning, the Lancastrians destroyed it and withdrew to the northern bank. King Edward calmly assessed the situation and sent a force to find a crossing-point up river, which they achieved 4 miles away at Castleford. The high water of the late winter must have made the crossing diffi-cult, for at least one chronicler asserts that a raft was used instead of merely fording, but the crossing was made. The crossing of the Aire was a major military achievement by Edward IV. A defended natural obstacle had been overcome, and some revenge had been gained, for in the fighting Lord Clifford was killed by an arrow. The river crossing was probably helped by a strange reluctance on the part of the huge Lancastrian army a few miles to the north to come to their comrades' assistance when they were needed. Memories of Blore Heath may have been awakened in certain hearts. The next major obstacle on the Great North Road was the River Wharfe, crossed by a bridge at Tadcaster some 20 miles to the north, but between Edward and Tadcaster lay the army he had been pursuing, deployed on a gentle ridge near the village of Towton.

The battlefield of Towton under snow, similar, but less severe conditions to those experienced by the opposing armies on Palm Sunday, 1461. This view is from beside the swollen River Cock, looking up towards the rear of the Lancastrian right flank. This area, known as Bloody Meadow, was the scene of the fiercest fighting in the largest pitched battle of the Wars of the Roses.

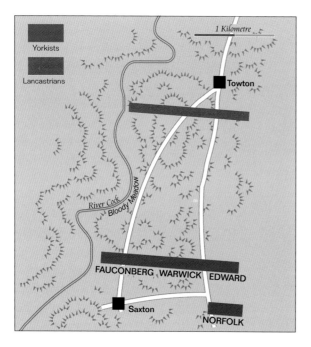

Yorkists

Lancastrians

1 Kilometre

Towton

River Cock

Bloody Meadow

FAUCONBERG WARWICK EDWARD

Saxton

NORFOLK

Map of the Battle of
Towton.

It is hardly surprising, in view of the local geography, the furious battling of the previous months, and the enmity built up since the deaths and executions at Wakefield and Mortimer's Cross, that the Battle of Towton should prove to be the biggest, bloodiest and most decisive battle of the Wars of the Roses, bringing this particular phase of events to a dramatic close. It is unfortunate that we have so few contemporary accounts of it. The numbers involved are known, the positions are clear, but there is little else. Perhaps the remoteness of the location and the sheer horror at so many lives being lost conspired to reduce the commentaries we have available. It is possible, however, to compensate for this lack of source material by visiting the atmospheric site itself, which is remarkably unchanged from that fateful Palm Sunday in 1461. The Yorkist army would have been strung along the southern end of the ridge, its flank resting on a small wood. The Lancastrians lined up to the north, straddling the two roads which join at Towton for Tadcaster. They must all have spent an uncomfortable night, bivouacked on the exposed ground, with the threat of snow.

On Palm Sunday morning, as villagers in nearby Saxton went to Mass, a sharp, cold south wind began to blow. No advance was made by York, as Edward was awaiting the arrival of John Howard, Duke of Norfolk, who was to take the right flank. Warwick was in the centre, and his uncle, Lord Fauconberg, on the left. At about eleven o'clock it began to snow. Taking advantage of this Lord Fauconberg ordered his archers to fire one arrow each, and then fall back out of range. The wind carried the arrows farther than normal into the Lancastrian lines, who were now almost invisible in the snow. But the taunt had the desired effect. Volley after volley of arrows were returned, falling short of the gleeful Yorkists who ran to retrieve them. It was a tremendous barrage, but little damage was done, as the Lancastrians were to discover when they advanced across the snowy ground to be met by hard-hitting salvos of arrows from the Yorkists. But the line came on, and on both sides archers were replaced by swordsmen and billmen who began to hack furiously at one another. As the men in the front line died or became exhausted fresh reserves from behind took their place. It may be that the opposing commanders organized some form of constant reinforcement, for it is known that the slaughter was so great that a wall of dead built up between the opposing men-at-arms. One major Lancastrian leader, Lord Dacres, was killed during a break in the fighting. Withdrawing from the line he sat down to refresh himself, removed his helmet, and was struck in the neck by a crossbow bolt which killed him instantly.

When Norfolk's troops arrived on the right flank, the battle began to turn in favour of the Yorkists, but the tide was a long time on the ebb. Eventually the Lancastrians began to fall back, and at this point the lie of the land started to tell against them. The flat ridge on which the battle was fought slopes gently down on its eastern side where the Duke of Norfolk was beginning to apply increased pressure. But on the western side the slope is steep, a fact that is not immediately apparent from the centre of the field. At the foot of this steep slope flows the little River Cock, about 10 feet in width and in summer not more than 2 feet deep. In March 1461 it was in spate, and its banks are steep. The retreating Lancastrians were funnelled back along 'Bloody Meadow' towards the only reliable crossing-point, a wooden bridge at the bottom of a deep slope, which carried the then Great North Road. Once the possibility of safe retreat became unlikely, panic swept through the ranks and was exploited by the pursuers. The River Cock claimed many who tried to force their way across it. The little bridge

The Battle of Towton. The Lancastrians have been driven down the slope in the driving snow, and the swollen River Cock begins to claim its dead.

Monumental effigy of Lionel, Lord Welles, a Lancastrian knight who was killed at the Battle of Towton in 1461. His body was conveyed in secret to this tomb in Methley, West Yorkshire. The sculpture is very striking, showing clearly the fashionable hairstyle of the period, and is very detailed in its representation of a contemporary style of armour.

is said to have collapsed under the weight of armoured men, to be replaced by a ghastly dam of human corpses, packed so solidly that the luckier escapers could scramble across it. On and on they came, slithering down the snowy, muddy, and bloody slopes leading to the river, until as darkness began to fall probably 30,000 Lancastrians lay dead. In fact Towton claimed more lives than any other battle in England, at any time.

Being in relatively undeveloped countryside, the battlefield of Towton is able to exert a strange effect upon the imagination. Even in the height of summer, wandering by the lazy River Cock, it is possible to conjure up images of the thousands of dead. In winter, to leave the path beside the monument, and walk down the slope to Bloody Meadow, slithering as the snow whips one's face, is to become one with the victims of that awful Palm Sunday, 1461, where Edward IV bloodily confirmed his throne.

Most of the slain found anonymous graves in huge pits dug nearby, while the nobles had grander resting places. Lord Dacres was buried with his horse in the churchyard at nearby Saxton. Henry Percy, third Earl of Northumberland and grandson of Henry Hotspur, was buried in York; one Lionel, Lord Welles, had his body secretly conveyed to the church at Methley, where his first wife's body already lay. His effigy now crowns the tomb, resplendent in armour, but denied a representation in alabaster of the Lancastrian collar formed by the letter 'S'. The memory of the total defeat was too strong to risk that.

THE WAR IN THE NORTH

The Battle of Towton established the Yorkist dynasty, and effectively neutralized their opponents for the next twenty years. Opposition, if it can be so called, continued, but minimally and at the extremities of Edward's new kingdom. We will study it in some detail, because the way Edward and his powerful cousin, the Kingmaker, dealt with such opposition illustrates just how well English knights were adapting to changed situations.

Resistance to the Yorkists in Wales was quickly dealt with. The Herberts, who had joined Edward before Mortimer's Cross, used their Welsh connections and military skills to wrest Pembroke Castle from Jasper Tudor. Along with the castle they captured Jasper's nephew, Henry Tudor, but the Herberts were merciful victors and took the little boy into their care, a policy they may later have regretted . . .

Lancastrian resistance was much stronger on the Scottish border. Despite the deaths of the second Earl of Northumberland at St Albans and the third earl at Towton, the Percys remained stout Lancastrians. As Warwick the Kingmaker was mainly concerned with fighting Margaret and her allies, the period added a new dimension to the long Neville/Percy rivalry for control of the Marches. Throughout these years, however, there was no York/Neville rivalry. Warwick served his cousin well in the harsh, unglamorous business of border warfare. In fact, Warwick's harrying of the Lancastrians in the north was very much a family affair. His second in command was his brother, John Neville, Lord Montague, and he was also assisted by his uncle William Neville, Lord Fauconberg, one of the few remaining veterans of the French wars.

Gaining castles, only to lose them again, was to become a feature of this new phase of the Wars of the Roses. The sense of urgency, which had characterized the earlier, battle-hungry times of St Albans and Towton, seems to have been replaced on both sides by a more desperate retrenchment, motivated by the same concern over uncertainty of supplies and doubtful loyalty of troops. In May 1461 Queen Margaret led a siege of Carlisle by a Scottish army, to which the Neville brothers responded by taking the Percy castles of Alnwick and Dunstanburgh, only to lose them again in the winter.

Of course, only places which had fortifications, or could have them quickly built, were liable to siege, and few places had any fortifications at all. The great Northumbrian castles were extremely formidable, as was Kenilworth with its vast artificial lake. London had imposing walls and the Tower, but of the hundred or so English towns which still had walls in the fifteenth century, many had fallen into disrepair. The reader will recall that neither at Northampton nor Ludlow

Dunstanburgh Castle, built on the rocky cliffs on the Northumberland coast. Much work was done on Dunstanburgh by John of Gaunt in the 1370s and 1380s. The castle was severely damaged during the Northern War of the Wars of the Roses, when it was bombarded by the Earl of Warwick.

The huge fortress of
Bamburgh, Northumberland.
From the end of 1463
Lancastrian hopes centred
on this castle, where Henry VI
held solitary state, but in 1464
it fell to a fierce artillery
bombardment conducted by
the Earl of Warwick.

The Lion Tower at Warkworth Castle, which was built in the latter half of the fourteenth century as the grand entrance to the Great Hall.

were the existing town walls used for defensive purposes, but that artificial palisades were erected elsewhere.

Control of castles was nonetheless important. They provided a military base with storage facilities, and the heraldic symbols on the flags flying from the battlements were an uncompromising statement of ownership, but after the catastrophe of Towton, castles were all the Lancastrians had. What they needed in addition were allies, which Margaret sought in her native France. Louis XI's terms were strict (he demanded a mortgage on Calais) but with Margaret's readiness to agree to practically anything if it would ensure her son's succession, a small French expedition under Margaret and her friend Piers de Breze collected King Henry from Scotland and landed at Bamburgh Castle in Northumberland on 25 October 1462. Dunstanburgh was already theirs, and Alnwick soon fell. An elated queen led her army south in much the same spirit as she had advanced on St Albans the previous year, but this time the impetus quickly faded. So few men joined her that the expedition was hurriedly abandoned and 400 French soldiers were left on Holy Island, where they were killed or captured by Warwick.

Warwick was nearby because he had recently recommenced the sieges of the Lancastrian castles of Bamburgh, Dunstanburgh (held respectively by a Percy and a Beaufort) and Alnwick. Seven thousand Yorkist troops took part in the three sieges, controlled by Warwick from nearby Warkworth Castle. As was so common during the Wars of the Roses, none had been garrisoned or victualled for a long siege – there just had not been the time, so Lancastrian hopes rested on the arrival of a Scottish relieving force. In addition to supplying reserves, Warkworth was a useful base from which to launch an attack on any Scots attempting to relieve the besieged. It was tedious work, and one of the towers of Warkworth bears possible evidence of the boredom experienced by a lonely sentry with an artistic flair.

A Scottish army arrived on 5 January 1463, but Bamburgh and Dunstanburgh had already surrendered. Had the Scottish leaders acted more readily they could have changed the whole course of the Wars of the Roses, for Warwick reacted to their appearance as if in total surprise, and withdrew his men from outside Alnwick in a hasty retreat. The Scots, however, did not take full advantage of the situation, and like Queen Margaret at St Albans, failed to ensure that Warwick's indecision was the end of him. Instead the garrison of Alnwick abandoned the castle and joined the Scottish army. Next day Warwick occupied the property – with vacant possession.

Being short of volunteers for the lonely life of garrisoning a Northumbrian castle, Warwick handed Bamburgh and Dunstanburgh over to the safe-keeping of Sir Ralph Percy, who had suddenly developed staunch pro-Yorkist sympathies. A few months later an army of Scots, French and Lancastrians reappeared in Northumberland, whereupon Percy promptly surrendered the castles back to the House of Lancaster! Nothing daunted, the Neville brothers returned and all the fortresses were recaptured except for mighty Bamburgh, and most importantly of all, negotiations began between King Edward and the Scots in the hope of neutralizing Lancastrian support from across the border.

From the end of 1463 Lancastrian hopes centred on the massive, gloomy fortress of Bamburgh, blasted by the east wind whipping over the sand dunes of its lonely beach. Here, in the one-time capital of the ancient kingdom of Northumbria, the pathetic King Henry VI held solitary state. Early in 1464 he was cheered by the arrival of Henry Beaufort, third Duke of Somerset, to join him in his exile. This young man, the son of the duke who died beside the Castle Inn at St Albans, had been pardoned by Edward after the siege of Dunstanburgh, and was actively courted by him on behalf of the Yorkist cause. But he was a Beaufort, and that was enough to make him quit the pleasures of Edward's lively and fashionable Court for life in the Scottish Marches.

A raid in 1464 broke the tedium of endless, unfruitful besieging. Warwick's brother, John Neville, Lord Montagu, was on his way to Norham Castle where he was to meet Scottish ambassadors and escort them safely to York for negotiations with Edward. Realizing that this conference could finally settle any Lancastrian hopes of a Scottish alliance, Henry Beaufort attempted to ambush him near Newcastle. Lord Montagu had only a small force, 'fourscore spears and bows too', but managed to evade capture and proceeded on his way, only to be met near Morpeth by another Lancastrian force under the command of Sir Ralph Percy. The resulting Battle of Hedgeley Moor, on 25 April 1464, though a footnote to the main conflict, is interesting as a purely Neville/Percy affair, from which the Neville side emerged victorious, leaving Sir Ralph Percy lying dead. His last words are supposed to have been, 'I have saved the bird in my bosom', presumably referring to the Percys' long-standing loyalty to Henry VI. His nephew, another Henry Percy, was imprisoned by Edward IV, and only later restored to his rightful title when Edward needed a Percy as a counterbalance to Neville domination of the north. Incidentally, it was this Percy that was fated to die at Barnet fighting the Nevilles, both families having changed sides since Hedgeley Moor – so much for the notion of York and Lancaster!

Within the recess of one of the crossbow loops in the Grey Mare's Tail Tower at Warkworth Castle is this crude carving of a crucifix. Perhaps it was carved by a prisoner, or by a sentry bored with his duties during the castle's long and eventful history.

These two boulders on the site of the Battle of Hedgeley Moor (1464) are known as Percy's leap, and tradition has it that Sir Ralph Percy, mortally wounded, jumped his horse the distance that the stones represent. They probably predate the battle considerably, but remain a curious monument to this little-known struggle which added another chapter to the long rivalry between the Percy and the Neville families for control of the Border country.

If Neville honour had been satisfied against the Percys at Hedgeley Moor, it was soon to be additionally satisfied against the Beauforts. Lord Montagu escorted the Scots ambassadors safely to York, then hurried back north. Early in the morning of 15 May he smashed into the camp of Beaufort's raiding party beside the Devilswater, south of Hexham. Henry Beaufort, third Duke of Somerset, was captured, together with Lords Hungerford and Roos, and was beheaded shortly afterwards.

Two weeks later, as a gift from a grateful king, John Neville, Lord Montagu, was created Earl of Northumberland, the title having been vacant since Towton. For the old Neville/Percy rivalry, it was the Nevilles' high-water mark. Filled with renewed vigour, the Neville brothers flung their energies into reducing the Northumbrian castles once and for all. The Scottish negotiations, which John had laboured so hard to bring about, had been successful, leaving the three castles ill-prepared and garrisoned by demoralized survivors of Hedgeley Moor and Hexham. Alnwick and Dunstanburgh quickly surrendered before the new Earl of Northumberland. Only mighty Bamburgh held out under the keeping of Sir Ralph Grey, and Warwick was determined to have it this time 'even if the siege should take seven years', as his messenger grimly reported to Grey. To the message was added a curious rider, that for every shot by the besiegers that damaged Bamburgh, a Lancastrian head would fall. Apparently Edward wanted Bamburgh intact, but it was unusual that such an intention should have been conveyed to the defending lord, particularly one who had already been refused a pardon! Nevertheless, in the belief that anything that could be damaged could as readily be repaired, Warwick opened

The Devilswater, near Hexham in Northumberland, the site of the Battle of Hexham in 1464 where Henry Beaufort, third Duke of Somerset, was surprised in camp by John Neville, Lord Montagu, and killed.

Map of the Battle of Hexham.

up on Bamburgh with the fiercest artillery bombardment England had ever known. From positions among the sand dunes and from inland, the king's great guns, laboriously transported north for the business, blasted away at the fortress. The recoil, absorbed to some extent by a block of lead against timber, and the resulting sideways movement, threw the guns out of alignment each time they fired, so perhaps the capacity of the sand dunes around Bamburgh to absorb recoil was exploited.

The guns, each with a nickname, such as 'Newcastle', 'London' and 'Edward', rained iron and stone shot on the defenders. Chunks of the stone ramparts splintered off and were sent flying into the sea. One gun, called 'Dijon', was particularly successful in precision work. Once the gunners had got the range they were able to fire repeatedly on Sir Ralph Grey's personal apartments, which one presumes were in the splendid Norman keep, and succeeded in loosening masonry which fell on his head and concussed him, so that he was for a while given up for dead. To the accompaniment of gunfire and a constant barrage of arrows at the ramparts to keep the defenders heads down, the castle was assaulted, but the guns had already won the day. Before the attack could be

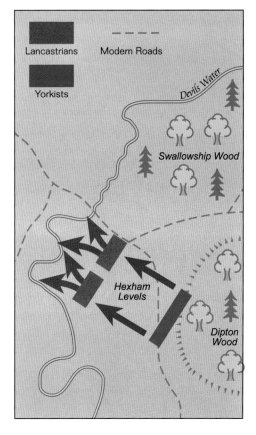

Lancastrians

Yorkists

Modern Roads

Devils Water

Swallowship Wood

Hexham Levels

Dipton Wood

fully pressed home the garrison negotiated a surrender. Bamburgh thus became the first castle in English history to succumb to gunfire. Grey was dragged unconscious from where the 'Dijon' had felled him, and was later beheaded at Doncaster.

MEN OF HARLECH

There is one more siege to consider. We last heard of Harlech during the rebellion of Glyndwr. During the War of the Roses it was held for the Lancastrians by Dafydd ap Ievan ap Einion, whose local influence had counteracted Yorkist domination in north Wales. 'King Edward,' wrote the chronicler Warkworth, 'was possessed of all England except a castle in north Wales called Harlech.' Gregory wrote that it was 'so strong that men said it was impossible to get it'. In the autumn of 1464 Sir William Herbert, Earl of Pembroke since the taking of that formidable castle from the Tudors, was granted its constableship and began a long siege. Despite a grant of £2,000 from King Edward towards the costs of besieging, and the supply of various guns, Harlech held out for four years. Notwithstanding the fact that the defenders used firearms, Edward must have concentrated as much effort on Harlech as he had on Bamburgh, and their topographical situations were not dissimilar. The new weapon technology could be devastating, but it was not infallible.

It was only in the sieges of the Wars of the Roses that cannon played a serious part, but there is ample evidence that they featured high in the preparations for war. As early as 1456, a royal warrant was issued appointing a certain John Judde, merchant of London, as Master of the King's Ordnance. The warrant plainly admitted that 'we be not yet sufficiently furnished of guns, gunpowder and other habiliments of war'. Judde was required to make field guns. Within a year he had supplied twenty-six serpentines, which were field guns mounted on mobile carriages, with a calibre of between 2 and 6 inches, and between 3 and 7 feet long. He had also made one culverin. They were transported to Kenilworth, whence they were probably taken to the Battle of Northampton, where Judde's careful work was brought to no effect by the mud and rain.

Field guns were sometimes a hindrance. At St Albans the queen's flank attack so surprised the Yorkist gunners that they succeeded in

Harlech Castle, which is built on a naturally strong position, managed to hold out for four years against the sophisticated techniques of siege warfare conducted by Edward IV. This brave resistance, led by one Dafydd ap Ievan ap Einion on behalf of the Lancastrian cause, forms the factual basis behind the song 'Men of Harlech'.

shooting each other! We know from Waurin's *Chronicle* that Edward took guns with him on the march north which ended at Towton but, as in the Northampton campaign, the weather was against their use, and the destruction of the bridge over the Aire prevented any heavy pieces being moved further than Pontefract. As for weapons of smaller calibre, I noted earlier the use of handguns by the Burgundian mercenaries at St Albans, but such weapons were not confined to foreigners. One of the Paston letters contains a vivid eyewitness record of defenders making a hole in the wall at knee height to shoot their handguns.

THE STEEL CROSSBOW

Artillery may have been the most visible development in military technology during the Wars of the Roses, but it was by no means the only one. Other tried and tested weapons were improved and expanded in their use, often following developments on the mainland of Europe. The commanders of the Wars of the Roses, far from being parochial and unimaginative, were eager to acquire any new technology and put it to use.

To begin with the crossbow, to the English a much-despised weapon, it was given a whole new lease of life in the mid-fifteenth century by the invention of the steel crossbow. Not surprisingly this packed a tremendous punch, doubling the range of the composite wooden crossbow's 200 yards to perhaps 450 yards, if modern tests are an accurate reflection of fifteenth-century practice. Steel crossbows probably started arriving in England in the late 1450s or 1460s. The more expensive variety were cocked by a rack and pinion activated by a crank. The speedy operation of this crannequin, as it was called, enabled a trained man to fire three times a minute, a considerable improvement on earlier practice.

With the universality of plate armour a new type of crossbow bolt was introduced. Its head was of square cross-section, the blunt force of its impact being sufficient to unhorse a man, particularly if it caught in his armour. At short range (and the crossbow had always been a short-range weapon), they could crack armour plate if delivered almost at right-angles to the surface – an effect similar to hitting the armour with a powerful hammer blow. Like artillery, however, cost was the factor that kept such deadly weapons in short supply, and most knights in the Wars of the Roses were reasonably safe from the old-style composite bow with its bolts designed for mail.

The English longbow remained the force it had always been, although mitigated by the difficulty of deploying it tactically because both sides used many archers. We have already seen how the Yorkist supremacy in archery at Towton was due to the good sense of Lord Fauconberg in exploiting a natural advantage, rather than any superiority of the archers themselves.

Overleaf: Pontefract Castle. A painting attributed to Alexander Keirinex, who produced it for King Charles I some time between 1625 and 1630. It is the best extant illustration of this once formidable castle, and hangs in Pontefract Museum. The painting is reproduced by kind permission of Wakefield Art Gallery and Museums Service.

The Faded Roses   12

It is perhaps no more than stubborn tradition that uses the term 'The Wars of the Roses' for the events subsequent to 1464. Words like treachery and turncoat become meaningless when the knightly families of the fifteenth century put their own survival above all other considerations. Thus the two remaining battles of the Wars of the Roses, Barnet and Tewkesbury, are worth studying from points of view other than purely military history. Barnet is particularly fascinating in that it was an engagement fought between two commanders who had hitherto fought side by side: King Edward IV and his cousin, Warwick the Kingmaker. The background to this strange reversal of loyalties, whereby the 'proud putter up and puller down of kings', as Shakespeare calls him, met his death at the hands of his king, is a very complicated one.

THE BATTLE OF BARNET

Edward IV's impulsive marriage to Elizabeth Woodville, which ruined all the plans Warwick had for him, so curtailed Warwick's position in the country that he used his immense influence to depose Edward and put the wretched King Henry back on the throne. At the Battle of Edgecote in 1469 Warwick defeated Edward's allies the Herberts and the Woodvilles, and to a background of local rebellions, the most serious of which was the Lincolnshire rising, Edward's power declined enough to cause him to flee temporarily to Burgundy.

He returned to England in March 1471, and landed at Ravenspur on the Humber. Bluffing his way through Yorkshire by claiming that he had come back merely to claim his dukedom of York and that he was a loyal subject of King Henry, he managed to evade three separate Lancastrian armies and entered London in safety. Warwick pursued him southwards, reaching St Albans on Good Friday, 12 April 1471. Taking with him as a hostage King Henry VI, who had previous experience of being forcibly taken along to battles, Edward advanced from London to meet him, and the following day Warwick continued his advance almost to Barnet, halting on the cross ridge just north of Barnet at Hadley Green. Both commanders knew the lie of the land well. There was some skirmishing as the two advance forces met, and as night fell both pulled back to their respective main bodies and battle lines were formed. As both sides

According to legend there lived one Arthal, Earl of Warwick, whose name meant 'bear'. A later legendary earl, Morvidus, slew a giant with a young ash tree torn up by the roots. Combining these two symbols, the historical Earls of Warwick arrived at their crest of the bear and ragged staff, seen here beautifully depicted on the wall of Lord Leicester's Hospital, Warwick.

Opposite: Gothic armour for man and horse, German, about 1475-80 The fluting on the outside surfaces was designed to deflect blows and is particularly attractive. (Board of the Trustees of the Royal Armouries II 3, VI 379)

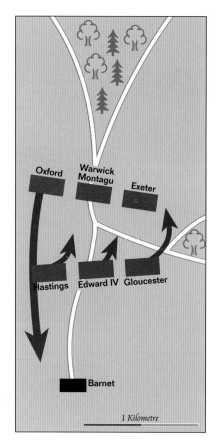

Map of the Battle of Barnet.

drew up their forces in the dark it is not surprising that the opposing lines did not coincide, and the right of one over-lapped the left of the other. That night Warwick kept up a barrage from field guns hoping, as the chronicler puts it, to 'annoy the King'. Edward, however, did not return the fire, for he observed that his cousin's army had assumed that he was further from their lines than was the case, and the balls were passing harmlessly overhead.

Dawn on Easter morning of 1471 revealed a dense mist that clung to the ground, muffling the sounds from the opposing armies. Then suddenly arrows began descending in random showers through the white blanket as Edward launched his attack. Guns fired, arrows and quarrels flew, as the two lines, at first grey and indistinct, plodded forward with eyes straining through helmet slits to catch a glimpse of the enemy. Suddenly the mysterious grey shapes became a splash of brilliant colour as the battle ranks materialized. Screaming war cries, the two armies flung themselves at each other. It was a mêlée of Towton proportions, but unlike Towton, where the narrowness of front channelled the opponents together, the extreme right on each side marched forward to encounter – nothing. The enemy were not there! In the dark the opposing troops had been drawn up out of line. On Warwick's right was the Earl of Oxford, an experienced soldier who immediately saw the possibility for a flank attack, wherever that flank might be.

Meanwhile the centre companies were furiously engaged. Edward and his brother George, Duke of Clarence, were hacking furiously at the Neville lines, where the centre was commanded by Warwick's brother John, Lord Montagu, whom Edward had deprived of his hard-won title of Earl of Northumberland at the time of Warwick's rebellion. On the Yorkist right Edward's other brother, Richard, Duke of Gloucester, was making good progress against Warwick's own division. The young man, who had accompanied his brother in exile, was only eighteen, younger than Edward had been at Northampton, and was serving in his first major military command. Perhaps Richard's inexperience prevented him from duplicating on his wing the bold, thrusting flank attack which Oxford was delivering against the Yorkist left, three-quarters of a mile away through the mist. In view of what was to happen next Edward must have thanked God for Richard's caution. Oxford's enthusiastic column hit the flank of Lord Hastings's division and knocked them sideways. Sensing victory, Oxford's men pursued them through Barnet and out towards London, where many began looting the neighbourhood. With great difficulty Oxford rallied his troops to lead them back. It would have been far better for the fortunes of Lancaster if he had let them continue looting. Instead he carefully, but hurriedly, retraced his steps with the remnants of his excited army.

The temporary absence of the Earl of Oxford's division had allowed Montagu's centre company to spread out to the right in an attempted envelopment of the Yorkists, when what should they see but a flying column of troops bearing down upon them slightly to their right. The first thing that caught their eye was the livery badge sewn on to the front and back of every tunic. It was the white star of Oxford, but in the thick mist, and to excited troops on their guard for an attack out of nowhere, it appeared to be the Yorkist white rose *en soleil*, the memorial of Mortimer's Cross, and the emblem at which they had hacked and beaten for the past hour. Arrows and bolts were discharged at the newcomers, who, under no illusions as to the identity of their attackers, drew the obvious conclusion: Montagu's men had turned traitor. The cry of treason went up, sending a chill through Warwick's army that even his presence could not allay. From that moment the day was lost. Edward brought up his reserves and Warwick's army broke. The Kingmaker was killed by an unknown hand as he tried to reach his horse, left at the rear as was the custom of the English knights.

The site of the Yorkist right wing at the Battle of Barnet, where Richard Duke of Gloucester, later King Richard III, was in command.

Heraldry has been called the shorthand of history, and nowhere is the allusion better illustrated than in the coat of arms of Richard Neville, Earl of Warwick and Salisbury, called The Kingmaker. On this one shield we see combined the previous arms of noble knights acquired by inheritance and marriage. In the second quarter are the quartered arms of Montagu and Monthermer, borne by his grandfather Thomas, Earl of Salisbury, killed at the siege of Orléans. In the first quarter are the quartered arms of his father-in-law, Richard Beauchamp, Earl of Warwick, which Beauchamp bore after 1423 with an inescutcheon of Clare quartering Despenser, now seen in the Kingmaker's fourth quarter. The third quarter displays the arms of Neville differenced by a label for Lancaster.

TEWKESBURY – THE SECOND TOWTON

On the very day that Warwick the Kingmaker died in the name of the House of Lancaster, Prince Edward, the heir of that House, accompanied by his formidable mother, landed at Weymouth. Among the deals which Warwick had struck with Queen Margaret was the marriage of the Prince of Wales to Warwick's daughter – what a weapon marriage was in the Middle Ages! The royal party received the news of Warwick's death the next day and were inclined to return to France, but the two Lancastrian lords who had met them at Weymouth persuaded them to stay. One of the pair was Thomas Courtenay, the Earl of Devon. The other was the latest of a long line of Beauforts to serve the House of Lancaster. Edmund Beaufort, fourth Duke of Somerset, bore the same name as his father, who had been killed in the first engagement of the war. His younger brother John accompanied him.

Margaret's strategic problem was as follows. Not as many West Country troops had joined her ranks as had been expected, and as the victorious Edward was no doubt advancing to engage her it was vital that she reached Wales, where the ever-loyal Jasper Tudor was enthusiastically raising an army. She first sent scouts towards the east, to make Edward think she was moving on London, and then, pausing briefly at Bristol to collect supplies and a badly needed, but slow-moving, artillery train, rushed her army towards the lowest bridge on the River Severn, at the city of Gloucester.

While the queen was still in Bath and intending to make for Bristol, Edward was at Cirencester, and would soon cut across her path. Somehow he had to be fooled into changing the direction of his advance. If Edward could be made to think that the queen intended to stand and fight, then as a good general he would probably choose the nearest natural strongpoint possible – which was Sodbury Hill, on the southern spur of the Cotswolds. Taking the initiative, and a great gamble, Queen Margaret sent her vanguard towards Sodbury Hill. Edward's scouts observed the move, and the scouts of both sides met by chance. In the ensuing skirmish some Yorkists were captured. This convinced Edward that battle was imminent, so he cautiously slowed his advance, and thus gave the Lancastrian army time to get clear of the vicinity. All that afternoon (2 May) and throughout the night, King Edward sat on Sodbury Hill, while his baffled scouts tried in vain to find the army that had seemed so ready for a decisive encounter.

That army had trudged wearily into Berkeley the same night, having gained a lead of 12 miles in the race for the river-crossing and the comparative safety of Wales. There were only 14 miles to go, and very early next morning the Lancastrians hurried on their way. By the time the news reached Edward only one thing could prevent them crossing the Severn and that was if the walled city of

The abbey of Tewkesbury, as seen from the field formerly known as the Gastons, which was the site of the Lancastrian left flank during the Battle of Tewkesbury in 1471.

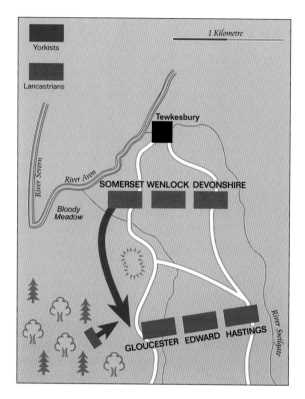

Map of the Battle of
Tewkesbury.

Gloucester refused the queen admittance. In that case she would have to march upstream to the next crossing point: a ferry just south of Tewkesbury, where the Avon joined the Severn. Tewkesbury was undefended and had no wall, but a ferry crossing would take much longer than a bridge, and time was the major factor in this campaign.

If it was to be Tewkesbury there would be a battle. Edward was sure of that, so he deployed his army in three divisions and a fast-moving detachment went on ahead to Gloucester. They won the race, and after hurried consultations with the governor the gates of the city were slammed in the queen's face when she arrived. After two hours of demands, pleas, and threats of assault which the governor knew she had no time to carry out, Margaret gave the reluctant order to move on to Tewkesbury. They arrived at the ferry at four o'clock in the afternoon, tired out after a 24-mile march in fifteen hours. The slow ferry crossing could not be risked. Edward would be upon them while half their army was on the far bank. Nor did they dare withdraw across the Avon into Tewkesbury itself. It would have been a better defensive position, but they would then have lost the ferry to Edward. No, here they had to stay.

The Yorkist army were as tired as their enemies. That night both hosts rested within sight of the beautiful Tewkesbury Abbey, and waited for morning. Queen Margaret had achieved so much in a remarkable strategic operation from which she emerges with much credit, but it was just too late.

The morning of 4 May 1471 found the two armies about 400 yards apart, and between them were 'foul lanes, and deep ditches and many hedges . . . a right evil place to approach'. The battle opened with a barrage of arrows and artillery. Then Edmund Beaufort, fourth Duke of Somerset, showed himself a worthy inheritor of his family's fighting tradition. He observed that the Yorkist left wing, under Edward's talented brother Richard of Gloucester, came to an end some 500 yards short of a round, densely wooded hill. It should be possible, Beaufort reckoned, to sweep his right wing out and advance unseen to attack the enemy's flank from the advantage of the hill. But this was not to be an isolated move. At the appropriate moment Lord Wenlock and the Prince of Wales would advance and engage the centre, catching the Yorkist left and centre from opposite sides. The Earl of Devon would take care of the Yorkist right, which was slightly detached from the rest of the army.

It was a plan that deserved to succeed, and it would have done had not the good generalship of King Edward foreseen the very danger which Beaufort planned to exploit. Not wishing to risk his brother's division by stretching it too thinly towards the hill, he had detached a band of 200 spearmen who were now lying in wait. As the chronicler quaintly puts it: '. . . charging them to keep a close watch on that part of the wood, and to do what was necessary if the need should arise, and if they saw no such need . . . to employ themselves in the best way they could'. This was a sensible delegation of responsibility by a commander who knew what he was doing.

So the spearmen waited, and along came Beaufort's division. Waiting until the bulk of the Lancastrians had passed them by, the small force hit them in the flank. It was a complete surprise, but need not have been a disaster if the centre

Bloody Meadow, Tewkesbury. Like its namesake at Towton, Bloody Meadow saw the fiercest fighting of the battle which finally sealed the fate of the Lancastrian dynasty.

THE BLOODY MEADOW
THE SCENE OF ONE OF THE FIERCEST
COMBATS OF THE BATTLE ᵒᶠ TEWKESBURY
4ᵗʰ MAY 1471

attack had been carried out. But there were no signs of movement from Lord Wenlock and the prince. Angry at what he thought was an almost treasonable lack of support by Wenlock (who had fought for the Yorkists at Towton) Beaufort spurred his horse back and remonstrated with the inactive lord. He called him coward, and traitor, and was obviously convinced that the latter accusation was the correct one, because, before Wenlock could protest his innocence, Beaufort lifted his battleaxe and smashed it down on Wenlock's head.

Northampton had been lost by the act of treason. Barnet had been lost by the suspicion of treason. Now Tewkesbury was to be lost by the presumption of treason. Beaufort's furious murder of his ally split the Lancastrian army in two, and the Yorkists rapidly took advantage of the situation. Hundreds of Lancastrian knights were driven back to the low-lying field by the river called Bloody Meadow, as at Towton. Many were drowned trying to cross the Severn where it is joined by the Avon at Abbey Mill. Many others scrambled across the Avon, or ran over the bridge to seek sanctuary in the abbey. But sanctuary meant little to Edward IV. His younger brother had almost gained sanctuary after Wakefield in the little chapel on the bridge, so there was to be no hiding-place in Tewkesbury Abbey for Edward's enemies. The chronicler Warkworth provides a list of those taken from the abbey and beheaded. Edmund Beaufort, Duke of Somerset, who had already acted as executioner himself that day, heads the list. His brother John already lay dead somewhere in Bloody Meadow.

Different battlefields have their special atmospheres under different conditions. Towton on a cold winter's day with a wind blowing and snow falling has its own ghosts. Barnet's ghosts linger in the morning mist on Hadley Green, beside the hedge which sheltered the Earl of Oxford before his fateful flank attack. Tewkesbury's ghosts are the products of a contrast, brought about on a sunny day. They come alive when one leaves the bright sunlight for the chill of the ancient abbey, desecrated by King Edward's revengeful presence on that distant May morning.

His noblest victim lies beneath the choir: Edward, Prince of Wales, son of Queen Margaret and Henry VI, or, if Yorkist propaganda is to be believed, Edmund Beaufort the Elder, father of the other Edmund who had been torn from sanctuary to meet his fate. But exactly what was the fate of the Prince of Wales? In all probability he died fighting in the thick of the battle, a worthy descendant of his grandfather, Henry V. The four earliest chronicles all state that this is how he met his death. A later, Tudor account has the prince taken alive and brought before Edward by Sir Richard Croft, the veteran of Mortimer's Cross, where he speaks defiantly to the king and receives a slap in the face from the king's gauntlet. At this point he is set upon by the Yorkists standing by and speedily done to death.

Opposite: Rear view of a Gothic armour for man and horse in the Wallace Collection, London. The visible rivets are in most places fitted into slots, so that pieces can slide freely across one another, providing a perfect protection. This armour was made in Landshut, Germany, between 1475 and 1485.

Sir Ralph Fitzherbert, from his tomb in Norbury Church, Derbyshire. His collar bears a pendant of a white boar, granted by Richard III. Fitzherbert died in 1483.

RICHARD OF GLOUCESTER

Richard of Gloucester, who became Richard III, always acted with exemplary loyalty towards the House of York and the person of his brother the king. He also acquired a fine reputation as a soldier at Barnet and Tewkesbury, after which he was rewarded by being made effectively Viceroy of the North, exercising a devolved government of northern Britain from his favourite castle of Middleham in Wensleydale. He was given a supervisory role over the latest Percy, Earl of Northumberland, who had fought beside him at Barnet, and in the absence of any Nevilles a peace descended upon the border Marches which stood in marked contrast to the years of disorder which had preceded it.

As for the threat from across the border, relations with Scotland had been cordial since 1464 as a result of Edward's peaceful diplomacy designed to neutralize Lancastrian support from that direction. The battles of Hedgeley Moor and Hexham had both arisen from those diplomatic manoeuvres. Now that the Lancastrian threat had shrunk to the fugitive Henry Tudor in Brittany, Edward was able to seize the initiative against the Scots and maybe even recapture Berwick, which had been surrendered to the Scots when Henry VI fled across the border after Towton. Richard of Gloucester was appointed commander-in-chief on 12 May 1480, and in June the Scots responded to the English build-up by raiding across the border as far as Bamburgh. Richard chased them back, and hostilities were suspended until 1482, when parliament voted a considerable sum for war against the Scots. The Scottish government was in turmoil. The country was threatened with an imminent incursion of an English army consisting of between 6,000 and 10,000 men under Richard of Gloucester, and with a vanguard led by Percy, Earl of Northumberland, and Lord Scrope of Bolton, two families of immense experience in border warfare.

Berwick was Richard's first objective, and the town soon fell. Leaving a detachment to continue the siege of the castle, he continued through Berwickshire on a *chevauchée*, while one wing of his army burned Roxburghshire as far as Jedburgh. Richard may have reached the outskirts of Edinburgh when the Scots came to negotiate. In any event, the two armies entered Edinburgh together the following day, an armistice having been agreed. Berwick surrendered as Richard marched south again, and the six-week-long campaign came to a triumphant end.

BOSWORTH FIELD

The subsequent events concerned with the untimely death of Edward IV, the accession of his twelve-year-old son, Edward V, and the sudden assumption of power by Richard III, are sufficiently well known in their outline to require no

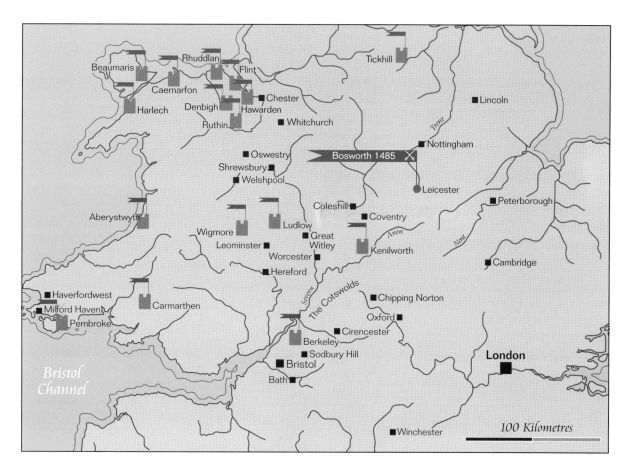

repetition here. As to the conduct of Richard with regard to the mysterious disappearance of his nephews, Edward V and Richard, Duke of York, it is now the unorthodox view to suggest that Richard had some part in their murder. The prospect of a boy king, with the likelihood of friction between the late king's family on one side and Queen Elizabeth's on the other, boded ill for the future of the Yorkist dynasty while Henry Tudor was waiting in Brittany and providing a focus for all renegade or dispossessed Lancastrians. It was, therefore, in the best interests of the House for Richard, an excellent administrator and accomplished soldier, to become king. But were the boys murdered, and if so on whose orders? We will never know.

Whatever the fate of the princes, the greatest threat to the House of York was the man in Brittany. Henry Tudor had been captured at the fall of Pembroke Castle in 1461 and had stayed an exile since 1471, since when both Yorkist kings had attempted to have him returned. He had been absent from England for fifteen years, a period of time which moulded his view of himself and also of the country whose throne he claimed. Henry's later opinion, that it

The Fort la Latte in Brittany, which has been much restored, gives the visitor an excellent impression of a medieval castle. It is built on rocky cliffs that tower over the sea – the perfect romantic situation!

Standard of Henry Tudor, Earl of Richmond, later to become Henry VII. This is the standard which Henry would have displayed at Bosworth.

The Battlefield of Bosworth, now carefully preserved and open to the public, where a reproduction of the standard of Richard III again flies.

was he who united the warring factions and restored peace to the realm, is often put down to Tudor propaganda, and his own consummate statecraft, yet this view of himself as a king in exile coming to bring a new era is probably an accurate reflection of the opinion he had of himself.

On Christmas Day, 1483, Duke Francis II of Brittany proclaimed Henry King of England at Rennes Cathedral. At the same time, Henry pledged himself to marry Elizabeth of York, Edward IV's daughter whom that monarch had always intended for the dauphin, but he was by now King Charles VIII and married to someone else. Henry clearly saw his union with Elizabeth as a symbolic act, over and above the purely political result of neutralizing any future opposition. Even more symbolic was the naming of their first-born son, Arthur. This was a break with a tradition of two centuries that had produced a succession of Edwards, Henrys and Richards. But what a choice! It was a return to an even greater tradition, to Geoffrey of Monmouth's tales of the legendary Arthur, king of the Britons. Is this how Henry saw himself and his successors, as a divinely ordained prince returning from exile? We do know that Henry believed firmly in his descent from Cadwallader, the last of the British kings, and lost no opportunity to proclaim it. It was a conviction strengthened by his early years in Wales under the care of his indestructible uncle Jasper, and reinforced by thirteen years in Brittany, where the independent Celtic spirit of the Bretons cherished the legends of Arthur.

In 1484 Richard III's final attempt to secure Henry's extradition failed when he slipped across the border into France to enjoy a last year of exile at the French court. The new king welcomed him, and did all in his power to strengthen Henry's belief that he was to overcome the apparent readiness with which the English deposed their kings, in contrast to the civilized state of things in France.

When Henry Tudor landed at Milford Haven in August 1485 he shared an identical concern with the reigning English sovereign. Neither knew exactly on whose support they could rely. Both sides had their passionate loyalists, but beyond them there was a grey area of doubt. For example, the Tudors were traditionally strong in Wales. Richard III's representative there was Sir Walter Herbert, of the Yorkist family of Earls of Pembroke. He had been sounded out by the Tudor faction, but had apparently not committed himself. The two brothers of the Stanley family of Cheshire (of whom the elder, Lord Thomas Stanley, was Henry Tudor's stepfather), had supposedly committed themselves to the Tudor cause. So had Gilbert Talbot, son of the glorious Lancastrian Talbot, whose actions had crushed the first flames of Yorkist revolt in 1451. The Percy family, of whom the Earl of Northumberland had marched with Richard to Scotland, were expected to follow the king, but the Percys could be unreliable.

Both rivals followed a predictable course once the landing had taken place. Henry Tudor proceeded to raise support, and Richard began to raise troops. The latter may have experienced some relief in the thought that the hour had come, for he was a born soldier, and in his element with the arrangements that now to be made. His plan was to collect his northern supporters, the Percys, and, he hoped, the Stanleys at Nottingham, and then march south to join the southern contingent at Leicester. These would include the forces of John Howard, the Duke of Norfolk, who had been knighted by Edward IV on the field of Towton.

Henry Percy took a long time to reach Nottingham, and it was with some haste that Richard took him to Leicester on the evening of 20 August, where they joined the Duke of Norfolk. The following morning the army left Leicester to take up its position at Bosworth Field. At sunrise on the morning of 22 August the absence of Stanley, the one fact which had puzzled Richard, was immediately explained. To the north lay Lord Stanley's forces with their white buck's head badges on red coats. They did not appear inclined towards either army, but Richard took the sensible precaution of assuming they were hostile, and arranged his forces accordingly. He placed the equally doubtful Earl of Northumberland at his rear. Henry's army moved up to the attack in battle formation: Talbot on the right wing, Oxford in the centre, and Henry Tudor himself on the left. To reach Richard's army they had to wheel round a large marshy area to their right, leaving their left flank exposed to a possible attack from the Stanleys, who had advanced towards the

Henry VII, victor of the Battle of Bosworth, and founder of the Tudor dynasty. This impressive sculpture by Pietro Torrigiano (1472–1528) is of painted and gilded terracotta. (Victoria and Albert Museum)

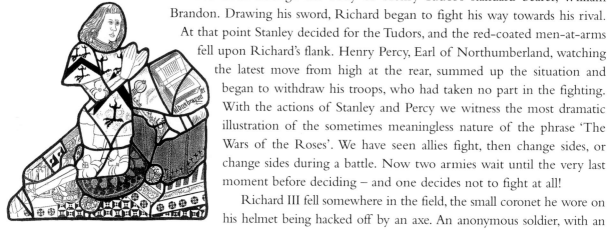

John Howard, Duke of Norfolk, who was knighted by Edward IV on the field of Towton in 1461 and was killed at Bosworth in 1485.

Sir Reginald Bray, who is traditionally credited with having found Richard III's crown in a hawthorn bush after the Battle of Bosworth. Bray took it to Lord Stanley, who placed it upon the head of Henry Tudor.

centre of the action. Richard ordered an advance downhill against the Tudor army, who were still dressing their ranks, and the assault was led by the Duke of Norfolk. It was a sensible move. To have hesitated would have exposed Richard's vanguard to the French and Burgundian gunners whom Henry had brought with him. But Oxford's men held firm, and packed themselves more tightly together to resist Norfolk's attack, whose advance was being slowly split in two. At this point the duke himself was killed.

By now there was something of a stalemate, and the decision which the Stanleys must soon be forced to take would decide the battle. Henry took the initiative and, with banners flying, rode over towards the Stanleys to beg their assistance. From Richard's vantage point he could see their every move, and as they showed their flanks to him he knew the moment was ripe for a cavalry charge. All his experience, of Barnet and Tewkesbury, of the lessons he had been taught of Agincourt and Formigny, showed him that here was the perfect target for a knight's move.

Of what would such a move consist? To charge, certainly, but with what? The hitting power of the armoured knight depended upon penetration as well as speed, and the penetrating object was the lance. This weapon, clumsy and heavy, had to be lowered to the horizontal and held there while the horse worked up to the gallop. A century earlier it had been held beneath the right arm, with the attendant danger of breaking that arm when the impact took place. Suits of armour were now fitted with a strong lance rest on the right breast, and we may imagine 1,000 heavy lances descending from the vertical to brace against the rest, as the force gained speed downhill. The knight was now a form of human projectile. There appeared to be no foot soldiers in his way, and if any were they were ridden down, their arrows bouncing harmlessly off his armour, as the knights recaptured their chivalric traditions.

Such was the force of the charge at Bosworth that King Richard's lance was rammed clean through the body of Henry Tudor's standard bearer, William Brandon. Drawing his sword, Richard began to fight his way towards his rival. At that point Stanley decided for the Tudors, and the red-coated men-at-arms fell upon Richard's flank. Henry Percy, Earl of Northumberland, watching the latest move from high at the rear, summed up the situation and began to withdraw his troops, who had taken no part in the fighting. With the actions of Stanley and Percy we witness the most dramatic illustration of the sometimes meaningless nature of the phrase 'The Wars of the Roses'. We have seen allies fight, then change sides, or change sides during a battle. Now two armies wait until the very last moment before deciding – and one decides not to fight at all!

Richard III fell somewhere in the field, the small coronet he wore on his helmet being hacked off by an axe. An anonymous soldier, with an eye for the chivalric prize of booty, stuck it into a hawthorn bush, hoping to retrieve it later. It was found there by Sir Reginald Bray, who brought it to Lord Stanley. Henry Tudor, ever the one for symbolism, accepted the coronet as a crown.

Bosworth was not, in fact, the last battle of the Wars of the Roses. That honour goes to the Battle of Stoke in 1487. Here Henry VII crushed the Simnel conspiracy by defeating a strong army that included 2,000 German mercenaries in an engagement that lasted longer than Bosworth. But Bosworth had seen the death of the last Yorkist King of England, whose family had done so much to keep England at the forefront of military development. Richard III had led what was to prove to be the last charge by mounted knights in English history, but similar events would be seen on the continent of Europe in the years to come as the knight constant lived on. The knight triumphant was now being used at the peak of his perfection, encased in armour, and impervious to hand weapons, the consummation of all he had believed in at Crécy, Tannenberg, Otterburn or the Battle of the Thirty.

King Dick's Well, on the battlefield of Bosworth, where Richard III is said to have refreshed himself prior to the battle which ended his brief reign. (Photograph by courtesy of Leicestershire County Council, who maintain the battlefield.)

index

Figures in **bold** refer to illustrations

Aberystwyth Castle 145
Agache, Gobin 43
Agincourt, battle of, 22nd
    October 1415 **152**(map),
    153–156, **154**(map)
Aire, River 218–219
Alençon, Duke of 175, 183
Alnwick Castle 223, 226, 227,
    228
Angevin Empire, the 29–31
Anghiari, battle of, 1440 117,
    126, 126–127
Anglo-Burgundian alliance 162
Anglo-Scottish border **12**(map)
Anjou, Duke of 92
Aquitaine 29, 62, 92, 94, 115,
    151, 184–185
archers 37, 44, **45**, 231
    at Agincourt 154, 155
armour **25, 47**
    at Agincourt **151**, 155
    gothic **234, 242**
    mail 46–47, 65
    plate **46**, 47–48, 65–66, **107,
    151**, 155, **176, 179, 216**,
    216–217, 231
    tilting **56, 57**
    Wars of the Roses 216–217
assassination 117
Astley, Sir John **215**
Auberoche, battle of, 21st
    October 1345 42
Audley, Sir James 63, 69
Auray, battle of, 29th
    September 1364 84–88,
    85, 86

Balliol, Edward (c 1283–1364),
    King of Scots 15–16,
    17–18, 24, 49
Bamburgh Castle 21, 23,
    224–225, 226, 227,
    228–230
Bannockburn, battle of 24th
    June 1314 9, 15, 47
Barnet, battle of, 14th April
    1471 235–237, **236**(map),
    237
bastides 115, **117**
Battle of the Thirty 58–60, **60**
Battlefield Church,
    Shrewsbury 141, **142**
battles 36, 37
Beauchamp, Sir Richard, Earl
    of Warwick **177, 179**
Beaufort family 189

Beaufort, Edmund, 2nd Duke
    of Somerset (c1406–55)
    181–182, 189
Beaufort, Edmund, 4th Duke
    of Somerset 238, 240, 243
Beaufort, Henry, Duke of
    Somerset 207, 227, 228
Beaufort, Margaret
    (1443–1509) 189
Beaugency 168, 177
Beaumanoir, Jean de 59, 60, 86
Bécherel Castle 73, 74, **76**, 85,
    95
Bembro, Richard 59
Bembro, Robert 72
Benhale, Robert 25
Bentley, Sir William 59, 61, 81
Berwick upon Tweed 9, 10,
    18, 193, 244
    siege of, 1333 18–21, 23, 27
Black Prince, the. see Edward
    the Black Prince
Blanchetaque, ford at 43–44
Blois, Charles de 33, **33**, 34,
    35, 36, 51, 59, 86, 88
    ransom of 74, 76
Blore Heath, battle of, 22nd
    September 1459 **197**,
    197–198
Bolingbroke, Henry, Earl of
    Derby. see Henry IV, King
    of England
Bonaguil, Château de **195**
Bonet, Honor 53, 58
Bordeaux, Truce of 82
Borgoforte Castle 121
Bosworth Field, battle of, 22nd
    August 1485 **245**(map),
    248, 249–251, **251**
Boucicault, Marshal of France
    104
Bramham Moor, battle of,
    19th February 1408 **145**,
    146
Brandon, William 250
Bray, Sir Reginald **250**, 251
Brétigny, Treaty of, 1360 82,
    92, 115
brigands 115
Brittany 50–51, 58–59, 61, 74,
    80–81, 84–85, 88, 96, 182
    English garrisons 95
    succession 33
Brougham, castle **208**
Bruce, Robert (1274–1329),
    King of Scots 9, **9**, 10, 15

Bryn Glas, battle of, 1402 136
Buckingham, Henry, Second
    Duke of **191**
Buckingham, Humphrey
    Stafford, Duke of 191,
    202, 205
Bureau, Jean 184
Burgundy 84, 178
Burgundy, Duke of 102

Caen 39–40, **41**, 156, 184
Caerlaverock Castle **16**
Caernarfon Castle 142
Caerphilly Castle **19**
Calais **39**, 50, 193, 197
caltrops 217
Calveley, Sir Hugh 60, 74, **77**,
    87, 88, 96, **96**, 115
Cambridge, Richard, Earl of
    150
cannon 104, 156, 170, 184,
    184–185, **201**, 229–230,
    230–231
Canterbury Tales (Chaucer)
    103, **103**
Captal de Buch, Jean de
    Grailly 57, 58, 62, 69, 84,
    90, 94
Caravaggio, battle of 128
Carcossone 63
Carlisle 193, 223
Castagnaro, battle of 125
Castilian forces, at Nájera 90
Castillon, battle of 184–185,
    185(map), 188
casualties
    Agincourt 155
    Auray 88
    condottieri warfare 116–117
    Crécy 46
    Halidon Hill 26, 27
    Towton 222
Catherine of Valois
    (1484–1536), Queen of
    England 162
Cesena 123–124
Chandos, Sir John (?–1370)
    37, 63, 86, 87, 90, 94, 191
Charles V (1337–80), King of
    France **74**, 77, 82, 84, 91,
    92, 95, 96
Charles VI (1368–1422), King
    of France **55**, 149, 162, 163
Charles VII (1403–61), King of
    France 163, 164, 165, 168,
    180, 181, 182

coronation of 178
    as Dauphin 162, 163
    and Jeanne d'Arc 174, 178,
    180
Charles VIII (1470–98), King
    of France 115–116
Charles the Bad, King of
    Navarre 84
Châteauneuf de Randon 96
Chepstow Castle **140–141**
Cherbourg 184
Cheshire 196
chevauchée 38–40, 42, 53, 57, 62
Cheyne, Thomas **46**
Chinon Castle 170, **172–173**
chivalry 53, 56–57, 60
    and the Black Prince 62
    and crusading 99, 102
    internationalism of 57–58
    and the pursuit of gain 58
    and warfare 57
chroniclers 36
Chronique de Bertrand du
    Guesclin (Cuvelier) 71–72
civilians 37, 38, **118**, 160
Clarence, Thomas, Duke of
    162, 163, **163**
Clement V, Pope 101
Clermont, Count of 183,
    183–184
Clifford, Robert de 10
Clisson, Olivier de 35, 86, 87,
    87, 88, 92, 95, 96
Cocherel, battle of, 16th May
    1364 84
Cock, River **218, 219**, 221
Colleoni, Bartolomeo 126,
    127–128, **129**
commissions of array 37, 194
Compiègne 180
condottieri 116–117, 118,
    120–121, 122, 125–129
contracts, recruiting 37, 191,
    193
Conwy Castle 136, 142
Courtney, Thomas, Earl of
    Devon 238, 240–241
Crabb, John 19
Cravant, siege of 163–164
Crécy, battle of, 26th August
    1346 42–46, **43**(map), **44**,
    45, 58, 99
criminals, pardons for service
    37
Croft, Sir Richard **210**, 213,
    214

crusader tourism 102–104,
103, 107
crusades 99, 102, 103; *see also*
Lithuanian Crusade, the
Cumberland 9

Dacres, Lord 220–221, 222
Dagworth, Sir Thomas 50–51,
58
d'Artois, Robert 35
D'Aubernoun, Sir John **25**
d'Audrehem, Marshal 58, 65,
73, 74, 89, 90
David II (1324–71), King of
Scots 15, 48, 50
'Day of the Herrings', the
170–171
Despenser, Edward le **67**
Despenser, Sir Hugh **47**
d'Este castle, Ferrara 118, **119**
d'Hesdin, Enguerrand 74
Dinan **73**, 77, 79, **88**
d'Ingham, Sir Oliver **31**, 32
Douglas, Sir Archibald 20, 23,
23–24, 26–27
Douglas, Archibald 136, 163,
164, 165
Douglas, George, Earl of
Angus 193
Douglas, Sir James 9, 10, 15, 20
Douglas, James, second Earl of
132, 133, 134
drawbridges **165**, **192**
du Guesclin, Bertrand. *see*
Guesclin, Bertrand du
Dunois of Orléans 175, 176,
182
Dunstanburgh Castle 223,
223, 226, 227, 228
Dupplin Moor, battle of, 11th
August 1332 16–17
Durham 13, 48, **49**
Durham, Bishop of 9, 46, 49

Edgecote, battle of, 1469 235
Edinburgh 244
Edward II (1284–1327), King
of England 9, 10, 11
Edward III (1312–77), King of
England **8**, 10, 13, 29, 82,
190–191
arrival in France 35–36
and Berwick 18, 21, 23
and Brittany 33, 33–34
and Caen 40
and Calais 50
claim to the French throne
31, 32, 58
at Crécy 37–38, 42, 42–43,
44, **44**, 46

and crusading 99
death of 96
at Halidon Hill 23, 24–25
illness 91
and the Order of the Garter
57
and Philip VI of France 31,
32
precautions against the Scots
49
revenue 31
ruthlessness of 21, 27
sends the Black Prince to
Aquitaine 62
standard **38**
and the Weardale campaign 15
Edward IV (1442–83), King of
England 206, 215, 219,
238–239
at Barnet 236, 237
coronation of 218
death of 244
as Earl of March 202, 210
marriage 235
at Mortimer's Cross 213,
213–214
at Northampton 203, 205
at Tewkesbury 239–240,
241, 243
at Towton 220
Warwick's treachery 235
Edward V (1470–83), King of
England 244–245
Edward, Prince of Wales
(1453–71) 238, 243
Edward the Black Prince
(1330–76) 31, 42–43, 46,
60, **64**, **90**, 115
and Aquitaine 62–63
at Crécy 44–45
death of 96
dysentery 91
at Limoges 94
at Nájera 90
personification of chivalry 62
at Poitiers 65, 69
in Spain 88, 89
Eleanor of Aquitaine
(1122–1204), Queen of
England 29
Elizabeth of York 187, 248
England 9, 31, 149–150
and France 31
Glyndwr's revolt **137**(map)
permanent military forces 193
Scots border **12**(map)
Scots raids 9, 9–10, **15**,
48–49, 132
and the Wars of the Roses
187–188

English forces 36, 37, 57, 180
at Agincourt 153, 154–155
at Auberoche 42
at Auray 86, 87
the Battle of the Thirty
59–60
at Berwick 10, 18–20
in Brittany 34, 50–51
at Castillon 185
at Cocherel 84
at Cravant 163–164
at Crécy 42, 43–44, 44–45,
45–46
defence of York 10
at Dupplin Moor 16–17
fleet 39–40
at Formigny 183, 184
in Gascony 32, 184–185
at Halidon Hill 23, 24–25,
26
at Harfleur 151
Henry V's *chevauchée* 152
at Mauron 61, 61–62
at Nájera 90
at Neville's Cross 49–50
in Normandy 183, 184
at Orléans 168–169, 170, 176
at Otterburn 133
at Patay 178
at Poitiers 65, 66, 67, 69
at Rennes 77, 79, 80
at Rouen 157
at Saint-Malo 95
and the Scots **14**
in Spain 88
at Verneuil 164–165
and the Weardale campaign
13, 14, 15

Falaise 156, **182**, 184
Fastolf, Sir John 170–171, 178
Fauconberg, William Neville,
Lord 203, 220
Felbrygge, Sir Simon **151**
Fenis castle **127**
Ferrara 118, **119**
Fitzherbert, Sir Ralph **244**
Flanders 32
Flemish forces, and the Crécy
campaign 42
Florence 122
Formigny, battle of, 15th April
1450 183–184
Fort la Latte **192**, **246–247**
Fougères, castle of **181**, 182,
204
France 29, **30**(map), 149, 162
and Gascony 31
revival of 71, 91–92, 94–97
succession 31

Free Companies 88, 115
French forces 57
at Agincourt **152**(map), 153,
154, 155
at Auberoche 42
at Auray 86–87, 88
the Battle of the Thirty 59,
60
in Brittany 51
at Castillon 184, 185
at Cocherel 84
at Crécy 42, 44, 45, 46
at Formigny 183–184
and Gascony 32
at Harleur 151
Henry V's *chevauchée* 152
at Mauron 61, 62
at Nájera 90
in Normandy 183
at Orléans 169–170, 171,
174–176
at Patay 178
at Poitiers 65, 66–67, 69
at Rennes 77, 80
revival of 91
at Rouen 160
support for Glyndwr's revolt
141–142, **144**, 144–145
at Verneuil 164, 165
and the Wars of the Roses
226
Froissart, Jean
(c1335–1404/10) 36
on Auray 87
on Caen 40
on the Scots 13
on Sir John Hawkwood 121

garrisons 60, 81
Gascoigne, Sir William **209**
Gascony 29–32, **30**(map), 42,
62, 82, 92, 94, 184
George, Duke of Clarence
237
Glendower, Owen. *see*
Glyndwr, Owen
Gloucester, Humphrey, Duke
of 155
Glyndwr, Owen (c1355–c1416)
136, **136**, 138, 142–143,
144, 145, 147
Golden Ambrosia Republic,
the 127–129
Grailly, Jean de. *see* Captal de
Buch, Jean de Grailly
Grand Fougeray, castle of 72
Grey, Sir Edward 191
Grey, Sir Ralph 228, 229, 230
Grunwald, battle of. *see*
Tannenberg, battle of

Guesclin, Bertrand du **70**, 71–72, 82, **97**
  achievement 97
  at Auray 85, 87, 88
  in Brittany 96
  brokers truce 95–96
  burial 96
  capture and ransom 81, 90
  at Châteauneuf de Randon 96
  coat of arms **72**
  at Cocherel 84
  death of 96
  guerrilla campaign 72–73
  knighted 74
  at Montmuran 73–74, **77**
  at Nájera 90
  promotion to Constable 92
  at Rennes 77, 79, 80
  at Saint-Malo 95
  in Spain 88, 89
  worth 90

Hainault, mercenaries from 13, 15
Halidon Hill, battle of, 19th July 1333 23–27, **26–27**, 48
Harcla, Sir Andrew 13
Harcourt, Godfrey de 40, 45, 46
Hardreshull, Sir John de **36**
Harfleur 92, 151, 156, 183
Harlech Castle **230**, 230–231
Hastings, Sir Lawrence de **52**
Hawkwood, Sir John 121–125, **123**, 129
Hedgeley Moor, battle of, 25th April 1464 227, **228**
helmets **24**, **57**, **92**, **151**, 155, **176**, 216, **217**
Hennebont 33, **34**
Henry II (1133–89), King of England 29
Henry IV (1366–1413), King of England **98**, **130**, 134, 135, 144
  as Bolingbroke, Earl of Derby 102–103, 108, 134–135
  French policy 149
  and Glyndwr's revolt 136, **137**(map), 145, 147
  at Shrewsbury 139
  standard **134**
Henry V (1387–1422), King of England **150**, 162, 163
  at Agincourt 153, 153–154, 155
  chevauchée of 151–152

consequences of Agincourt 156
  crosses the Somme 152–153
  French policy 149–150, 162
  at Harfleur 151
  invasion of Normandy 150–151
  Prince of Wales 135, 136, 139
  at Rouen 157, 160, 161
  second French campaign 156
Henry VI (1421–71), King of England 163, 177, 180, 184, **187**, 193, 194, 196, 199, 202, 227, 235
  at First St Albans 190
  marriage of 181
Henry VII (1457–1509), King of England 196, 222, 244, 245, 248, 248–249, **249**
  badge 187
  at Bosworth Field 250, 251
  and the Simnel conspiracy 251
  standard **248**
Henry of Lancaster (c1310–61) 42
Henry of Trastamare 88, 89, 89–90
heraldry **238**
Herbert, Sir Walter 249
Herbert, Sir William, Earl of Pembroke 213, 230
Hermitage Castle **17**
Hexham, battle of, 15th May 1464 228, **229**, **229**(map)
Hitler, Adolph (1889–1945) 112
Holland, Sir Thomas 40
Holy Trinity, banner of the **55**
Homildon Hill, battle of, 14th September 1402 136, **138**, **139**
hostages 20, 21
Hundred Years' War, the 29, 38, 40, 58, 69, 102, 103–104, 131, 149, 165, 167, **169**(map), 185, 191, 193
Hyddgen, battle of, 1401 136

Isabella of France (1293–1358), Queen of England 10, 10–11, 13
Italy 115–116, 129

Janville 168
Jargeau 168, 168–169, 177
Jeanne d'Arc (1412–31) 71, 171, 174, **174**, **175**, **178**
  attitudes towards 177

at Beaugency 177
  capture of 180
  contribution 176
  at Jargeau 177
  at Orléans 175, 176
  at Patay 178
  role 175
  trial and execution 180
  wounding of 178
Joan, Countess of Flanders 76
John II (1319–64), King of France 61, 69, **69**, 82
John II, Duke of Brittany **61**
John III, Duke of Brittany **32**, 33
John, King of Bohemia 45, 46, 58, 102
John of Gaunt (1340–99) 90, 92, 95, 96, 151
Josselin Castle 59, **59**
Judde, John 230
Jungingen, Conrad von, Grand Master of the Teutonic Knights 108
Jungingen, Ulrich von, Grand Master of the Teutonic Knights 108, 109, **109**, 111

Kenilworth Castle 202, **202–203**
knighthood, bestowing of **156**, 177
knights 36–37
  brotherhood of 102
  discipline exerted by 53
  international brotherhood of 57–58
  last charge of 250, 251
  and looting 53
  perfection of 251
  reconstruction of **148**
  role 57, 69
Knights Hospitaller 100
Knights Templar 100
Kniprode, Winrich von, Grand Master of the Teutonic Knights 104
Knowles, Sir Robert 60, 86, 87, 88, 92, 115
Kyriell, Sir Thomas 183, 184

La Roche-Derrien 51
La Rochelle 94
Lancaster, Earl of 65
Lancaster, Henry of 76, 77, 79, 80
Lancaster, House of 189
  red rose of 187
Lancastrian forces 207, 210, 226

at Barnet 236, 237
at Bosworth Field 250
at Ludlow 199
at Mortimer's Cross 213, 214
at Northampton 202–203, 205
at Second St Albans 217–218
at Tewkesbury 240–241, 243
at Towton 219, 220, 220–221, **221**, 221–222
at Wakefield 207
Landal, castle of 73
Languedoc 96
Le Mans 167, 181
Les Tourelles 176
Limoges 94
literature, themes of 56
Lithuania 100, 107–108
Lithuanian crusade, the 100–102, **101**(map), 104–106, 107–108, 111–112
  battle of Tannenberg **12**, **108**, 108–111, **109**
  and crusader tourism 102–104
Loire, River 168
London, Tower of 205
Longueil 57
Longueville, Jean Dunois, Count of 167, **168**
looting 40, 53, 120, 122
Loryng, Sir Nele **67**
Louis XI (1423–83), King of France 226
loyalty 191, 193
Lübeck Chronicle, the 112
Lucca 120, **120**
Ludford Bridge 199, **199**
Ludlow 199–201, **200**, 205
Ludlow Castle 198, **198**

Machiavelli, Niccolò (1469–1527) 116, 116–117, 129
Maine 182
Malestroit, Truce of 36
Manny, Sir Walter 34, 42, 58
Mar, Earl of 17
Marcher Lords, the 131–134
Mares, Eslatre des 74
Margaret of Anjou (1430–82), Queen of England 181, 196, 197, 201, 205, 206, 210, 217, 218, 223, 226, 238, 240
Marienburg Castle 101, 111
Marienwerder, castle of 104

Mauron, battle of, 14th August 1352 **60**, 60–62
Meaux 163
Melun, siege of, 1420 162
mercenaries 13, 15, 88, 104, 108, 115
  condottieri 116–117, 118, 120–121, 122, 125–129
  in France 180–181
  and the Lithuanian Crusade 111–112
  looting 120
  loyalty 116
  Wars of the Roses 193
  the White Company 121–125
Merlin, prophecies of 142
Meung 168, 177
Milan 126, 127, 128, 129
military orders 100; *see also* Teutonic Knights
miners 37
Molinella, battle of, 1467 117
monarchs, dependence on loyalty 40, 42
Monmouth, castle **150**
Mont Saint Michel **158–159**, **160**
Montagnana **114**, **126**
Montague, John Neville, Lord 223, 227, 228, 237
Montargis, siege of 167
Montecastrese Castle **105**
Montfort, John de, Duke of Brittany 76, 80, 86, 87, 88, 95
Montfort, John de, the elder 33, 59
Montmuran, castle of 73–74, **75**, **77**
Montpazier **117**
monumental brasses **25**, **46**, **151**
Moray, John Randolf, Earl of 10
Morlaix, battle of, 30th September 1342 34–35
Mortimer, Edmund 134, 135, 147, 150, 188
Mortimer, Edmund, the Elder 136, 138, 143, 146
Mortimer, Roger (1287–1330) 11
Mortimer's Cross, battle of, 2nd February 1461 213, **214**
mounted infantry 13
Myton-on-Swale, battle of, 20th September 1319 10

Nájera, battle of, 2nd April 1367 89–90, 91
Nantes 33, 35, 36
Naples 115–116
Narbonne 63
Nene, River 202–203
Nesle, Guy de 61
Neville, family 131, 132
Neville, Cecily 189
Neville, Sir Ralph 49, 134
Neville's Cross, battle of, 17th October 1346 **49**, 49–50, **50–51**
Nicopolis, battle of, 1396 103
Norfolk, John Howard, Duke of 220, 221, 249, 250, **250**
Norham Castle 11, **11**
Normandy 65, 150–151
Northampton, battle of, 10th July 1460 202–203, 205, 230, 231
Northampton, Earl of 34, 35, 45
Northumberland, Earls of. *see* Percy

Order of the Garter 56, 57, **67**, 99
Order of the Star 61, 62
Oriflamme, the 69
Orléans, city of 165, 168–171, **170**(map), 174–176
Orléans, Duke of 66
Orléans, Louis, Duke of 149, 155–156
Otterburn, battle of, 5th August 1388 132–134
Oxford, Earl of 236, 237

Page, John 157
Paimpont, forest of 72
Paris 11, 65, 180
Patay, battle of, 18th June 1429 178
pay, rates of 37
Pedro the Cruel, King of Spain 88, **90**
Pembroke, Earl of 94
Pembroke Castle 222
Penhoet, Lord of 77, 80
Percy, family 131–132, 134, **134**, 138, 206, 222–223, 249
Percy, Sir Henry 49
Percy, Henry, Earl of Northumberland 134, 139, 143, 145–146, 249, 250
Percy, Henry Hotspur (1364–1403) 132, 133, 136, 138, 139–140

Percy, Sir Ralph 227
Percy, Thomas, Earl of Worcester 139
Peronne 153
Philip (of Valois) VI (1293–1350), King of France 31, 36, 48
  and the Crécy campaign 42, 44
  and Gascony 32
  and the siege of Calais 50
Philippa of Hainault (?1314–69), Queen of England 21, 50
Piccinino 126, 127
pillaging 39
Pisa 120, 121
Plantagenet, House of 147
Ploermel Castle 59
Poitiers, battle of, 19th September 1356 58, **65**(map), 65–67, **66**, 69
Poland, kingdom of 100, 107
Pole, Sir William de la 169
Polish forces, at Tannenberg 108–109, 110–111, **111**, **112**
Pommiers, Sir Aymenion de 99
Pontefract Castle 135, **135**, **232–233**
Pontorson 167
Pontvallain 92
prisoners 57, 58, 168
  at Agincourt 155
  the Lithuanian crusade 101, 106, 107–108, 111
property, destruction of 38
Prussia, conquest of 100
psychological warfare 77

Raglan Castle **186**
ransom 58, 87, 106
recruitment 37, 190–191, 193–194
Redman, Sir Richard **176**
Rennes 36, 61, 72, **78**, **80**
  siege of 76–77, **79**, 79–80
retainers fees 191
Richard II (1367–1400), King of England 125, 131, **132**, 134, 135, 138
Richard III (1452–85), King of England 244, 248, 249
  at Barnet 237
  at Bosworth Field 249, 250
  death of 250–251
  murder of the princes 244–245
  standard 215

Richard, Duke of York (1411–60) 147, 155, **188**, 188–189, 194, 202, 205
  Act of Attainder against 201, 205
  death of 209
  disposition of forces 196
  and First St Albans 188
  at Ludlow 199, 200
  at Sandal Castle 206–207
Richemont, Arthur de, Constable of France **166**, 167, 177, 183, 184
Ripon 9–10
Robert I, King of Scots. *see* Bruce, Robert
Robert of Geneva, Cardinal 123–124
Rokeby, Sir Thomas 14, 146
Rouen **161**, 183
  siege of, 1418–19 156–157, 160–161
Rouvray 171
Rudolph IV of Baden-Durlach (d1348) **113**
Rutland, Edmund, Earl of 209

Saint-Loup, fort of 176
Saint-Malo 95, **95**
Saint-Pern, Bertrand de 77
Saint Pol de Léon, battle of, 9th June 1346 51
Salisbury, Earl of 162, 163, 164
Salisbury, Richard Neville, Earl of 196, 197, 202, 205, 209
Salisbury, Thomas Montague, Earl of 168, 170
Sandal Castle **206**, 206–207
Scala, Can Signorio della (d 1375) **116**
Scala, Cangrande della **121**
Scala, Mastino Il della **122**
Scales, Lord 205
Schwarzburg, Gunther von 102
Scotland **12**(map), 15–17, 16
Scots, the **14**, 131, 244
  at Berwick 9, 18, 19, 20, 23
  at Dupplin Moor 15, 16
  in France 162, 163, 164, 165
  at Halidon Hill 24, 25, 25–26, 27
  military techniques 13
  at Neville's Cross 49–50
  at Norham Castle 11
  at Orléans 171
  at Otterburn 133
  raids 9, 9–10, **15**, 18, 38, 48–49, 132

and the Wars of the Roses 193, 226, 226–227
and the Weardale campaign 13, 13–14, 14–15
Seton, Thomas 21, 27
Sforza, Francesco 125–129, **128**
Sforza Castle, Milan **128**
shields 25
Shrewsbury, battle of, 21st July 1403 139–141
siege tactics 19–20, **20**, **21**, **22**, **63**, 79–80, **104**, **105**
Simnel conspiracy, the 251
single combat 25
Skenfrith Castle **81**, **82**, **83**
Skipton 10
Skipton Castle **10**
slaves and slavery 108
Sluys, battle of, 24th June 1340 38
Sodbury Hill 239
Spanish Campaigns, the **89**(map)
Spofforth Castle 132, **133**
squires **215**
St Albans
  First battle of, 22nd May 1455 188, 189–190, **190**
  Second battle of, 17th February 1461 217–218, 230, 231
St Catherine of Siena 122
St Fermo Maggiore, church of 118
Stalin, Joseph (1879–1953) 112
standards **38**, **134**, **248**
Stanley, Lord Thomas 249, 250
Stewart, Sir John, of Darnley 163, 164, 171
Stirling 9
Stoke, battle of, 1487 251
Suffolk, Earl of 170, 177
supplies 38–39
surcoats 48, **102**
Surenne, François de 182

tactics 17, 24–25, 46, 62, 69
  Wars of the Roses 194, 196
Talbot, Gilbert 249
Talbot, Sir John (c1384–1453) 145

Talbot, Sir John, Earl of Shrewsbury 167, 170, 178, 180, 183, 184, **184**, 185, 188
Tannenberg, battle of, 15th July 1410 **108**, 108–111, **109**, **110**, **112**
Teutonic Knights 100, **100**, 101–102, **107**
  and crusader tourism 102–103
  and the Lithuanian Crusade 100, 101, 102, 104–105, 107, 108
  myths of 112
  reputation 105–106
  at Tannenberg 109, **109**, 110, 111
  weakness after Tannenberg 111–112
Tewkesbury, battle of, 4th May 1471 238–241, **239**, **240**(map), **241**, 243
Thomas of Canterbury 79
Thomas, Hopkin ap 142–143
Thomas, Sir William ap **153**
Thorn, Treaty of (1411) 111
total war 38
tournaments **54**–**55**, **56**, 58, **58**
Tours, Treaty of, 1444 181
Towton, battle of, 29th March 1461 217, **218**, 218–222, **219**, **220**(map), **221**, 231
trade 30–31
trebuchets 19, **19**, **20**, **21**
Tree of Battles, the (Bonet) 53
Trollope, Andrew 200, 207, 218
Troyes, Treaty of, 1420 162, 163
truces 20
Tudor, Edmund, Earl of Richmond (1430–56) 196
Tudor, Henry. see Henry VII
Tudor, House of 196
  Rose of 187
Tudor, Jasper, Earl of Pembroke (c1431–95) 196, 201, 213, 214, 215, 222
Tudor, Owen 189, 196, 213, 214–215
Tuscany 122

Ulrech, Heinrich **106**
Umfraville, Sir Thomas 133

Urslingen, Werner von 120–121

Valognes 183
Vannes 28, 35, **35**, 36
Vaughan, Sir Roger 213
Venice 126, 127, 129
Verneuil, battle of, 17th August 1424 **164**(map), 164–165
Verona **124**–**125**
Vignolles, Etienne, called La Hire 167, 178
Vilnius, siege of 103
Visconti, Bernabo, Duke of Milan 121–122, 126–127
Visconti, Bianca 127
Vitre Castle **91**, **93**
volunteers 37

wages 193
Wakefield, battle of, 30th December 1460 **206**, 207, **207**, 208
Wales 249
  Glyndwr's revolt 136, **137**(map), 138, 141–142
  and the Wars of the Roses 196, 205, 213, 222, 230–231
Warden of the Northern Marches 132
warfare 36–37
  chivalry and 57
  condottieri 116–117
Warkworth Castle **146**–**147**, 226, **226**, **227**
Wars of the Roses 184, 187, 187–188, 191, 193, 210, **212**(map), 235, 251
  castles and 223, 226
Warwick, Richard Neville, 'the Kingmaker', Earl of (1428–71) 189, 196, 197, 198, 201, 202, 210, 213, 218, 222–223, 226, 226–227, 228
  at Barnet 236, 237
  coat of arms **238**
  crest **235**
  death of 237
  and Edward's marriage 235
  at First St Albans 190
  at Ludlow 200
  at Northampton 203, 205

at Second St Albans 217
  support for Henry VI 235
  at Towton 220
Warwick Castle **6**, **68**
Waterton, Sir Robert **135**
weapons 217
  crossbows 44, 47, 118, 231
  longbows 44, 46–47, 231
  shortages of 65
  swords **24**, 47
Weardale campaign, the 13–15
weather 31
Welles, Lionel, Lord 222, **222**
Wenlock, Lord 240, 243
White Castle, the **165**
White Company, the 121–125
Wigmore Castle **143**
Wiltshire, James Butler, Earl of 213, 214
Wisby 47, **48**, **62**
Wladyslaw Jagiello (1351–1434), King of Poland 107, 108, 111
Wodehouse, John de **55**
Woodbury Hill, battle of, 1405 **144**, 145
Woodville, Elizabeth (?1437–92), Queen of England 235

Xaintrailles, Poton de 167, 178, 184

Yonne, River 163–164
York 10, 13, 18–19, 209
York, Archbishop of 49, 144
York, House of 210, 245
  white rose of 187
Yorkist forces 196
  at Barnet 236–237
  at Bosworth Field 249–250
  at Ludlow 198, 199–201
  at Mortimer's Cross 213–214
  at Northampton 203, 205
  at Second St Albans 217
  at Tewkesbury 240, 241, 243
  at Towton 220, 221
  at Wakefield 207, 209
Yorkshire 206

DATE DUE

High Meadows School
Library Media Center
1055 Willeo Road
Roswell, GA 30075